WINNING
AGAINST THE ODDS

WINNING
AGAINST THE ODDS

My Life in Gambling and Politics

STUART WHEELER

Quiller

*To Tessa, without whom I would never
have been anything*

First published in the UK in 2019
by Quiller, an imprint of Quiller Publishing Ltd.

British Library Cataloguing-in-Publication Data
A catalogue record for this book is available from
the British Library.

ISBN 978-1-84689-295-0

Design by Guy Callaby

Printed in the Czech Republic

Quiller
An imprint of Quiller Publishing Ltd

Wykey House, Wykey,
Shrewsbury SY4 1JA
Tel: 01939 261616
Email: info@quillerbooks.com
Website: www.quillerpublishing.com

CONTENTS

INTRODUCTION

A bullet whizzed over my head. God, I thought to myself, it is getting a bit dangerous here. It was 1954, Egypt, and I was in the middle of my National Service. I was the officer in charge of the guardsmen who raised and lowered the targets on the firing range. At that moment I was standing on the 'wrong' side of the targets; past them from the point of view of those who were firing their guns. I was below the flight path of the bullets and so I thought I was safe.

Wrong, of course: a ricochet hit me. My instantaneous reaction was not that I had been hit, but that it was getting dangerous. The bullet removed half my upper lip, and broke six of my front teeth. Naturally there was a huge palaver and I was surrounded by soldiers and, soon afterwards, medics. It did not hurt all that much, and yet I have a distinct memory of asking for more morphine as I was rushed by car to the hospital. Perhaps I enjoyed my first hit of the drug.

If the bullet had gone half an inch away in one direction, I would have been dead – half an inch in the other, and it would have missed. A fairly average sort of result, I suppose.

Luck has played a big part in my life: this was an early example.

If I had died when I was thirty-five, I would have had a highly orthodox career: Eton, the Welsh Guards, Oxford, a few years as a barrister, a few more in merchant banking. Perhaps, though, there were a couple of things that might have caught the reader's eye as they read my obituary.

First, I was adopted, and grew up not knowing who my natural parents were. And, secondly, I liked to gamble. I still do. I play blackjack, backgammon, poker and bridge; I have placed bets on everything from horse races to elections to the sex of my first child; and I have gambled everywhere from exclusive Mayfair clubs to the World Poker Championships in Las Vegas. If I am in a café, I will make a bet with myself about how long it will take the waitress to make my coffee. Each morning, before I weigh myself, I will try to work out the odds of me being lighter or heavier than the day before. There is no point in it, but I find myself doing it automatically.

I do not do this because I am addicted. I gamble because I am fairly good at it. I gamble because I have a very strong desire to succeed. Most of all, I gamble because I am fascinated by probability and odds.

It was, in a sense, my love of gambling, and my fascination with odds, that led to the second, rather less reputable, phase of my career: as a bookie. This is the point when my CV suddenly becomes a lot more interesting. I set up my company, IG Index, in 1975 in the attic of my house, to take advantage of a boom in gold trading that never actually took place. It was either, as someone I know once put it, 'the greatest idea of our generation', or, as most other people felt, an act of madness. Almost thirty years later I sold my shares and made a fortune. (Not as clever as it sounds; had I held on for a bit longer, I would have been fifteen times richer.)

In *Winning Against the Odds*, I shall tell you how I made a success of IG Index, and became a major figure in UK politics. I will talk about the many celebrities I have encountered – from P.G. Wodehouse to Princess Margaret; Nigel Farage to Omar Sharif – and try to answer some important questions. What was I doing with Lord Lucan two days before the murder of his nanny and his disappearance? What could have possessed a small boy to biff me over the head at the 1966 World Cup Final? How did I find myself being thrown out of Las Vegas's Caesars Palace at six o'clock on a Sunday morning? How on earth did 9/11 make me a million pounds richer? Why did I become the biggest donor in British political history? And for what possible reason could the party, to whom I had given so many millions of pounds, have expelled me only a few years later?

I have tried to be honest in this story of my life, though, as I see it, there are two objections to speaking plainly. One is the looming threat of a libel suit. The other thing is: how many enemies for life am I prepared to make?

What follows is, then, something of a gamble. I hope you enjoy it.

CHAPTER 1

A CURIOUS START IN LIFE

I was born on 30 January 1935 in Enfield in a hospital that no longer exists. It seems that I entered an adoption society home within a very small number of weeks, or even days, of my birth. I stayed in this home for longer than average, because I had a club foot[1] – I suspect that the staff thought they needed to deal with this before I could be adopted – though naturally I have no recollections of this time. Most people grow up being told about things they did when they were only a couple of months old; there are photographs, videos and shared memories. I have none of these: my first two years on the planet are essentially a blank.

Fate's first real intervention in my story occurred some months after I was born, when Betty Wheeler came through the doors of the home, accompanied by her sister Vera, who had come with her because my adoptive father had said he was too busy that day (though his definition of 'busy' was eccentric). A

---

1 I have never, until writing this, bothered to find out what a club foot is, but apparently it is not very interesting.

few hours later they left, having decided that I was the child that Betty should adopt.

There was nothing inevitable about the choice. Betty rather fancied a very good-looking baby (obviously not me). But then Vera drew her sister's attention to another baby (me), who was making a nuisance of himself. 'This one might be more interesting in the long run,' she suggested. I am extremely grateful that she did.

What I believe happened next is that when I was around a year old, I went to live with Betty and her husband; and approximately twelve months later, on 4 January 1937, the day that our adoption orders were formally signed, I was joined by my adoptive sister, Susan, eleven months younger than me. For much of my life, this was as much as I knew about the circumstances of my birth: I did not even know my birth mother's name, nor whether she was still alive or if she wanted to be contacted.

The second major stroke of luck in my life was the kind, loving nature of the two people who brought me into their home.

My new father, Alexander Hamilton Wheeler, known as Alec, was born in 1880 in Pennsylvania in the United States, one of eight children of a rich banker. So he grew up with plenty of money, but by the time he inherited anything, his father's fortune had been divided by eight. This did not seem to bother him unduly. He lived in some style, and never did a stroke of work in his life, except that he fought bravely in the First World War (where he got an MC). So there was not a lot left when he died.

Alec was one of those Americans who embrace their adoptive country so tightly – he had been naturalised by the time he had adopted me – that they become 'more English than the English', and he divided his time between hunting with the Quorn, shooting and fishing. So he considered himself very busy.

The pictures I have of him show a stern face framed by a bristly moustache and wavy hair, only just disciplined by the combined efforts of comb and some oil; but there is also much tenderness in one photograph, which shows him balancing me on his knee as I stare back at the camera.

Alec was a country gentleman, who behaved in the same way as all the other country gentlemen around him. I doubt that he thought for a moment that living the way he did might not be an ideal way to spend one's life; he loved his existence, and I imagine that, almost unthinkingly, he did and said the sorts of things his peers did and said. He was prone to saying ghastly things like, 'There are two problems in the country, the Jewish problem and the servant problem.' I distinctly recall one day when I was six, I was a bit put out when he said, 'Now, Stuart, you've reached the kind of age when from time to time I'll need to give you a good licking.' I was not too sure what a good licking was, but it sounded none too desirable. Perhaps he felt he had to say something like that, but I doubt that he either wanted or expected to beat me.

Although, on the one hand, I am very much of the opinion that one should never trust a man who claims he is honest, on the other, it is also true that I am sometimes accused of being too honest for my own good. I think this characteristic must have come from my father. Certainly, it would not have been something my mother instilled in me: while extremely kind, she was the type of person who would have been happy to indulge in minor dishonesties such as bringing items through customs without declaring them.

Alec also taught me to ride. I doubt you would find many others using the method he employed, which was to tie his horse to mine and gallop off. I did not like this much and when he died, I took the decision that it was the end of riding for me.

My father was kind and well-intentioned, but he was not always very effective. Soon after my sister and I had been adopted, he put some of his diminishing inheritance into a trust for us. He chose something that he considered dead safe – Chinese bonds.

Before long, they were worthless.

Alec had had a fairly short-lived marriage earlier in life – so it seems likely that he was the one unable to have children, though I do not think he ever quite gave up hope of being able to do so. In his will, he stipulated that his adoptive children should be treated in precisely the same way as any natural offspring *except* in one respect: an adoptive son was not to inherit his pair of Purdey guns. I never did find out what happened to them.

I have vague recollections of Alec behaving quite badly, from time to time, to my mother. I can just about remember the two of them becoming cross with each other over tea, and my father even had a woman to stay; it was never clear (to me at least) what their relationship was, but it seemed to make my mother unhappy.

Of course, it is hardly a surprise that I sometimes struggle to recall much about my father because, as was customary for children of our time and social position, we rarely saw our parents, except when we were taken for walks by them, and when we joined them at tea time. We were looked after in the main by our nanny[2] in the nursery – she was like a second mother to us, really – and only occasionally would we receive visits there from my mother or father. We also got on very well with the cook, the butler, the groom and the scullery maid.

Betty Lydia Gibbons, my adoptive mother, was well meaning and kind, and very *laissez-faire* – inclined to let us get on with our lives and not interfere unless it was necessary. She was the kind of person who took life as it came.

Betty was the daughter of Gladys Constance Mostyn Watkins and a baronet – an old-fashioned, slightly impoverished gentleman called Sir Alexander Doran Gibbons. Like my father, he led a leisurely existence largely concerned with outdoor pursuits. He

---

2 She would become a beauty queen after leaving our employment, and was featured in the *Daily Mirror*.

was the one who taught me to shoot, and to play bridge, as well as passing on other pieces of less useful knowledge, which demonstrated the firm but illogical opinions that men like him used to hold. He told me, 'You can be as cruel as you like to a rat!'

After Alec's death, we would often stay with my grandparents and their only unmarried daughter, Joan (who, because she was especially interested in, and kind to, my sister and me, became our favourite aunt),[3] in their house on the border between Somerset and Dorset. The visits were a source of great pleasure to us all, but Gladys, a charming old lady who was always very kind to us, died in 1945 when I was only ten.

Betty was the second of four daughters (her parents' first child had been a boy, who died aged just five months) and she felt put down for the rest of her life because of the family reaction to her last sister's birth. When the news came back from the nursing home, it was not a case of 'mother and daughter are both well: isn't it great', but a terribly depressed, 'it's *another* girl'.

There is something tentative about my mother in the photographs I have of her. In one, which must have been taken one summer in Connemara, Southern Ireland (my mother is posed in front of a painting of a particularly large fish caught by my father), she is dressed in a cardigan and houndstooth skirt; in another, a single delicate string of pearls encircles her neck. But what both have in common is the way her gaze is averted: she seems unable, or unwilling, to look directly at whoever was taking the picture.

Eventually a boy, John, did arrive, but he turned out to be another disappointment in spite of the fact that he alone got a

---

3 Joan had, incidentally, been working in the British Embassy in Berlin when war was declared. A fortnight before that, she had said in a letter to my mother, 'Please tell Stuart [I was four at this time] that I have not met Mr Hitler yet.' What is of rather more historical interest is that she told of lots of rumours of war, but said it was not likely to happen. She and the rest of the staff had a tough time making it back to England.

proper education, another fact that my mother unsurprisingly resented. John was captured during the Second World War and was held for several years in a prisoner-of-war camp. That may begin to explain why he spent part of his life later in a mental institution. But he did retain his sense of humour. One day, probably when I was ten or eleven, my mother and I took him out on a walk to Port Meadow, near us in North Oxford, and he expressed an opinion with which I happened to disagree. 'You must be *mad*,' I said, without thinking. Luckily, he saw the funny side and laughed.

Betty was just as keen on riding and hunting as Alec – she rode side-saddle – and perhaps it was their love of hunting that brought them together. I know that my mother was always terribly proud of having, as she put it, *got* my father, whom she considered, despite the twenty-six-year age gap between them, to be a great catch that many others were after. He appeared to be quite rich, was a desirable character, and possessed the added attraction of being the sort of fellow who hunted with the Quorn, the poshest of the hunts. Although they must have been greatly disappointed to discover that they were not able to have children naturally, they were unfailingly kind and loving parents to Susan and me.

If I was lucky in the terms of the personalities of the two people who adopted me, I was also lucky in their circumstances. It is possible that I might have been just as happy had I been brought up in an ordinary middle- or working-class household, but there were undeniably many advantages to joining a family somewhat further up the social and financial scale. My father's private income meant that there was no need for him or my mother to work. It also meant that we had a good start in life. We lived in an atmosphere of comfort and plenty, and in due course I, at least, was sent to excellent schools, though my mother, perhaps displaying some of the prejudice in favour of the male sex that had distressed her when she was young, was less generous with Susan, my sister.

The home into which I was taken was called Leighon, a large, handsome house in Manaton, on Dartmoor, which my father rented, with the full complement of servants that people of my parents' background were accustomed to employ at the time. It was surrounded by a beautiful garden and plenty of land. Close by were ponds that we walked to for picnics and in which we swam, and it was here that my father tried to teach me to fish. Until I was four, when the war began, we spent the summers in Connemara, Ireland, where we had another house. This sat, rather splendidly, in the middle of a lake that one had to row across. I was proud to be handed the oars.

The house in Manaton is my earliest recollection. Memory does play tricks, but I claim to remember being warmly congratulated as, aged about fifteen months, I suppose, I took three steps from one grown-up to another. Beyond this I can recall only flashes from this happy, contended period in my life; though I do also have a memory of saying to myself that it was about time I implanted something inside my brain that I would remember.

I got along with my sister about as well as most brothers and sisters do, although one day I boasted to my parents that I had made her cry six times before breakfast. When I was four, I was sent to Miss Bodkin's kindergarten in nearby Bovey Tracey. I do not think she was a very sensitive lady. For some reason I really struggled at reading, and I dreaded those moments when we would be called upon to read out loud and she would mock me for my inadequacy. It is interesting that I had no trouble when it came to reading the problems set in our maths books.

When I turned seven, I gave Susan my much-loved teddy bear and gollywog. I felt too grown up to keep them. It was at this age that I first put on a bet. I placed a shilling on a hot favourite, Brighter Days II, which was running in a point to point, where I had been taken by my mother and my aunt. (I had, of course, studied the form, shown in the local newspaper.) Brighter Days II obliged, as they say, which was tremendous, though to this day I remain conscious that I should have gone round the betting ring and got odds of 5 to 4, instead of the 'evens' I did get.

I went on to place a series of successful bets that day, coming home seven shillings up, a nice boost to my spending power at the time, but in its small way it could have led me to the false conclusion that I was good at picking winners: a dangerous delusion for a gambler to entertain.

In the summer of 1939, as tensions grew in Europe, my father took me on his knee and told me that if a bad man called Hitler did not start behaving himself, there was going to be a war: I did not know what a war was, but it was obvious from my father's concern that it was something pretty serious.

Like other families in the early months of the war, we took in evacuees, in our case a pair of cockney children called Mavis and Trevor. I do not think Susan and I realised quite why they were with us, but we enjoyed having other children to play with.

On one occasion I was in a hotel in London with my mother and an air-raid warning sounded. That was exciting, but nothing came of it. We were not even sent to air-raid shelters. Another incident was more interesting. We were on holiday at St Ives in Cornwall, and we were splashing around in the sea when a German bomber appeared. I had no idea what was happening, but we all rushed back from the sea onto the sand. The pilot had presumably got lost – certainly he had no reason to be there – but he evidently thought he might as well drop a bomb. So he did and one very unlucky man in the gas-works was killed.

Really, the only major inconvenience the conflict with Germany caused was to my diet. We ate what seemed like endless quantities of semolina and parsnips, and while rabbit makes a perfectly nice lunch, you do not want it five times a week.

What I do remember very distinctly is a day when I was seven, and I lay in bed thinking to myself, I am really enjoying myself right this minute; I should think that if I spent my whole life feeling as happy as I do now, it would be a good thing to settle for.

You can read two things into this curious reflection: that I was very content as a young boy, but also perhaps that I was a rather odd child.

I might also suggest that it was an early example of the unusual way in which my mind works. Even then I instinctively saw every decision, even the most mundane, in terms of odds. This is something that everyone does, to a greater or lesser degree; I am simply more conscious of this process, and perhaps approach things a bit more rationally than the majority of people. The world is chaotic and unpredictable. Counting, looking at things in terms of odds, helps me to restore a bit of order and clarity. I might put it like this: some feel their way through life; I prefer to count.

It was while I was still seven that my father died. Perhaps it was because he was rather a distant, though benevolent, figure in my life, that when I was told he had died, I did not feel the great wrench one might expect. He had leukaemia and for six months we would go to visit him in hospital once a week, until one day we were told that we would not be going to see him that week. A couple of days later (while Aunt Joan was staying with us), after my sister Susan and I had been read a story and she had gone to bed, my mother told me, tearfully, that my father had died.

Betty said to me that they were not going to tell my sister yet, for they feared she would be too upset, and I replied with a solemnity that I now find rather ridiculous that I agreed this was a good idea, for otherwise she might start screaming.

I am afraid I was terribly matter of fact about it. It does not figure as a horrific incident in my life; perhaps I was too young to appreciate how tragic and sad the situation was, and certainly my emotions then do not bear any comparison whatsoever to the shattering grief I felt after the death of my wife Tessa in 2016.

Curiously, my mother told me, some time after Alec's death, that his doctors had at one point suspected her of poisoning him. I have not the slightest idea what gave her that impression. She is highly unlikely to have made it up. On the other hand, she was about the most unlikely person to commit such a crime that you could possibly think of. It was very strange. Maybe she got the wrong end of the stick.

It may also show something about me that I have very little memory of the moment a couple of years later, after we had moved to Oxford, when I was told, with my sister, that we had both been adopted. I believe that most adopted children find that when they are told they were adopted, it is a disturbing emotional experience: but not in my case. People often ask me how I felt when I was told. The answer, typical of me but odd, was that I did not feel anything much about it, but it made me feel rather important.

Betty moved from Leighon soon after Alec's death. She had bought a house in Oxford, only a couple of hundred yards from where her delightful sister, Vera, and her family lived.

My sister remembers this period as being one of complete turmoil, but I do not think I found it difficult, which you might say is a tribute to my mother's ability to keep everything afloat. It was only occasionally that we saw glimpses of the strain she must have been under. One moment in particular has stayed with me: on the journey from Dartmoor to Oxford, I recall watching another family led by a mother who seemed to me so cheerful and happy. I wished that my own mother could be like her.

Our new home was a fairly ordinary townhouse. It was fine, but it bore no comparison with Leighon. Instead of a cluster of servants, we simply had Olive, a very nice cook and cleaner. My mother never said so to me, but I had a feeling money was fairly tight. We had more than one paying guest (PGs, as they were known). But there was never anything dramatic, like meals missed or moneylenders hammering on the front door; it was simply that we were living life on a smaller scale than before.

Living so close to our cousins was lovely. We played endless games of Monopoly, and also of a board game called Attack – which suited a boy like me who was never much good at sport. My family was also very keen on cards, and I learned to play games like Hearts, Beggar My Neighbour, Oh Hell and Racing Demon.[4]

In the summer of 1943, I went to a private boarding school called St Aubyns, which had been evacuated from its peacetime home in Rottingdean, just outside Brighton, to North Wales. The twenty-eight of us – the school must have been very near to closing, though I doubt that we knew at the time – were lodged in a large house in Betws y Coed, where we also had our lessons. Life was wonderful. We went on long walks in the hills and the war was invisible.

There was a lot else that I enjoyed about St Aubyns, including the two years after we had returned to Rottingdean at the end of the war. I enjoyed the lessons, particularly maths – I had always been keen on puzzles, especially numerical ones, and so it became my favourite subject and would continue to be so until halfway through my time at Eton. I liked the rigour of maths, the way in which, if one followed its rules, one could produce intellectually satisfying solutions to problems.

When I became head boy, however, I did not enjoy the school so much. I was a terrible goody-goody, but when it came to

---

4 I taught all of my daughters to play the card games that I had been brought up with when I was young, except that I did not include bridge. I think parents who shove bridge down their children's throats are apt to put them off the game for ever.

stopping the other boys talking after lights out and that kind of thing, I was very ineffective and that bothered me.

The headmaster very oddly made me captain of cricket – a game at which I was useless. The previous captain, who was a genuinely gifted player, had the unfortunate defect (at least as far as the headmaster was concerned) of knowing his own mind, and he had been too reluctant to bring on the bowlers that the headmaster wanted. I was far more amenable, though this rearrangement did little to improve our team's fortunes.

Seventy years later, I was asked to return to my old school to give a talk to its pupils. Afterwards, when it was time for questions, I was expecting them to be about the speech I had just given. On the contrary, I was asked what my highest score as a batsman had been when I was playing for the school. I replied quite honestly that I could not remember. 'Well, we know,' the boys pointed out triumphantly, 'four!'

While my sister and I were away at school, my mother led her own life. This included volunteering for the Red Cross, helping them run a car service that took people, who would not have been able to afford it otherwise, to and from hospital. And from 1947 onwards, once we had returned to Dartmoor (and a house that was situated under Hound Tor, a collection of rocks that is believed by some to have inspired the setting for Arthur Conan Doyle's terrifying book *The Hound of the Baskervilles*), she delivered books from libraries into prisons.

I once accompanied her to Dartmoor prison. It thoroughly deserves its grim reputation. It is usually covered in mist and looks as forbidding as it is, often in the middle of rain and dark weather. Nowadays you might say that she had a social conscience, but she would never have talked about it in those terms. Apart from the early death of her husband, life had dealt her a pretty decent hand – she never needed to work after she married – so she was just doing what she thought was the right thing.

I remember one event very well. We happened to have a much older cousin staying with us, who was a nurse. News came from the rocks that a boy had fallen and was injured. So my cousin went up to the rocks to help. But the curious point was that she seemed relaxed and took her time, and by the time she had arrived the boy had died. It appears to be a rule among most medical people that it is almost always inappropriate to hurry. I doubt very much whether my cousin could have saved him, but the incident left a vivid impression on me.

Many parents have strong ideas about where they want their children to go to school, but my mother did not.[5] I do not think she had given the matter much thought until the headmaster at St Aubyns, W.H. Gervis (or Gervy, as we knew him), who had very good contacts in a particular house at Eton, indicated that he was keen I should go there. I believe he rather fancied my mother, and perhaps he liked me; you never quite knew with masters in those days. In our final term, each of us leaving boys was invited into the headmaster's office to have the mechanics of sex explained. I knew nothing of the subject, but I doubt that Gervy, who never married, knew a great deal more. I think he also took a moment to warn us against the attentions other boys might pay us once we got to Eton.

At first, it did not seem that there was a place in the house for me, but then came another of the little twists of fate that do so much to affect our lives: at almost the last minute, a place did become free. The Common Entrance (CE) exam had already been taken, but St Aubyns always used that year's CE papers for

---

5 In some ways, however, she was not so unconcerned. She was quite keen that my sister, who had quite a few boyfriends when she was young, should marry well. 'If only he had played his cards right,' she once said of a naval officer who had courted my sister unsuccessfully, 'he might have got her.' I am not sure it had crossed her mind that my sister might have had her own opinion on the matter.

its own exams as a matter of routine, and so Eton was shown my answers and I was accepted.

I was of above average intelligence without being a genius, and by the time I had got into the top form at St Aubyns, there was still a year to go before I was due to leave. What this meant in practice was that I barely learned anything new for twelve months, and I suppose it set me back a bit, so that I am not sure I was equipped intellectually to deal with the work I would be tackling at Eton. This academic impediment was made worse by a social one.

I think that if my father had been alive, I would have been better prepared. Partly because he might have taught me a thing or two about life, but also we would have mixed more with the type of people who sent their sons to Eton, so that I would have found life there easier. I believe much of the naïvety and foolishness I have often displayed would have been avoided if there had been a father figure to put me right.

There was nobody on hand to tell me how to handle Eton's unique rules and customs, or what I needed to do to make myself popular with other boys; and I did not possess the confidence to be able to stick up for myself.

In many ways chance dealt me a good hand after my adoption, but sometimes I do wish I had had somebody around to tell me how best to play it.

CHAPTER 2

YOU'LL FIND IT GETS BETTER NEXT HALF

I arrived at Eton in May 1947, shy, nervous, and with a complete lack of *savoir-faire*. I knew very little about what to expect, and the one thing I did know would happen filled me with dread.

Almost as soon as you arrived at the school, you were tested to see whether you could sing well. I was then, and still am, absolutely useless at singing, and the mere thought of doing so in public was a nightmare. The only good thing about it was that I was so bad that it was clear very quickly that I was not the sort of boy who would end up performing solos in front of the rest of the school. So the test did not take long.

I am not a typical Etonian. I do not think like one, and I do not believe I am usually taken as one by those who do not know. All the same, I am proud of my old school, and my experiences there had a large effect on me; shaping my personality and also, I think, the direction that my life would later take.

When I arrived, I found myself surrounded by boys whose families had taught them that it was their place to be in command:

they were the ruling class; that is how it was and always had been, and, I am sure they believed, how it always would be. I did not possess their easy charm, or their belief that, ultimately, they knew best.

I am a far cry from someone like David Cameron, who wanted to be prime minister because he thought he would be 'rather good at it'. It is often because of comments like this that people run down Eton. I contrast this with the attitude of someone like the grammar-school-educated Mrs Thatcher, who had wanted the same job because she had an ambition for what she wanted to *do* with it.

One of the first things I noticed about Eton, apart from its sheer size, was that life there was governed by a great range of rules. On arrival, we had to learn the 'colours' of each of the houses, and to try to get our heads around the school's unique vocabulary. At Eton, they said half instead of term, beak instead of master, dame instead of matron. If in the summer you played cricket, you were a dry bob; if you rowed, you were a wet bob. It was rather like London taxi drivers having to do 'The Knowledge'.

Many of these rules involved the matter of how senior or popular you were. For instance, there was one side of Eton High Street that only members of the Eton Society, an exclusive club known to the boys as 'Pop', could walk down. And only members of Pop were entitled to sport spongebag trousers and a fancy waistcoat with the traditional Eton uniform of black tailcoat, stiff white collar and white bow-tie.

During your first years, you had to be alert in case any of the members of the 'Library' in your house (other schools call them prefects, but at Eton there was actually a room called the Library, which its members were allowed to use) should yell 'Fag!' at the top of his voice. At this, you all had to rush to wherever he happened to be, and whoever arrived last had to perform the task he wanted doing. Often this involved taking a message to a boy in another house. If the boy to whom you were taking the message was very popular, this was exciting.

You also had a fag master, whose bed you were supposed to turn down each evening, along with other minor chores. I was so absent-minded that I forgot to do even these small things half the time. So I was lucky that my own fag master tended to be relaxed about my forgetfulness.

This was a good thing, since I had started Eton as a scared and lonely boy and things soon became worse. Because I had done well in the Common Entrance, I was put initially into the upper fourth, but after three or four weeks moved up into what was called 'remove', the class reserved for the brightest pupils. There were two problems with this. The first was that showing academic ability was one of the worst things to do if you wanted to be liked (people like me were called 'Saps', short for sapiens, the Latin for 'wise'). The other was that although I had found work in the upper fourth relatively easy, I really struggled in remove.

This alone would have given my self-confidence a dent, but worse was to come. It was made clear to me by some of the other boys that, while in the eyes of the vast majority of the country's population my background would have been quite upper class, it was not, as far as they were concerned, what was expected at Eton. I was not 'out of the top drawer', and they saw me merely as a boy living with a single mother in an ordinary home in Oxford. Perhaps I did not suffer as much as the seventy scholars.[6] We scoffed slightly at those boys, who were dismissively called Tugs, as well as those who genuinely hailed from further down the social scale – 'oiks'.

While I was reasonably bright, my abilities were as nothing

---

6 The seventy scholars lived in a house known as 'College'. The rest of the boys at Eton – about 1100 – were known as Oppidans, from the Latin word 'oppidum', meaning town, as they lived in boarding houses within the town of Eton.

compared to those of one of the scholars, a boy called Stephen Hugh-Jones. He was really brilliant and although that year contained a group of scholars who were even cleverer than usual, he was, without exception, top in every subject at the end of every half. I can remember thinking that he was so phenomenal that he would either become prime minister or go to prison. He certainly did not become prime minister and, as far as I know, he never got anywhere near prison, but he did become editor of *The Economist*.

So there I was, younger, studious and (in the eyes of some of my contemporaries at least) rather common. The boys who persecuted me were pitiless as they homed in on my innocence and embarrassment about sex: 'What's down there, Wetty Wheeler?' they would ask. 'Cock and balls! Cock and balls!' It sounds extremely silly now, so many years on, but at the time it was agony. Two of my principal tormentors were a pair of identical twins called Nick and Tim Dawson who, even then, at the age of fourteen, knew that what they wanted to do more than anything else in life was to run a private school, which they did – they acquired Sunningdale in 1967 and proceeded to run it extremely successfully for thirty-six years.

One forgets a lot as time passes, but I can still recall the names of these boys and those others who temporarily made my life a misery. I also remember saying to myself, 'I am not going to make the mistake of forgiving these people in forty years' time.' Forty years later I had still *not* forgiven them. It is only now, sixty years on, that I have.

None of the bullying was ever physical – I never had my head forced into the loo or anything like that – and yet it was a very big thing for me. For instance, one had to go to chapel every day, and each boy would sit in a fixed place. For one half I had to sit directly opposite one of the Dawson twins, and in every service I would feel ridiculously embarrassed as I tried to avoid his eyes.

Occasionally, when a bully needed help with his maths homework, there would be a sort of truce, which would only last until I had done his work for him. The other way I could get into their good books was to take advantage of the fuel shortage that afflicted Eton at the time, and left all of our rooms damp and horribly cold. Each boy's room had a small fireplace. Instead of eking out my supply of fuel over the course of a week, I would burn it all in two evenings, thus ensuring my room would be full of boys being nice to me as they warmed themselves beside my lovely fire. I was then forced to shiver until our next delivery of fuel, but it was a small price to pay.

I did have one notable experience in that otherwise miserable first year. I was given a ticket to Lords to watch a Test match between England and Australia – I was in semi-disgrace for some reason that I cannot now remember, but nevertheless I was permitted to go to Lords to watch the match – a great treat.

My housemaster, Dick Routh, knew I was having a hard time, probably because I had written to his friend, my headmaster at St Aubyns, and in an ineffectual way Routh did try to help. For the next half, I was moved a little away from the rest of the boys and closer to his private quarters – I think he believed this would offer me some protection. He did once say, 'You'll find it gets better next half.' It did not, but I never complained – after all, what would I have been complaining about, that some boys were saying rude things to me?

Routh, who taught history, was widely thought of as being a very good chap. He, like a maths teacher called Hope-Jones (or HoJo), was one of those very self-confident masters who were liked by all the boys. But there were plenty of others who were far from self-confident and easily lost control. I behaved very nastily to one such master in class, making jokes and so on to get the other boys to laugh. I am ashamed of that now.

Eton was divided, as far as younger boys were concerned,

largely into two groups: those who bullied, and those who were bullied. Perhaps in a way the same applied to masters. Routh seemed to understand this. He could be highly sarcastic about those of his colleagues who did not know enough about cultural matters. I remember his withering comments about a master who pronounced the word 'campanile' as 'camp-oh-nile'.

In 1949, when I had been at Eton for two years, Routh came to the end of his fifteen years as housemaster and was therefore automatically replaced by another. His successor was 'Fishy' Williams. Fishy (I never found out quite how he acquired this nickname) was a very inhibited bachelor who lived with his ancient mother and a feeble sister; the latter of a character so depressing that she was known as 'Death'. He was a kind, innocent man, who did not understand boys or very much else, and he was not equipped to control the house. This was in part because of the deficiencies in his personality, but also because of the new arrangements he introduced.

One was that boys who the House Captain had decided should be beaten had the right to appeal to him. On one occasion when I was House Captain, I decided that a particular boy needed to be beaten – you could be beaten for everything from so-called mobbing, which involved making a racket with other boys and throwing things around in your own room, or generally behaving in an uncivilised manner, to simply being rude to the wrong person.

I was confident of his 'guilt', but I was just as confident that he would invoke his right of appeal, and also about what his grounds for appeal would be. So I went to Fishy, told him that I intended to beat this boy, and that I was sure he would appeal. I then provided him with my responses to his grounds of appeal. It all happened exactly as I predicted, and the boy was left to my tender mercies.

It is obvious that Fishy should never have been made a

housemaster. On one occasion, after we had all had supper, he made a little speech about the great effort he was making. He knew he was unpopular and that things were going badly. He finished by saying, with great feeling, 'God knows I do my best!' before stalking out of the room, followed so quickly that he cannot have failed to have heard it, by a gale of laughter. Boys can be very cruel.

A year after I left Eton, things really collapsed in our house and Fishy lost control completely. He had to retire for what were euphemistically described as 'health reasons'.

The bullying ended after my first two years, I do not know quite why. I suppose it fizzled out, and after that, since I found I was good at work and enjoyed it, I began to have a nice time.

Outside the classroom I played a lot of chess with a boy from my house, Calvert, whose Christian name I no longer remember. My enthusiasm for the game may have been the result of an early triumph. In my very first half I had entered the school chess competition, and in the first round I found myself drawn against the head of the school, Stephen Willink. I was not much good, but he was even worse, and so I began my campaign – which did not last long – with a notable scalp, and felt very proud of myself.

I played a lot of both Eton Fives (an excellent game) and tennis, which was just as well, since there was not much else to entertain us: no films, no trips to the theatre. A couple of times each half my mother would come to take me out to lunch at one of the two hotels by the river in Windsor – the most notable outing being one when we found ourselves next to a table occupied by Laurence Olivier and Vivien Leigh, whose son was also at Eton.

Otherwise we were very much left to our own devices. Sundays in particular were very boring. Nobody knew what to get the boys to do, and I cannot now recall much of how we filled the long hours between the two mandatory visits to chapel.

We were forbidden to play cards anywhere other than in the dame's room; so I would sometimes go there to play bridge. Gambling was not exactly encouraged, but I do remember being very anxious to listen on the dame's radio to a boxing match on which I had somehow managed to bet half a crown on one of the fighters.

I also ran a book on the Derby one year. Everything was going well, except that by the evening before the race I had taken bets on all the main fancied horses except Galcador. That night I dreamt that Galcador won the race, and so the next day, seeking to balance my books, I said to one of the boys, 'Why don't you put some money on Galcador?' Of course, Galcador then did win, so my dream cost me a packet!

The truth is that though I was no longer being bullied, I remained very shy. I still did not know the right people, I was hopeless at sport, and the things I was good at like classwork, and following rules, did not count for anything amongst my peers. I was quite lively – as long as I felt reasonably confident in the company I was in, I was talkative and apt to express my opinions quite firmly. But I was young for my age, inclined to behave in a childish, slightly bolshie way, and to make more of a fuss about things than necessary.

I was eventually appointed Captain of the House, largely because, having joined the school when I was so young, I stayed there for longer than most of my contemporaries, which meant that when I finally got into the Library, it was only six weeks from the end of the half when all the other Library members would be leaving, and so my appointment was almost automatic.

The other point in my favour was that it was looking likely that I was going to become Captain of the Oppidans.[7] Since you could only be Captain of the Oppidans if you were also Captain of your House, and every housemaster wanted one of his boys to be Captain of the Oppidans, it gave Fishy a strong reason for selecting me.

The Captain of the Oppidans was supposed to get automatic membership of Pop, but at least two of its members decided to blackball me, which I am not sure had ever happened before. But since the rules made it obligatory that I be 'elected', I was put up again and elected (a good thing too: I had already been to the tailors to get my spongebag trousers made). I actually discovered in a surreptitious way that I had been blackballed: when no one else was around, I crept into the special room that was reserved for members of Pop, and looked through the election book until I had found what I was looking for.

The normal thing, once you were elected, was for two or three of the existing members to rush round to your room to congratulate you. Because I had convinced myself (rightly) that their 'welcome' would not be genuine, I made myself scarce until I could be sure that I had avoided this humiliation.

We never stopped to wonder whether there was anything curious or unusual about the school's culture and rules. The sixth form consisted of ten scholars and ten Oppidans. At chapel each morning, we twenty would enter together after all the other boys. The scholars would then wheel off to their places, leaving the Oppidans to march right up to the centre of the chapel where our seats were.

The convention was that we should go in very slowly. I maintained an ostentatiously leisurely pace. By contrast, we were

---

7 The Captain of the Oppidans was the boy who, as long as he was captain of his house, was the senior boy in the school academically. Your academic position depended upon how you had done in the exams immediately before you specialised in one subject. I did quite well in those exams but, more importantly, I stayed on at Eton until I was about eighteen and a half, so that most of those who might otherwise have been ahead of me academically had left the school.

allowed to leave first, and, leading the rest of the Oppidans, I would dash off at top speed. A master came up to me once and suggested that I was leaving at an inappropriate speed. My only thought in response to this was: how dare he? Of course he was right.

I was still no better at trying to keep order than I had been at St Aubyns. For instance, I made a complete fool of myself when a rude note, saying 'Piffle', was added to the bottom of a notice another member of the Library had put up on the board. I summoned the boys together and told them that I wanted to know who was responsible, and until somebody owned up, nobody would be able to share a room with anybody else during the ninety-minute work period that took place every evening. Naturally no one did own up and so, after a fortnight, I had to back down.

There was a book called the Oppidan Book, kept by the Captain of the Oppidans. I read it very carefully and it emphasised how desirable it was thought to be that the Captain of the Oppidans should try to improve his authority. One day four boys, about fifteen or sixteen years old, all from different houses, were caught smoking. So it was decided that they should all be 'Pop-tanned', which meant being beaten in the presence of the members of Pop. This, it seemed to me (idiotically), was an ideal opportunity to enhance the standing of the Captain of the Oppidans.

Unfortunately, the President of Pop thought the job should be his. This led to a shaming argument between the two of us about who should do the beating. In the end a compromise was reached: the President of Pop beat two of the boys and I beat the other two. It was only much later that I realised both how terrifying the experience must have been for the four victims, and also that many of the Pop members who were there to enjoy seeing the boys beaten probably smoked themselves.

I had myself been beaten only once. Several boys, me among them, had gone out, against the rules, onto the fire escape at night. We were all summoned to the Library and told that the miscreants must own up. I was the only boy that did, and was beaten: a well-deserved fate, I now realise, not for going onto the fire escape, but for my foolishness in confessing.

As Captain of the Oppidans, one was also in charge of some more special events. The fourth of June, when parents and friends come down and everyone has a good time and a picnic, is a very important date in the Eton calendar. In the summer of 1953, it fell to me to organise fireworks and to get a military band to play at that event. On this particular year, the Royal Family was going to be at Windsor Castle shortly after the fourth of June for Windsor races, and so the celebration was held later than normal.

I got the Band of the Welsh Guards to come. What I did not know was that I should have told them that the Royal Family would be there – because, when royalty is present, the band wears a different uniform. Luckily for me, when I joined that regiment as a raw recruit only a few weeks later, no one put two and two together.

The mix-up over the band was not my only faux pas that evening. I was seated, during the fireworks, between the Queen Mother and Princess Margaret. Conversation between Princess Margaret and me was not going strong, and so in an attempt to give it a bit of a lift, I took it upon myself to ask her, 'Were the fields today good?' There was a long silence, after which she eventually realised that I was asking her whether there were a decent number of horses in each race, and she said something bland in response. It was only later that I was told that it is quite wrong, in conversation with a member of the Royal Family, ever to change the subject.

During that summer half, the captain of the school, John Jolliffe, and I had the pleasure of showing the then crown prince

Akihito of Japan around the school. He was about the same age as us and very agreeable. He is now the Emperor Emeritus Akihito, having abdicated in April 2019.

As soon as you had taken your school certificate – the equivalent of what would now be called GCSEs – you were allowed to specialise in a single subject. I passed the exam when I was still just under sixteen. It was then discovered that one was not eligible to sit the exam until the age of sixteen. So I had to wait another half before I could take the exam. In some senses I am a sort of dilettante. My great friend Rodney Leach once said that when I had mastered a subject, I was good at speaking about it, but too often I have not made the effort to learn as much as I should. I am inclined to spend too much time on trivial matters. If I am not interested in something, I find it hard to devote much time to it.

Subjects like maths I could cope with easily because I found them interesting, but not so English literature. Luckily, although I was not particularly interested in Shakespeare, I did have a very good memory at the time of the school certificate. We were all expected to read a Shakespeare play, and then comment on it. I left my reading to the last minute, so late in fact that I only got through fifty-two per cent of the text (I am ashamed to say I cannot recall now which play it was). Enough, however, had stuck and it was okay. A similar thing happened with my history exam. We were supposed to have read a 400-page book called *The Age of Drake*, but I did not start it until two hours before the test. I found the sixty pages I managed to get through extremely interesting, and they yielded sufficient information to allow me to pass.

It was obvious that I would, when the time came, specialise in maths. If you understand maths, there is no reason why you should not get 100 per cent in an exam. Until the school certificate I *did* understand the subject, which meant that in the exams I got 100 per cent in arithmetic, 100 per cent in algebra, and 99 per cent in geometry. But as soon as I reached the next stage, and I found myself in the company of extremely clever boys, many of them scholars, I found that I could not understand a word. Take calculus, which includes the concept of 'i', which is the so-called square root of minus one. The problem, as far as I was concerned, was that you could not have the square root of a minus number. So what was it all about?

When I found that I could not understand something, I would put my hand up and ask the master to explain. I would then listen while he politely took me through the point in question, but I would often be left just as baffled as I had been before. I did not have the guts to admit that I still did not follow it. I got nowhere. The only good thing was that it ensured that I did not make the mistake of reading maths at Oxford.

My time at Eton finished in 1953, with me getting deliberately drunk for the first time. Faced with the prospect of singing a verse, solo, in front of the whole school, which was a tradition expected from the four most important boys in the school, I went for dinner with a great friend, Timothy Gooch, who had already left for his National Service, and I drank a great deal of wine. I was so drunk that I do not remember much about it, but I am told that my effort was hilarious.

I do wonder sometimes how different my life would have been had I gone to another school. In the six years I spent at Eton, I had at different stages been utterly miserable and quite content. I had been the victim of bullying, but I also became a top person. I had received a good education, academically speaking, but I was in many ways unprepared for life outside Eton.

I have three daughters and I am often asked whether, if I had had a son, I would have sent him to Eton. I am clear about the answer. If he were an extrovert, and self-confident (and if I could afford it) I certainly would. Eton had excellent teachers when I was there and probably still does, and the facilities of all kinds are superb. So, if you want to excel academically, Eton is one of the best schools to go to. I have to say also, though it is fashionable to say that class no longer matters in life and that one succeeds or fails on merit, I do not believe it: many of the friends you make at Eton will, even now, help you in later life.

On the other hand, if my son were shy and lacking in self-confidence, Eton would not be right for him. Things have probably changed for the better, but I am inclined to think not all that much: Eton is a tough place for the shy boy.

It was customary for the headmaster, when a boy was about to leave the school, to give him a book of Keats's poems. But Robert Birley, the headmaster in my time, had got to know me quite well as I was Captain of the Oppidans, and he told me he had decided to give me a special present instead. The result? He remembered not to give me Keats's poems, but he forgot the special present. So I got nothing! Oh well – I did get a lot from Eton.

CHAPTER 3

PUT YOUR BOOTS ON YOUR HEAD!

I always knew, of course, that after Eton I would have to do National Service. But I did not really give it much thought until almost the last moment, when I had to decide which regiment to apply to join. This was the sort of thing that other families held enormously strong views about but – *laissez-faire* as ever – my mother had done nothing about it. In the end, I simply followed the advice of a serving officer called Vivian Wallace, who was at the time in charge of Eton's Combined Cadet Force. He purported to give me a balanced view about various regiments before, very flatteringly, suggesting I tried his own, the Welsh Guards.

I had hoped to fail my medical, the examination to decide whether one was physically good enough for the army (or navy, or air force). I failed to fail, and instead was left to count the days before I would join the army – 4 September 1953 – with mounting dread.

My mother realised how nervous I was and, before I went off, she told me, 'Just let life flow over you.' It was excellent advice, but not something I have ever managed to do.

The idea of having to do National Service was, in the words

of my friend Edward Cazalet, 'bloody irritating'. I was not particularly worried about having to go to war – I did not pay enough attention to what was going on in the world to alarm myself about it – it was more that the whole prospect was frightening to someone who had little sense of what it would be like.

When we became recruits at the Guards Depot in Caterham, we had to exchange our fairly luxurious lives as senior boys at Eton for an existence in which we found ourselves being shouted at by sergeants and forced to engage in all sorts of distasteful tasks, such as cleaning our own boots and making our own beds. It came as a very unwelcome surprise, although even then we continued to be privileged in one crucial way.

It was assumed that as former public-school boys we were officer material, and so we were separated from the rest of the men and put into what was known as the Brigade Squad. There were twenty-four people in the hut we shared and, astonishingly, twelve of them had left Eton the same day as I had. I feel great sympathy for the rest of the new recruits who had no such advantage, boys who might never have been away from home and really knew nothing about anything – suddenly they found themselves in barracks being bellowed at. They had an awful time.

At Eton we had our own rooms, but now we were spending twenty-four hours a day in each other's company: eating together, drilling together, sleeping together (and being forced out of bed at quarter to six in the morning). It was very hard work. When I joined the army, I was a tall thin weakling. In seven weeks of basic training, I put on half a stone – something due entirely to the amounts of exercise we were forced to take (it was certainly not because of the food).

One thing that emerged in these circumstances was a sense of camaraderie and I became a bit of a wag: I found it very easy to crack jokes about our grim situation. So, while I cannot say that

I enjoyed this spell, it was probably good for me.

After I had been there for little more than a week, a dance was held in the NAAFI, a kind of café for recruits and guardsmen. I was hopeless at dancing then,[8] as indeed I still am, and so I went back to our hut before anybody else. The Trained Soldier, who lived with us in our hut and supervised us, making sure we polished our boots and looked after our kit properly and so forth, had stayed out until late with my companions. When he had asked for beer, they had laced it with whisky. I was asleep by the time he returned, but was woken up by his drunken yells as he arrived back, rather unsteadily, in our hut.

'Wheeler! Wheeler!' he shouted in my general direction as I slowly awoke. The next thing I knew he had thrown a bayonet across the room: it stuck in the wall nine inches above my head.

Obviously delighted with his new game, he said, 'Give it back, Wheeler, and put your boots on your head!' Alert enough now to realise that he was planning to knock the boots off my head, and possessing less confidence than he did in his ability to do so without also causing me considerable damage, I returned the bayonet, but I did not stick around.

Still wearing only my pyjamas, I went out into the barracks, which must have done a lot to shock him into a more sober state: if anybody had found me there, and asked me what had driven me out into the night, he would have been in serious trouble. Luckily for him, I was not observed and, when I thought that enough time had passed and that he had probably calmed down, I returned to bed. Neither of us would ever mention the incident again.

The Trained Soldier was completely out of his depth. He was from a remote part of Wales and naturally had no experience of

---

8 A bit later on in life I thought to myself that I ought to do something about my dancing. I took innumerable lessons but never got any better.

coping with a group of arrogant eighteen-year-olds who had just swaggered out of Eton. We treated him horribly, and in turn he was difficult and tiresome with us. I suspect this was a sort of defence mechanism for him. Looking back on it, it is clear that he had no idea how to behave towards us, and we should have realised that and sympathised with him. The tradition was that at the end of one's eight weeks at Caterham, the group took the Trained Soldier, and the sergeant who was in charge of us, up to London for what was supposed to be a riotous evening. It is a shaming thing to admit, but we did not take the Trained Soldier.

Our initial training was followed by a few weeks at Pirbright, in the middle of which we spent a fortnight in Yorkshire, where we ran around the countryside pretending to fight. I have never really been able to see things as they are, and was always liable to do silly things such as taking the men away from the scene of the 'battle', where they should have been given their lunch, to somewhere that I thought would be safer from a military point of view. The senior officer that day said, 'You're such a fool, Wheeler,' in a particularly withering way. He was right.

After Pirbright I was sent, with the other prospective officers, to Eaton Hall in Cheshire. On our first day, an officer gave us a pep talk in which he laid it on thick about how hard we were going to have to work, and how important and difficult our job would be, so that we had better knuckle down to it right away. Within days, a boy (in the Welsh Guards as it happens but a few months ahead of me, so I had not met him) committed suicide. A few weeks later, another boy injured himself quite badly with a blank, i.e., a grenade that did not contain any explosives, we thought perhaps on purpose. So then the officer who had addressed us on our arrival got us all together. 'Now look, boys,' he said, talking far more emolliently this time round, 'you're only in the Army for two years, you really mustn't get too worried about things!'

The other great excitement of our time at Eaton Hall

concerned someone who was not even there. My bunk was next to that of Teddy Goldsmith. He was the elder brother of James Goldsmith. Jimmy was to play a very important part in my life, but at the time I did not know him.

Jimmy became the centre of a huge sensation. He was already notorious for having left Eton at the age of sixteen, after having won £8,000 (something over £200,000 in today's money) on a £10 three-horse accumulator at Lewes. He had announced to his housemaster, 'a man of my means should not remain a schoolboy', and he did not hang around much longer.

What catapulted him into the public eye was his elopement early in 1954 with Doña María Isabel Patiño y Borbón, the seventeen-year-old daughter of a Bolivian tin magnate. Her father had refused the pair permission to marry. (It is said that when Jimmy asked his putative father-in-law for Isabel's hand, Mr Patiño had told him, 'We are not in the habit of marrying Jews,' to which Jimmy is supposed to have replied, 'Well, I am not in the habit of marrying Indians.')

The affair completely dominated the front pages of the newspapers for ten days and so Teddy, even though only the brother of Jimmy, had to be taken away from Eaton Hall for a fortnight because the press were all over us, desperate to get an interview with him.

One of the things I did not enjoy at Caterham was the endless and tiring drill sessions. I was not good at them, but I did try hard, and the sergeant in charge of us realised that I was doing my best. At Eaton Hall, we did more interesting things like firing rifles and Bren guns, and I discovered that I was quite a good shot, good enough to be made part of the Eaton Hall shooting team.

This led to an amusing challenge when I was at Oxford University. My great friend Richard Creese-Parsons was also a good shot and he had been in the Harrow shooting team. We went to a fair together one day and came to a stall where you had to shoot down matchsticks. Each of us, unaware of the achievements of the other, was confident that he would win. As we were both gamblers, the stakes became high. I was up by quite a lot at one point but, fortunately for our friendship, he got it back and we finished all square.

At the end of our time at Eaton Hall, we became officers. I kept saying to myself in a mixture of pride and disbelief: 'I'm an officer in the Brigade of Guards.' After Eaton Hall, the next thing was to join my regiment, which in my case meant flying out to the Suez Canal Zone in Egypt in 1954. One afternoon, while I was waiting, I went by myself to the cinema. A very unsavoury-looking old man came and sat in the seat beside me, and draped his arm over my shoulders.

'I'd rather you didn't do that,' I told him.

He replied, 'Well, I like the position.'

'Still,' I said, 'I really would prefer it if you stopped.'

'Well, okay,' he said, 'would you care to take tea with me?'

Honest as ever, and delighted to have found a convincing and true excuse, I said, 'Actually, I've already had tea.' I got up and went to another part of the cinema, and he did not, thank goodness, follow me. Perhaps I should have been flattered.

Soon afterwards, with my innocence still remarkably intact, I travelled out to the Suez Canal. I was oblivious to the political landscape, and had no idea how tense the environment was that we were being sent into. While I was out there, Gamal Abdul Nasser, who was to become so famous later on, took over from General Muhammad Naguib, the man who had led the coup that had deposed King Farouk in 1952. It would have electrifying consequences – including the invasion of Egypt two years later after Nasser had seized the canal from us – but at the time it did not make any difference to us.

The British were far from popular in Egypt, which was hardly surprising, as we were effectively an occupying force. What this meant in practice was that we could not go to Alexandria or to Cairo. In fact, we could not do *anything* interesting. We were restricted to our camp, initially in El Ballah, beside the Suez Canal. One British soldier had gone into Ismailia and had been mobbed by a crowd of Egyptians. After that there was no question of any of us visiting the place other than on duty.

We were all nervous, trigger-happy, and suspicious of the 'wogs' that surrounded us on all sides. While I was in hospital (of which more later), an Arab woman was shot by the British in her stomach for not stopping when she should have. It was a stupid and cruel thing to have done to this poor woman, who probably did not understand the instructions that were being yelled at her.

Officers from other regiments tended to look upon the exclusive, upper-class Guards with a small measure of envy, and a far larger one of contempt. As far as they were concerned, we were useless for anything apart from putting on ridiculous hats and keeping watch on Buckingham Palace.

We had very little to do beyond trying to stop Egyptians from getting into our camp and pilfering. We led a pretty languid existence, but one thing that became clear very soon was that our training left us unprepared for anything much more than lying about. I was still lacking in any real confidence, and was unfortunate enough to be the officer of a platoon whose sergeant, known as Black Jack, was notorious for being extremely difficult and giving his officers a bad time. He was very bossy and flamboyant, and he showed me little or no respect, an attitude that soon filtered down to the guardsmen.

On a night soon after our arrival, I was sent out on patrol in a lorry with three soldiers to inspect the area around the canal – the Egyptians were forever pinching things like the lead from our pipelines. At one point there was a commotion and I thought I heard a noise that *could* have been a shot. Perhaps we were under fire? I gave the order to stop the lorry and we piled out into the desert.

When we had gone a few yards, I decided, as it was dark, to put up flares. This was effective in that the surrounding area was lit up, showing that we were in no danger. What I had failed to realise was the obvious point: if you fire flares directly up into the sky above you, rather than towards a point some distance in front, their casings naturally fall onto your heads. I was more of a threat to my men than any Egyptian could possibly hope to be. Luckily nobody was hurt.

Later that evening we went to inspect the Sweetwater Canal, which ran parallel to the Suez Canal, as well as connecting Ismailia to Cairo. It belied its name by being a revolting stretch of water, being full of dead camels and, some said, dead bodies. We came across a tiny boat piloted by a pair of ancient-looking Egyptians. I called them over and told them that we wished to inspect its contents.

One of them very generously put his arms out to help me onto the boat, but I slipped and fell into the wretched canal. I was then fished out pretty swiftly by the two nice old boys on the boat. I was, however, in the water long enough to get dysentery, which resulted in me spending two weeks in an appalling local hospital, which, with its filthy surfaces and overflowing toilets, seemed more likely to cause dysentery than to cure it.

It was not very long afterwards that I caught the ricochet in my face, and so found myself in hospital again. However, this hospital was okay – it was run by the British Army – and a surgeon very skilfully sewed my lip back on. While I recovered, I was struck by the fact that Brigadier Deakin, the officer in charge of the three battalions of which the Welsh Guards was one, visited me three times, but my battalion commander only once. For some reason, this has always stayed with me.

A court of inquiry was convened while I was still in hospital and it concluded, in my absence, that the injury was a result of my misconduct and/or negligence. I would probably have had a case then for appealing, on the ground that the inquiry should not have been held in my absence, but it may be a bit late to complain now …

When I got back to London, I visited my adjutant to ask if there was any chance of compensation. He was not sympathetic: 'Don't be so completely ridiculous!' I went away with my tail between my legs. One of the things that the army absolutely does not want to happen is for their soldiers to get shot. So I think they were all put out by how much effort I had made, at least as they saw it, to put myself in harm's way.

For a long time, my face was so swollen that people in the barracks would cross the road rather than have to look at it (or at least I convinced myself that this was what they were doing).[9] After my National Service finished, I went to the appropriate office in Oxford. I was awarded an index-linked pension that I still receive well over sixty years later. A more immediate result was the nickname some of my friends gave me: 'Bullets' Wheeler.

Some years later, I learned that you could apply for a bigger pension if you considered that you had been hard done by. Nothing to lose, I thought, I'll have a go. They asked me various questions, including, 'Do you think you've ever lost a marriage through this?' 'Well,' I said, 'there was one girl who declined to marry me. She didn't actually *say* that it was because of this …' It did not do me any good.

Years later, when I *was* married, a friend said, 'What would you say now?' I replied, 'I'd take Tessa down to see them and say

---

9 My daughter Charlotte suffered an awful car crash in Malawi once. The woman looking after her was a bit surprised that the first question I asked was if there were any scars to Charlotte's face, but I think Charlotte herself knew what lay behind my concern and was very touched.

that this was all I could get!' She did not find this very funny; but then women are odd sometimes.

A month after the incident on the firing range, I was put on a plane home to England, which was a far more hazardous experience than it is these days. Edward Cazalet, another old Etonian, and someone to whom I would become very close when we both got to Oxford, had also been out in Suez around this time. He was due to fly home, but a different soldier, who had been given compassionate leave so that he could visit his sick mother, took his place. Edward's flight was uneventful, but the one he was to have been on crashed without any survivors.

Once back, I was posted to Caterham, the place where I had experienced such a tough time as a recruit. Any gloom, however, was soon dispelled. Whereas first time around we had been subjected to constant physical ordeals, now that I was an officer, I had almost nothing to do and led a pleasant life. This comparative idyll was brought to a maddening end. One of my fellow officers in the Welsh Guards, who was stationed at Pirbright, threw a blank at a soldier while fooling about, and injured him. As a result, we were made to swap posts and I had to take up a position at the far less congenial Pirbright, which, as it was for battle training, actually required the officers to do some work.

If this move had a bright side, it was that Pirbright was closer to London. Most Guards officers of my age spent their weekends at deb dances – living up to their reputation as 'debs' delights' – whereas partly because I was not quite from that background, and also because my face was a bit of a mess, I was seldom invited.

Instead I would head up to the capital and play bridge at the New Acol Club in West Hampstead all day long, before returning to Pirbright first thing on Monday morning. My fellow officers, as far as I can remember, never asked me what I did at weekends and I suppose that, feeling I should perhaps have been at smart parties, I never volunteered the information.

My days at the barracks were dull and pretty much all ran into each other. I did not have the common touch and I was hopeless with the men, and my attempts to keep discipline and retain their respect were worryingly similar to my failures to do the same at school. Some officers tried to make their men like them; others attempted to make them fear them. I had little desire to do either, and I would not have known how to even if I had.

It was customary for those guardsmen who were charged with fairly serious offences to be defended at their court martial by an officer. This was less of an advantage than it might seem. The officers in question were not given the slightest help in this: they were not even taught the basics of cross-examination or anything like that. It was a most unfair system.

When I was called upon to represent a soldier who had returned to his home in Ireland without leave, I had no idea what to do, and was given no support. My soldier's case was due to be heard on 5 September 1955, actually the day after I was supposed to be leaving the army. 'Don't worry too much,' people said when I told them I was getting a bit worried, 'he'll only get three months.'

I was somehow able to find out the identity of his priest back in Ireland, and I procured some letters saying what a wonderful guy he was and so forth, but I did not even meet the chap I was supposed to be defending. It did not occur to me to do so, and nobody ever thought to suggest that I should.

Neither the letters in support of his character nor my own speech can have been very impressive, since he was sentenced to a year in prison. I did then write an appeal, which had the very marginal benefit of reducing his sentence to eleven months. It is a chapter in my life that I look back on with horror and shame. (Though I feel too that the army should also be ashamed of arranging for those at risk of being sent to prison to be defended by officers who had been given no training or advice on how to do the job.)

It was natural for people to expect that two years in the army would have taught me quite a bit about life, and that I would be going up to Oxford as a wiser man, who knew his way around a bit. That is not what happened.

My general lack of *savoir-faire* in those days is illustrated by what had happened at Caterham when I appeared before the Unit Selection Board (which determined whether you would go on to the War Office Selection Board to be tested as a potential officer), and they asked me whether I believed National Service was good for young men. I replied that I thought it did them some good, but not enough to compensate for the two years out of their lives they lost doing it. Perhaps that is a good example of me being too honest for my own good!

CHAPTER 4

YOU MUST STOP PLAYING BECAUSE YOU WILL LOSE

My application to Oxford University was made with the same lack of preparation as my entrance into the Welsh Guards. I knew that I wanted to go to university, but I did not know which one, beyond having a vague sense that Oxford might be a good choice. I wrote something along these lines to Thomas Norrington, the head of Trinity College, Oxford, and a great friend of my family. He told me that Christ Church's entrance exams were due to take place in a couple of weeks, and suggested that I should drop them a line. So I did.

Things were so much easier (for some) in those days. I went to Christ Church for the exams. I was given a brief maths paper, and a general paper, and was asked a handful of questions at an interview. That I had been Captain of the Oppidans at Eton very likely ensured that however I did in either of the tests, and whatever answers I gave during the interview, I was pretty certain to get a place.

At first, I was keen on reading history, but later I said that I would prefer to take PPE (Politics, Philosophy and Economics). I then changed my mind again and decided to study law. Sixty or so years on, I cannot remember why. Nobody seemed to mind my indecision.

When I was young, I was apt to dread some things and look forward to others. The former usually turned out not to be so bad after all and the latter were often a bit disappointing. But my three years at Oxford were an exception: I expected to enjoy them and I did.

I had a few weeks to spend between September, when I left the army, and the start of my first term at Oxford. So I put an advertisement in the personal column of *The Times* in which I said that I was looking for employment and that I was mathematically inclined. I got a reply from somebody who said that he had a very important mathematical job for me to do, and so I agreed to go to his house in Hastings to help him with it. It turned out that he was completely deluded.

This man thought he had a system for winning money by betting on dog racing (based on doubling up on certain types of bet until one came off): it was entirely fallacious, though of a kind that some people seem prone to getting mixed up in. I worked quite happily for him, recording the results of his bets, without quite telling him that I thought he was mad. I never got paid. Not long afterwards, someone told me that my former employer had indeed been sent to an asylum.

I got off to a good start once I finally reached Oxford. Somebody, it may even have been me, had the happy idea of setting up a roulette wheel, and I was the natural person to run the gambling. This had the effect of ensuring that I quickly became one of the 'in' crowd, which was important, as a number of my Oxford friendships have lasted to this day. I also found that I was mixing with people who I had been too shy to get to know while at Eton.

Running the roulette wheel enabled me to become a different, far less diffident, kind of personality for a couple of hours. I relished the chance to put on a flamboyant act, to be the man who shouted, 'Money for money and cash for cash!' I suppose I am rather like those people who are so shy they can barely speak in their day-to-day lives, but are then transformed when it is time to give a performance. The journalist Bernard Levin was a good example. He would tear into his victims on television every Saturday in the very popular television programme, *That Was The Week That Was*, but when I met him at a drinks party, he was so shy he could hardly speak.

There are still some environments and situations, such as at my bridge club, where I do find myself in uninhibited mode, often when I have had too much to drink.

More than anything, these roulette evenings, to which thirty or forty people would be invited, were glamorous and fun, but they were also designed to make us a bit of money. There were five of us, the most distinguished of them in years to come being David Scholey, who left Oxford after two terms, something that did not stop him becoming the chairman of Warburgs, the famous merchant bank. We each put up £12, which gave us a capital of £60. Unfortunately, we hit a run of bad luck and we had to dig into our pockets for another £5 each – if we had been a company, it would have been described as a rights issue.

I had played roulette in Monte Carlo (a pretty boring place, as by then, the rich and famous no longer gathered there) and so I realised that a comparatively small change in our rules would give us a substantial edge. We changed the rule that applied if zero came up when the punter had made an even money bet (red or black, odd or even, 1–18 or 19–36). Before then, bets went 'into prison' when zero came up and were returned to the punter if the next roll was in his favour. From that point on I laid down, they would be lost as soon as zero came up (as indeed they are in Las Vegas), and we began to make money.

After my first two terms, in which I had worked quite hard out of fear of failing my prelims (an exam you take after two terms) and being sent down, I was very idle. Luckily for me, my tutor, Edward 'Teddy' Burn, an extremely nice don who was not a great deal older than I was (he died in early 2019), was not strict. When Edward Cazalet came up to Oxford the following year, he warned Teddy that he would be spending a large portion of his time riding the horses trained by his father, Peter Cazalet (one of the era's most successful trainers, training, amongst others, many of the Queen Mother's steeplechasers). Teddy barely blinked and told Edward that as long as he delivered the essay expected of him at each week's tutorial, he saw no reason why he should be forced to stay in Oxford when he might be racing.

I often failed to produce my weekly essay, but Teddy did not seem to mind. I liked that at the time, but now I am inclined to think that it is a pity he was not tougher on me.

Edward's arrival at Oxford was far from helpful, as far as my academic progress was concerned, but it provided me with a life-long friendship. Even before I had met Edward, people were telling me how knowledgeable he was about his father's horses, and so, once we had run into each other – and quickly become close – we were bound to spend a lot of time together racing.

Although in the summer vacation after my first year at Christ Church I had managed to turn £10 into £100 betting at the races, I really knew nothing about horses. I am certainly not one of those people who can tell at a glance whether a horse is fit or in good form. Nor, even when I was betting quite seriously, was I much interested in the horse's recent performance. What *did* interest me was when people in the know – such as Edward – told me that they fancied one of the runners.

On our first outing at Newbury, I put £40 of my £100 on one of his father's fancied horses. It came sixth. That was worrying, but I persisted and backed another fancied Cazalet horse: Lolliono.

The bookmakers' odds were 8 to 1. In those days, however, there was an excellent device that showed how much money had been bet on each horse on the Tote, so that you could tell what odds the Tote would be paying out if the race were to be run that minute. On that particular afternoon, Lolliono, a French horse that Edward's father had just brought across the Channel, was showing 15 to 1 on the Tote. I bet £20 on a win and £5 on a place. (A bet on a place means you are betting that the horse will finish in the first three.)

It romped home and I won more than £300, a fantastic sum back then. The rest of our little group at Newbury had also won – though nobody had backed it as heavily as I had. A few days later, we celebrated our triumph at Chez Peter, a splendid restaurant in Henley, where I got so drunk that in trying to get out of the car as we drove home, I fell into a ditch. This was the beginning of what we called the Lolliono Club.

That was not the only dramatic day. Not long afterwards a Cazalet-trained horse called Flaming Star was strongly fancied by the stable. The odds were 6 to 1. We all backed it. I put on the bets for everyone, including, for myself, the largest bet I had made in my life: £140. Very late in the day, someone else asked if I could put a bet on for him. This led to a few minutes of near panic.

When I telephoned Ladbrokes, the lady on the line said that Flaming Star was doubly engaged (meaning that the horse had been entered for two races on the day concerned, and the trainer would decide in which race it would run) and she wanted to know for which race I wanted to back it. A check of the papers told me that she was wrong, and that it was another horse, a complete no-hoper called Flaming *East* that was doubly engaged. Terrified that we had all accidentally backed the wrong horse, I rang Ladbrokes back hurriedly. All was well and we sat back to wait for the race.

In the days before television coverage, we could follow the

race only by listening on the telephone to the unsatisfactory commentary provided by the bookmakers. It gave us information only at each fence, and left nail-biting silences between the updates.

Flaming Star went into an early lead, with the favourite, Piper, ridden by the famous Dick Winter, well behind. Three fences from the finish, the order was Flaming Star, another horse, another horse and Piper. An agonising pause. Two fences out, the order was: Flaming Star, another horse, and Piper. Another agonising pause. At the last fence: 'Flaming Star and Piper; these two.' The silence that followed seemed to last an eternity, and our anguish was heightened by the knowledge that Dick Winter, Piper's jockey, had a habit of just pipping the Cazalet horses at the post. At last the disembodied voice told us: 'Flaming Star the winner.' I had won £840, an unbelievable sum.

Soon afterwards we had an even more dramatic bet again involving Flaming Star. This time we had all gone to the races. Flaming Star was strongly fancied – so much so that I placed an even larger bet on him than I had before. But this time another horse, whose name I have forgotten, was the subject of a big gamble.

Flaming Star hit the front two fences from the finish and had a fair lead. But then the other horse started to make up ground. Flaming Star still led at the last fence, but on the run-in to the winning post, the other horse was closing with every stride. Three of us were standing at the winning post, so that we could see which horse had won should the finish be a close thing. With ten yards to go, Flaming Star and the other horse were virtually level. Flaming Star's jockey, Arthur Freeman, riding as if he had got his mortgage and his wife and everything else on his mount, almost threw the horse at the winning post.

One of us thought we had lost, one of us thought we had won, and I thought that it was a dead heat. There were no photographs in those days and after about a minute the decision was given: 'dead heat'. That rare result meant that one half of our bet was considered to have lost and the other half was considered to have won. Flaming Star was not at very long odds that day, but at least we had not lost and we came out with a bit of a profit.

It was soon after this that the manager at the Eton branch of the Westminster Bank, where I still had my account, wrote me a charming personal letter. He made the point that he had seen several young men have a run of success gambling, only to go overboard and get themselves into serious difficulty. I did not pay much attention to his warning, and I got myself into trouble playing bridge not all that long afterwards. I had to go to the bank begging for a loan for £50 – how little that seems these days.

I was pretty short of money during those years. My mother could offer only modest support, and my racing winnings helped me a lot at Oxford. So did poker. I was not, by a very long way, an expert at poker, but young men at Oxford were so foolish that as long as one threw away one's bad hands, one was highly likely to be a winner. The only real challenge was how to collect your winnings: people did intend to pay, but they were in no hurry to do so.

I spent much of the time I should have been working, chatting, backing horses, playing bridge and drinking and eating at places like the Gridiron club. Occasionally some of us would venture further afield. One day a young don, David Spencer-Brown, who held a licence to pilot small aeroplanes, asked several of us to come over to Paris in an aeroplane piloted by him. It was so long since he had last flown that he needed to do it to maintain his licence.

The journey to Paris was harrowing, not least as we watched him wrenching at various levers while we landed. We did land okay, but at the wrong airport. Once we had finally arrived at the right one, we spent an enjoyable day in Paris, but by the time we were due to take off back to London it was getting dark.

It was far from clear whether the plane possessed the lights that were needed to return home safely. The rest of my companions did brave it, but, always more willing to take on financial risks than physical ones, I joined Richard Creese-Parsons, who lived in Paris, and we went to a casino called, of all things, 'Le Club Anglais'. Pooling our resources, we played baccarat late into the night, and by phenomenal good luck we had amassed what was, for us, a considerable profit.

All this time a French-Canadian had been sitting behind us and offering us a stream of unsolicited and unwelcome advice. Though we had steadfastly ignored him, he nevertheless persisted and in the small hours said, 'At five o'clock the dealer will change and you must stop playing, because you will lose.' My friend, much wiser than I was, wanted to stop. With absurd arrogance, I thought there was no question of me losing and insisted on playing on. It was not until we had lost, without winning a single hand, about a third of our winnings, that I got the message and we stopped.

Just how he was cheating, I do not know, but I have learnt over the years that there is no point concerning myself with that. I would never be able to detect it and, even if I could, I would never be able to prove it.

A number of lifelong friendships began at Oxford. Rodney Leach was a tremendous friend and had a great influence on me over the years. I first met him through our bridge group at Oxford (he would go on to become chairman of the Portland Club, my bridge club). Rodney, who was two years ahead of me because he had not done National Service, having failed his medical, always seemed to have masses of time to play games or talk about anything under the sun, even when taking his finals. He had an absolute top-class mind, and attained a double first. Rodney told me that at his viva, instead of asking questions, the examiners just stood up and said, 'We enjoyed your papers, Mr Leach.'

He could speak on equal terms with me on the subjects about which I did know a little, but he would also be able to talk on equal terms with a hundred other people about *their* special subjects. He was clever, well-informed and quiet and, when he spoke, he always had something interesting to say. Despite his intelligence and formidable learning, I never heard him put anyone down – he was very considerate. He was one of those people who have a real gift for friendship.

In my third year at Oxford, I shared a flat with Robin Furneaux (Viscount Furneaux, who became the Earl of Birkenhead on the death of his father in 1975). This was almost by default, because neither of us had stirred ourselves sufficiently to arrange anything until the last minute. Robin was a year behind me at Eton and so, as often happened, we did not get to know each other until we were both up at Oxford. He was a great friend of Edward Cazalet and a keen bridge player, so it was sort of inevitable that we would meet.

Robin was prone to gaffes. Once, when I was quite young still but living in London, I was ill enough to have been confined to bed and my mother came to look after me. Robin popped over to see how I was. When my mother answered the door, he brushed past her and headed straight for my bedroom. We chatted about this and that for a couple of minutes and then he said, 'By the way, Stuart, who was that woman?'

'That's my mother,' I replied.

'Don't be silly, Stuart,' came the response. 'Who is she?'

Robin was quiet and very intelligent. His grandfather F.E. Smith, or Lord Birkenhead as he became, the great lawyer, politician and friend of Winston Churchill, had ruined the end of his life through drink, as did Robin's father, and Robin inherited the problem. He adored wine and knew a lot about it, but he used to get wildly drunk. He then gave it up for a while, before he decided to drink again 'in moderation'. This was disastrous. After another period of sobriety, he decided to repeat the experiment, with similar results. At that point he realised something about himself and never touched another drop.

Although we were both shy, and would never dream of talking about personal subjects, such as relationships with women, we were close. I saw him a great deal at Oxford and in the years that followed, probably more than I saw anyone else.

One day while we were sharing digs, we learned that there was going to be an election for the Bullingdon Club that same evening. Then, as until recently, the Bullingdon was considered to be a highly desirable club of which to be a member. It was not until later on that it evolved into the apparently very wild affair that David Cameron and Boris Johnson were involved in. As I cannot prove what went on, I shall not attempt to describe it.

At the time, I rather fancied my chances of being elected as a member of the Bullingdon, for one reason or another, and it had not crossed my mind that Robin, only fairly recently arrived at Oxford, could himself be elected. It was just as I was discussing with Robin my chances that a number of people came round to congratulate the club's newest member who, it turned out, was not me but him.

I do not know why, but this remains a source of great embarrassment to me, and I have hardly ever talked about it since. I did get into the Bullingdon in the end, for a single term.

Among other friends I made at Oxford were Paul Channon, Jacob Rothschild, and, as he then was, Jeremy Peel. Paul Channon was one year behind me, and extremely friendly and amusing. His father died after Paul had been at Oxford for only a year or so, and Paul in effect inherited his father's seat in Parliament. He left Oxford and became a very young MP, before marrying another member of the Guinness family. He later held two

Cabinet positions before falling out of favour with Mrs Thatcher and being returned to the back benches.

Jacob Rothschild, now Lord Rothschild, also a year behind me, had gone through quite a bad time doing National Service in one of the Guards regiments. When he was at Caterham as a recruit, the sergeant liked to shout out 'Mr fucking Rothschild' and give him a hard time generally. He worked very hard at Oxford, partly, I think, because his father, then Lord Rothschild, used to tell him that his intellect was not good enough. In the end, Jacob, who was famously shrewd and made a great success of life in the City later, did get a first, to his great credit.

Jeremy Peel was a close friend of Robin Furneaux, and they shared rooms in college for at least a year. At Oxford he was an exceptionally macho type, making appalling remarks such as, 'You should never serve a girl of your own class' – meaning you should only have sex with girls from the lower orders. Even so we got on well, though I was never as close to him as Robin was.

Soon after we had left Oxford, Jeremy was convicted of impersonating a woman in a cinema, something that I did not even know was an offence. We all rather thought, oh, what a laugh, good old Jeremy. It was, in fact, a sign of what was to come.

He had married soon after Oxford and had three children (I am the godfather of the eldest of them). In his late forties, however, he decided to change sex and went through with it. He wrote to Robin to tell him. Robin called me up. 'Jeremy's written me a rather *emotional* letter,' as if to imply: for God's sake, all he has done is change sex. (Robin later showed me Jeremy's letter. It was a very good one – whatever you think personally of his decision, he entered into it on very reasonable and rational grounds.)

Sadly, Jeremy died early. He had, as a woman, enjoyed a very successful career in the Post Office, and he never caused any embarrassment to his children.

I was lucky to have many good friends, and the confidence that had ebbed away at Eton was beginning to flow back into me, so although I remained shy, and in many respects awkward, I was happy at Oxford. I even started to do things that were really quite uncharacteristic.

CHAPTER 5

SOMETHING EVEN MORE
DISREPUTABLE

In December 1956, just after the Russians had moved into Hungary, I travelled with Richard Creese-Parsons to Vienna, where we drove an ambulance for the Red Cross. We wanted to help the Red Cross, but we were also motivated by curiosity – we wanted to see the refugees as they came over the border into Austria.

So we did the required driving, but when the Red Cross asked us to take the ambulance back to Vienna, we decided to head instead for the Hungarian border. It took us ages to find the place where people were crossing over from Hungary, and it was not until about three in the morning that we finally saw a stream of refugees. A striking sight was of mothers slapping their babies' faces – they had drugged their babies in order to prevent them from crying and being heard by the guards as they crossed the border, and if the babies were allowed to sleep for too long, it was explained to us, they were at risk of catching pneumonia.

The great majority of the Hungarians we saw were headed for

the horrors of a refugee camp. However, we were persuaded by eight men, who claimed in rudimentary English that they really did have somewhere to go in Vienna, to take them in our ambulance back to the Austrian capital.

Off we went in the middle of the night with me at the wheel. We made good progress, until about fifty miles from Vienna, when I turned our vehicle over as we were descending a snow-covered hill. 'Get out,' I told the refugees, 'and push the ambulance upright.' They did so, and our ambulance, which had luckily suffered only a small amount of damage, made it to Vienna.

By that stage, I was already as tired as I had ever been in my life. Worse, it had occurred to me that there was a worrying possibility that whatever these men might have said, we could not be sure that they did have any contacts in Vienna, and I did not know what to do in that case. Thank goodness they got off, each in turn, at various points in the city. I still do not know whether they really had anywhere to go.

When eventually I had steered our battered vehicle home, we both fell into a deep sleep, rudely interrupted when a lady brigadier from the Red Cross summoned us to come and explain ourselves. We were promptly sacked for having damaged the ambulance, which freed us up to spend three enjoyable days in Vienna that included seeing *Turandot* at the opera house, which had just been rebuilt. We caught a train home on Christmas Day.

Another occasion led me into something even more disreputable. I am a goody-goody but only in some, limited senses, and Richard was the kind of person to whom it was very difficult to say 'No' when he had what he thought was a good idea. Richard, who was an old Harrovian, came to me one day and said, 'It's Harrow Founders' Day tomorrow, and all the teams there have to play Harrow Football against the parents. What we'll do now is go to Harrow, to where they keep the footballs, and pinch the lot.'

So we motored down in his very old Rolls-Royce, found

where the footballs were stored, and put them all into the back of his car. Next, we drove to a spot close to Eton and chucked all of the balls into a stream. Nothing ever happened to us, but apparently they did have spare footballs, as despite our efforts the games went ahead. It was *almost* the perfect crime.

At the end of my second year, Edward Cazalet's first, he and I took a trip to North America, where we worked for a month at Pilkington Glass, in their Toronto factory. We were not being paid, but it was something that Christ Church, which arranged for a lot of our contemporaries to make similar expeditions, found for us.

I am appallingly bad at DIY now, and I was no better as a young man. So I was highly unsuited to the job. One of our main tasks was putting the glass made by the company into the window frames of newly built homes. Edward proved himself reasonably efficient, and was thus allowed to do quite important things on our visits. But the limit of what I was considered capable of doing was scraping the excess putty off the edges of the freshly assembled windows.

It was soon clear that our fellow workers were by no means on the side of their employers. We experienced, for the first time, men idling, or perhaps taking an entire day to load a lorry only to unload it again. They were all pretty jolly about the whole thing, and as we were spending so much of our time with them, we tended to sympathise with their point of view. Once they had got over their initial suspicion that we had been sent by the management to spy on them, we all got on well.

We then went to the home of P.G. Wodehouse in Long Island. Wodehouse was Edward's grandfather by adoption (Edward's grandmother Ethel had married P.G. Wodehouse in 1914 after her first husband had died. He adopted Ethel's daughter, Edward's mother). He and Ethel lived together with a Pekingese, which was given every possible luxury.

P.G. Wodehouse was one of those men who are extremely funny in writing, but do not purport to be a great wit in person. He was just a very nice man in his early seventies, who would have breakfast, do his exercises and write for three hours before lunch. His conversation gave no indication at all that he was the creator of Jeeves and Wooster, or the author of three simultaneous absolutely top hits on Broadway.

There was an attractive naïvety about him, which helped one to understand how he had got himself into such a terrible mess during the war. He made six broadcasts for the Germans in Berlin after he had, like many others, been captured when Germany conquered France. The broadcasts were not in the least pro-German, but the fact that Wodehouse had made them put him in danger of being arrested for treason if he ever visited England again. That was a tragedy, as it is obvious that he enjoyed England so much.

I thought of him as being incredibly old, though I realise now that he was seventy-five, nearly ten years younger than I am now.

Edward and I borrowed the great writer's car and drove right across North America as far as Vancouver, going through Canada for most of the way. We started in Maine and then went on to Eastern Canada, which is full of the most lovely lakes, and where we seldom saw another human being.

We would stop off to swim, and then sleep out in the open, with me on a camp bed, while Edward was in the car with the doors open. It was great fun, as long as one could ignore the bloodthirsty mosquitoes.

However, we were warned after a bit that what we were doing was dangerous – there were all sorts of nasty people about. It was a message that we heard regularly, and then one night, as we were driving back to the US, somebody made the point a bit more forcefully. So we thought that we should do something about it. We steered the car well off the road to a spot where we were convinced that nobody would see us. At about four in the morning, we were woken by a menacing growl: 'Here! I wanna have a word with you.'

Scared out of our wits, we stepped towards the flashlight being brandished in our direction, and were relieved to find it was only the police, who were *also* keen to tell us that what we were doing was dangerous.

As it turned out, we did get into a bit of trouble. On the journey back to Long Island, we drove over the Rockies on a series of rough roads. Occasionally we would wake to find a bear watching us from 100 yards or so away, and then as we passed through Yellowstone National Park we had an even closer encounter.

We had an informal rule that whoever was driving was also in charge of petrol. Edward was behind the wheel, and so, when we discovered we had run out, he was the one who had to flag down a motorist and ask for a lift to the nearest gas station.

Soon after Edward had left, three bears ambled over and began to clamber over the car. I am terrified of most animals, let alone bears, so I was far from happy. I locked the doors, shivered with fright and occasionally hooted the horn in an attempt to frighten them off.

Three hours later, Edward returned and shooed them away as if they were a trio of rabbits. 'I'm awfully sorry,' I then had to tell him, as he tried and failed to get the car started again, 'but it's just possible that I may have used the horn so much that the battery has gone flat.'

As well as lending us his car, Wodehouse paid for us to learn how to water-ski, on the Long Island Sound. I soon discovered that it is extremely easy to stay upright once you are actually standing – child's play in fact, unless you insist on going on one ski – but the difficulty is in getting to that point. There was one alarming ride when Edward was up in the boat with the very pretty divorcée who was teaching us. He fancied her, and I think she was keen on him, and they surged forward for about five miles without a single glance back at me. I hung on for dear life, hoping that they would remember my existence before I fell in and slipped beneath the waves, never to be seen again.

I do not like boats. I like looking at water, but I am less keen on being in it, or on it. But a few years later, Robin Furneaux hired a small yacht while a group of us, including my lovely Welsh girlfriend Anne Griffiths, flew to Rhodes, to wait for the yacht.

The boat was four days late, so we were stranded on the island. When it did arrive, I was so worried about being seasick that I took some very strong anti-seasickness pills. They did work, and I was not seasick, but there were side effects: every morning I woke up in a vile temper; except on one day, when they had such a powerful impact on me that I was found asleep under a card table.

Before the trip, I had asked Robin if there were sharks in the Mediterranean – I am even more scared of sharks than I am of bears. 'Oh no,' he said, with great confidence. So when we discovered that the yacht came with a tiny little boat that you could water-ski off, I took my turn. As I watched the girl ahead of me, Susie Aird, I could see the outline of a large shape in the water, not too far from where she was skiing.

'What's that thing in the sea?' I asked, when she climbed back on board. 'Don't worry about that,' I was told, 'that's not a shark; it's a dolphin.' But I was not so sure. I took no chances.

On our return, Robin gave me a book: *The Shark: Splendid Savage of the Sea*. I looked up the Mediterranean, and found a rather different story to the one Robin had told. My eyes were drawn to one sentence in particular: 'Shark attacks in the Mediterranean, being relatively rare, tend to attract a good deal of attention when they do occur.'

There was a sequel to the Rhodes trip. We were staying with

Torquil Norman in Marbella in 1963 and another guest, Jimmy Wilson, who at the time had a lot of money, took us in his yacht to Gibraltar, and then on to Tangier – my first visit there. I got it into my mind that the risk of seasickness on rough seas was increased if one had an empty stomach. I proceeded to stuff myself with fried eggs and coffee and goodness knows what, which was of course fatal, and I was violently sick on the way over.

Having loathed every minute of the crossing, I leapt into a taxi as soon as we docked in Tangier. I said, 'Airport, please!' and got the first plane out. I was back almost within the hour, and I have not been on a yacht since.

I convinced myself early on in my Oxford career that there was no point in going to lectures. They can give you the impression that you are working hard, but the time you spend travelling to and from the lecture, and the fact that once you are there you do not usually have the chance to ask any questions, means they are actually of little value. If you really want to learn a subject, you will be far better off reading about it. I thought that then, and nothing I have learned since has caused me to change my mind.

I go further than that. You do not need to read five or six books to make progress in a subject: if one is able to completely master the simplest book on the topic, one will already be way ahead of most people. I first came to this conclusion when we studied public international law one term. At the beginning of the following term we were given a test, based on a previous year's exam, which we were expected to deal with as best we could. My paper was hopeless. My tutor, who was beginning to lose patience with me, told me, 'Go away, use any books you like, but just give me a proper answer.'

I knew that there was a short and extremely good book on the subject and I decided on an experiment. We had been told that we need not even consider trying to get away with just relying on this book (whose name escapes me), but I thought I would try. I produced an answer that included nothing that was not contained within the short book. My paper was marked Alpha.

It was not until my third year that I realised it was time to start working properly. I even took my books away with me on holiday in the lead-up to the final exams. Although my contemporaries knew that I was reasonably intelligent, the consensus was that I had been so idle that I would be lucky to scrape a second. This meant that when I was summoned for a viva, they all thought I was somewhere between a second and a third, whereas I was pretty confident that I was actually between a first and a second.

I placed an advertisement in the personal column of *The Times*, stating that I was looking to engage, for about ten days, someone who had himself obtained a first in law at Oxford. I would double the fee if I got a first. I received twelve replies, only one of which came from somebody who actually had got a first in law at Oxford. So I took him on.

We met a couple of times, and he gave me some help, but not much. In the viva itself, the first question the examiners asked – perhaps because they had seen the advertisement I had placed in *The Times* – was whether I had received any help in my preparation. I played dumb and pretended I thought that they were asking about my tutor who, I pointed out, could not help me because he was himself an examiner and, of course, examiners were not allowed to help students to prepare for a viva.

They began the viva with the law of contract. I discovered later that I was still borderline after that. Next the examiners moved on to Roman Law II, the subject that above all I would have wished to avoid. I could see from the bored faces and glazed-over eyes that it was going badly.

Then they asked me what I thought the point was of a particular element of Roman Law. 'Well,' I told them, brightening as I thought I had something clever to offer, 'the orthodox response is as follows,' and gave a précis of it, 'but I don't happen to think that's a very good answer.' I could see that I had grabbed their attention, but although I had read an interesting article in a magazine that had made the criticism, I could not recall the point of it, and that was pretty much the end of me.

Although I feared that the viva had been a failure, I still thought there was a slim chance of a first. So when I learned that I had got only a second, I actually shed a tear or two.

Back then it was certainly a far greater thing than it is today to achieve a first. I had also had a silly, glamorous idea that if I was awarded a first, I might stay on to have fun with Edward Cazalet and those others of my friends who still had a year left. This, plainly, was no longer on the cards. I headed to London.

CHAPTER 6

I DON'T MIND PAYING FOR
A MAN'S RACEHORSES

Typically of me, I had arranged nothing in advance of my move
to London, and I had nowhere to live. I spent two days looking
around a series of gloomy one-bedroom flats, increasingly
depressed. Then I telephoned Rodney Leach. Typically of him, he
had a solution. 'Come and live with us,' he said. I moved into the
flat, 33 Colville Square in Notting Hill Gate, with Rodney and
his friends in autumn 1958.

Colville Square was at that time pretty run-down; it later
became, so I understand, one of the centres of the London drug
trade, before coming up in the world to become, first, acceptable,
and then rather smart. I shared a small room, in which our beds
were very close to each other, with Giles Fitzherbert. Also in the
flat was Antony Martin, whom Rodney described as being
cleverer than himself, which was certainly saying something.

One evening, everyone except Antony went out for a meal.
When we got back, Antony was sitting in a drunken stupor in a
chair in the living room. The rest of us went to bed. At two or
three o'clock in the morning, Antony came into the room I

shared with Giles and told him that he must have a doctor. Giles, who was half asleep, finally admitted that he was awake and said something along the lines of, 'Sorry I don't know where there is one.' I had been pretending to sleep, but in the end I also admitted to being awake.

When I opened my eyes, I saw Antony standing before me covered in blood. He had wandered out into Colville Square, pretty drunk as well as tired, and had been mugged. The muggers bundled him into a car and stole whatever they could before dumping him in the street.

A curious twist was that amongst the stolen items were the tickets he had bought for a holiday in Ireland. The muggers then extremely kindly sent the tickets back to him in the post in time for Antony to go on his trip. I thought about whether it would or would not have been right, if there had been something in the envelope by which one could track down the muggers, to use the information to catch them. After all, it was nice of them to send him the tickets. Quite a conundrum.

After a year I moved to a flat in Albert Hall Mansions, Kensington, with Edward Cazalet, who had just come down from Oxford. At Albert Hall Mansions we often gave dinner parties where the cooking was done by our daily, Mrs Lunn, the widow of a steeplechase jockey. I am told now that her food was appallingly overcooked, but nevertheless people came and must have enjoyed themselves, as they seldom refused the invitations.

At school I had tended to think that I was clever, and had believed that if I were to become a barrister, I would be a very good one. It was only once I had been called to the bar, and begun my pupillage, that I realised I had considerably overrated myself.

Becoming a barrister was very easy. I had been told by someone at Oxford that you did not have to do any work to pass the bar exams. I took this man at his word, did no work, and passed.

But my first six months in chambers, where I worked for the very eminent then (but forgotten now) Sir Frank Soskice, did not go as well as I had hoped. Luckily, I got an introduction to Mark Littman, a brilliant QC who had been the youngest person ever to become a silk. I became his pupil and was allowed, though with no formal agreement, to remain in his chambers after my pupillage.

The head of my new chambers was John Foster, QC, a flamboyant figure who was described in his obituary, rather wonderfully, as 'a genius Benthamite Utilitarian who believed in the maximisation of human pleasure'. He was very well known as a top silk, important politician, and prolific lover.

A serious problem was that Foster's chambers only dealt with big, complicated cases, so there was no way that I, being so junior, could get work for myself. What I should have done was make myself useful to the other barristers by doing research and so forth (devilling, as it is called), but what I actually did was gossip. For some reason they did not chuck me out.

The only jobs I got occasionally were low-paying ones, such as defending people facing minor motoring charges. Nevertheless, I was as shy and nervous as ever, and for no good reason I was in awe of the magistrates. After three years at the bar, I decided that it was not for me and at the age of twenty-six I went into the City.

I wonder now whether, if I had been able to conquer my diffidence, and also my indolence, I might have become a reasonable barrister; after all I have a logical mind. I was, however, rather hamstrung by the fact that Mark Littman, nice though he was, never really told me what to do, how to cross-examine a witness and so on.

I also had a sense that as a barrister, 'You earn money, but you don't *make* money.' You might get a very good income, but to make real money you need to own shares, preferably, though I was not at that time thinking of it, by starting your own business.

John Foster was very helpful. He introduced me to Eddie

Rothschild, the senior partner at Rothschilds; to Siegmund Warburg, the famous banker; and to Kenneth Keith, the head of Philip Hill, Higginson and Erlangers, which later merged with M. Samuel, to form Hill Samuel, a major merchant bank.[10]

Rothschilds offered me a job, as did Kenneth Keith, who told me to go and speak to his colleague Derek Palmer about the details. Palmer asked me what sort of salary I was expecting. Robin Furneaux had told me earlier that one would be very lucky to get into a merchant bank, but that although in the end one should do extremely well financially if one stuck with them, one could not expect to get paid anything significant to start with. So I replied, 'Would £1,000 a year be all right?' Palmer looked astonished and said, 'Well, I think we had better call it £1,250.' It was still a minuscule salary. I would probably have got three times as much if I had asked for it.

The last of the three bankers I saw was Siegmund Warburg, who talked to me for thirty seconds or so. 'It is not often,' he said, 'that I know exactly what a young man should do. You should be articled to a chartered accountant for three years and at the end of that period you may well be able to get a job at a thousand a year.' I thanked Warburg, and then called Kenneth Keith to accept his offer.

I started out in the investment department. I might have done better if I had even had any real idea about how normal banks operated, never mind knowing what a merchant bank did. Even if you had told me the simple fact that the fundamental thing that banks do is to take deposits from people at a low rate of interest,

10 When Philip Hill, Higginson, Erlangers and M. Samuel were negotiating their merger, there was the often contentious question of what the merged company should be called. Should it be Hill Samuel or Samuel Hill? I think that the way it was resolved was in fact inevitable. Philip Hill, Higginson, Erlangers had a very well-known investment trust called Philip Hill Investment Trust, very often known simply as PHIT. If the merged bank had been called Samuel Hill, the investment trust, PHIT, would have become SHIT.

and then lend them out at a higher rate, I would have been better informed.

The work itself was quite interesting: we selected investments and gave people advice on them. For some time I shared an office with David Stevens, now Lord Stevens, and until recently, one of Ukip's two members of the House of Lords. David and I had a bit of a row when an opportunity came up to go on a tour of the United States, designed to encourage British investors to buy US shares. Since my job involved American shares, and David's did not, I thought that if anybody was going to make this trip, it should be me. Our boss, Brian Whitmee, initially intended to send David, but I managed to get that changed.

It was highly enjoyable. We were whisked around the place by air to see the heads of very important companies. Normally we had a great time wherever we went and were given good food and a drink at dinner, but IBM was an unwelcome exception. We got there after a highly unpleasant bumpy flight, longing for a drink. That was out of the question, because IBM had a no alcohol policy. Instead, they forced us to sit through endless lectures.

After three years in the investment department, I realised I was getting nowhere. I asked for a change and was moved to the issues and mergers department, before returning to investments two years later. A good thing about being back in the investment department was that I was required to make about three trips to the US every year. This meant that I could plan my journey so that I would need to be in San Francisco or Los Angeles at the beginning or end of the week, and could spend the weekend playing blackjack and enjoying myself in Las Vegas.

The best weekends back in England were those when I was invited to stay in luxurious country houses. Paul Channon had a very grand house in Essex that I was invited to a couple of times, and a big group of us sometimes went to Robin Furneaux's family home.

My favourite place was Somerhill, the country house owned by Sir Henry (or Harry) d'Avigdor-Goldsmid, a Conservative MP, who was chairman of the Anglo–Israel Bank. I adored going there. The reason I was asked, more than any other, was that Edward Cazalet was immensely keen on his eldest daughter, Sarah. Edward was asked down there very frequently and I was quite often invited with him.

Somerhill was a large, rather dark and gloomy, house, but staying there was tremendous fun. Things were much more formal then than now. There was a butler and two footmen, and one always wore a dinner jacket in the evening. I think some guests found the whole set-up rather unnerving.

One Friday night when I was not there, around the time of Wimbledon, there was a young deb who was conscious that she had not contributed much to the conversation up to that point. She decided to rectify this over drinks by demonstrating a serve. Unfortunately, she did it so energetically that she smashed a priceless (both sentimentally and financially) chandelier that had been in Harry and his wife Rosie's bedroom, but which they had recently moved downstairs. Rosie burst into tears at the sight of the thousand shards of chandelier on the floor and Harry, who was not normally noted for his wit, boomed, 'GAME, SET and MATCH!' I never found out what happened to the poor girl.

The guests were of very mixed ages, and there were often some well-known people. One might run into the Conservative MP Duncan Sandys one week, Siegmund Warburg the next, or the writer Cyril Connolly another time. Godfrey Winn was sometimes there, too. He was a journalist and writer known as a great wit, and he used occasionally to invite me to dinner at his flat on Ebury Street before we then went on to play bridge at Crockford's. There would be music wafting down the stairs as I went up to his flat. I think he fancied young men, even ones as bad-looking as I was, if they could play bridge.

I liked Harry, though others found him somewhat dour, and I think he quite liked me. He said to somebody else that he thought that I would turn out to be the most influential of the young men and women of my generation who used to go there. I had no idea at the time why he said this, but I think I have at least exerted, in one way or another, a bit more influence than appeared likely then.

Harry had an off-hand, cynical manner, and was not, it seemed, a happy man. A few years before he died, he made it clear that he could not see any particular point in living much longer. He could never be said to have been full of the joys of life.

He loved playing bridge, though, and on one of the first times I stayed there I was invited to play. I was asked what stake I would like to play for. To Harry's considerable surprise I suggested £2 a 100, a very high stake in those days. I won £100, a big win, and the next week I took Edward, Sarah and four or five others out for dinner and to a performance of the Lionel Bart musical, *Fings Ain't Wot They Used T'Be*. I got a lot of Brownie points for that.

On the following weekend, however, Edward's father, Peter, came to dinner. He lived nearby, and he joined us for bridge. This time I lost almost exactly the same amount as I had won seven days earlier.

In the years that followed, I would often think of how wonderful it was to stay at Somerhill. I used to say to myself, 'I do not think I'll ever be able to afford something similar. But if I could …' And then, in 2002, I bought a big country house of my own, Chilham Castle. We had lived in the nearby village for a number of years, and then, by a great stroke of luck, at about the time when I had made a lot of money because my company had gone public, the castle came up for sale.

After a long refurbishment, we were able to move in. Tessa had been anxious that anything we did should look both tasteful and authentic, while I only really wanted the water to be as plentiful and hot as it is in the top Vegas hotels – to test this I had my daughters' friends scurry around the house ensuring that every tap was on simultaneously.

I am not interested in the things that the super-rich are after: I do not want a big yacht or a fast car or fancy clothes. But I do like to live in a lovely home. And Chilham is a lovely home. It is very beautiful and I am very proud of it. What I like most, however, is being able to invite lots of friends to come to stay and have a good time with excellent food and drink. I would hate to be alone in the castle with no guests. To some extent, I have recreated, several decades on, the sort of weekend that made Somerhill so special for me.

Tessa was always magnificent at playing a very active role in the local community. I have not been so good, but I do enjoy our arrangement with the Globe Theatre. For the last few years they have put on outdoor performances of Shakespeare plays in the grounds of Chilham. (Something that would not be possible without the support of Taittinger, who make a valuable financial contribution, as well as providing us with large quantities of their excellent champagne.)

It is good for the village, and good for the reputation of the castle. The cast gives every impression of enjoying it, the audience seem to love it, and it has taught me a little about Shakespeare too.

I was less keen on the theatre in my twenties, but one thing I did quite often was to go to watch Bill Nicholson's great double-winning football team, Tottenham Hotspur, when Spurs played at White Hart Lane. I also went with a group of a dozen or so friends to watch England in the final of the 1966 World Cup at Wembley. Curiously enough, it was easy to get tickets, because the fans of the other countries' teams, who had travelled to England so full of hope, had by that time gone home.

I had put a big bet on West Germany to win the World Cup.

On the day itself, I tried to buy a West German flag, but they refused to sell me one. When Germany scored the first goal, I leaped to my feet in excitement and a young boy gave me a bit of a biff on the head.

This was followed some time later by the most exciting thing I have ever seen in world sport: with England leading 2–1 and literally fifteen seconds to go, the largely English crowd were singing with joy, the way crowds do when they 'know' that their side is about to win an important match, when Wolfgang Weber of Germany smashed the ball into the back of the English net. It is hard to find the words to describe the change in atmosphere from ecstatic to horrified, but you can imagine it. England did win in extra time, so the fans' mortification did not last long.

I do rather enjoy being wicked and cheering on one side, when the rest of the crowd want the other side to win, but I cannot imagine that I would leap to my feet in similar circumstances nowadays. I would be lucky to escape with my life.

I did, however, place a bet of £5,000 on Croatia at 11 to 8 to win their 2018 World Cup semi-final against England. I do not usually put that big a bet on subjects I do not know much about. On the other hand, I am a contrarian and also it seemed clear to me that although England had deserved to beat Sweden in the previous round, Croatia were a better side. Another point was that the great majority of the British public would be backing England, and so the odds for those who wanted to back Croatia were probably generous. In case you are not a football fan, I must add that Croatia did indeed win, but only after a long period during which England were ahead, having scored a magnificent goal about five minutes into the game – an uncomfortable period for me.

In 1968, I left Hill Samuel to join a mini-merchant bank, J.H. Vavasseur. Getting the job involved a long series of interviews and so on. I wanted the job very badly, and the money that came with it, and I found the process stressful. I think my manner during the negotiations was calm, but once the agreement had finally been reached (over the telephone), I very nearly fainted.

I held this job until 1973, when I was sacked for my striking lack of success in managing an investment trust. I then applied for a job with a very thrusting company – well known for being aggressive and highly successful, thus far at least – called First National Finance Corporation (FNFC), run by a dynamic figure, Pat Matthews.

It seems odd that, having failed at Vavasseur, I then got a much higher salary – around £15,000, which was a lot at the time. On top of that, I was told that if I got the job, I would be lent £50,000 to invest on my own behalf. By this time, I had learned to be more pushy than I had been earlier, so I asked for a higher salary. Matthews refused, but when I asked whether he would lend me £75,000 rather than £50,000, he said, 'No problem.'

I was practically penniless, yet I had just been promised an enormous sum of money by a man who had no reason to think I could repay it if my investments did not pay off. In spite of my previous lack of success, I was confident that I would be able to turn it into a fortune – perhaps one day I shall finally realise that I am no good at picking shares!

Before I joined, Pat Matthews had signed an agreement with Hambros Bank to borrow £50 million (close to £1 billion now), intended to be used for a direct investment (i.e., buying a specific business). Until they found a company to buy, I was to use this loan to invest on behalf of FNFC.

But when I had been there just under three months, the so-called Secondary Banking Crisis struck. First National was all very well in good times, but ultimately it was a ropy business. Hambros got cold feet and gave Matthews to understand that although the deal had been signed, he should not try to touch the money.

One of the first things that Matthews did was to tell me, 'I'm afraid it doesn't look as if there's going to be a job for you to do.'

'Well, that's very unfair,' I replied.

'Don't worry,' he told me, 'I'm sure you'll get another job very soon.' With that he walked on.

I went home and looked at my contract. I found that I would get nothing if I were to be turfed out in less than three months, but if I lasted for three months, I was entitled to three months' tax-free pay. My conversation with Pat Matthews had taken place on a Thursday. I realised that if I survived the Friday and came into work on the following Monday, I would have crossed the magic three-month threshold.

Nowadays I would have enough sense to avoid the office entirely on the Friday, but, innocent as I was in those days, I went in, spending the whole day hoping desperately that Matthews would not notice me. He did not, and so, when I was made redundant on the Monday, I asked for my severance cheque. I had it specially cleared, because the secondary banks were all in danger of going bust. FNFC did (just) manage to survive, but my time as a banker was over.

I had no income, with the exception of a sinecure at Rothschilds (a sort-of job which did not really involve me doing anything at all) very kindly arranged for me by Rodney Leach. So, in order to keep myself afloat while I looked for a job, I turned to something that up until that point had only been a pastime: bridge.

The obvious bridge club for me to join when I came to London was Crockford's. Being a member at Crockford's gave me the chance to play with the top bridge players in England, some of whom were world class.

Two of the most notable, or notorious (depending on your perspective) figures I encountered were Terence Reese and Boris Schapiro, who in 1965 would both be convicted of cheating at the bridge world championships in Buenos Aires.

Schapiro, born in Latvia, was a swashbuckling character and thought he was incredibly funny. He made a habit of propositioning women on a regular basis. 'Fancy a spot of adultery?' he would ask them.

He was highly conceited. I remember going to a drinks party some years before the scandal in Argentina. Everyone there was playing canasta – there was a sort of craze for it at the time, though I never got on with it. Schapiro was boasting about how he and Reese, as well as being the best bridge partnership in the world, were probably the best canasta partnership, too.

He also had a terrible temper. On one occasion at Crockford's, when I was his partner, I made some error. Schapiro took up the cards that had already been played and plucked one out to show me how stupid I had been. Shy as I was, I was stung into action. I shouted back at him, 'You're impossible to play with, absolutely impossible, and that's why you do so badly.'

Schapiro, who was now puzzled as well as angry, said, 'Me, do badly? I don't do so badly,' but that was the last time he ever lost his temper with me.

Reese, by contrast, was the quiet, intense type. He had got a double first in classics at Oxford, and was extremely intelligent. He was an even better bridge player than Schapiro, perhaps even the best in the world.

There are, as I see it, two types of expert bridge player. One has an instinct and is able to pick up inferences and work out, from the manner in which his opponent plays, where the cards are. Schapiro was this sort of player.

Reese was the opposite. He was totally analytical, and worked everything out. He was also a brilliant writer about bridge, perhaps the best ever, able to get points over in an acerbic, witty and lucid way.

Reese, though generally far less expressive than Schapiro,

could be equally fierce. I played with him once in my mid-twenties, some years before the 1965 cheating scandal. I was already quite nervous as the partner of a man whose play I respected so greatly when, in the course of playing a hand, I made a mistake. Reese hissed, under his breath, but quite audibly, 'How can a man be such a *cunt* and live.'

For me it was like being reprimanded by God, and I lapsed into a stunned silence. I would eventually get to know Reese quite well, and we used to play backgammon with each other.

People who see bridge as a sleepy activity for retirees in the Home Counties may not realise how worked-up players can get. It amuses me to see a player fly into a tremendous rage at the bridge table, when nothing that has happened, of course, is of the remotest importance compared to real life. It is such an absorbing game that, while one is playing, it is as if the outside world does not exist. One thing to bear in mind: arguments between married couples arising from bridge disputes have led to at least five murders.

I remained a member of Crockford's for five years, but in 1963 I joined the Portland Club. It was prestigious, and, while the standard was lower than at Crockford's, the stakes were higher, so that my chances of winning, and winning well, were much greater. I did not, however, get elected the first time I was put up.

My proposer was Harry d'Avigdor-Goldsmid. The club's chairman, Quinnie Hoare, who was also the chairman of Hoare's bank, asked Harry, 'Has he a regular source of income and can he, without undue distress, write a cheque for £1,000?' The answers were, in both cases, No. I had to wait and try again later.

There was an understanding at the Portland that 'professionals' were not to become members. People wanted to come in, drink a lot, play pretty badly and either win or lose at high stakes. There was also, as there is now, a lack of younger players. So when I finally got in, at the age of twenty-eight, I was put straight onto the club's committee. Soon afterwards a candidate was proposed for election. One of the committee suggested that he was a pro, which led to a discussion about what exactly it meant to be a professional.

Another committee member hit the nail on the head: 'I don't mind paying for a man's racehorses,' he said, 'but I don't want to pay for his rent.' The point is that if the expert in question is rich, or has some source of income to support him, then it does not matter to him if he wins or loses. What we objected to was people coming to the club who needed to win to stay afloat, because it is no fun playing against a desperate opponent. If you know that the person across the table from you will have to take his children out of school if the cards do not go his way, then you cannot really enjoy either winning or losing and it would be a mistake to elect him.

After I lost my job at FNFC, I became very close to being that kind of undesirable element myself: though certainly no expert,[11] I was relying on my winnings to keep going from one week to the next. I do not think that any of the Portland's members knew quite how precarious my finances were. It was only when a small newspaper piece came out about me, saying that I was surviving on what I could win at the club, that Philip Colville, who was quite a successful player, approached me shortly after and told me that he had been amazed to read it. This worried me. Were other members likely also to be amazed or worse? I need not have worried. It seems he was the only one to have noticed the article.

---

11 I am often asked whether luck or skill plays the greater part in bridge – a difficult question. In a given evening at my bridge club, the cards will have a greater impact on my fortunes than anything else. But over the course of a year it will be my skill, or lack of it, that will determine the outcome. Luck is likely to even out roughly over a year, but my skill, or the lack of it, will not.

Left: My sister Susan and me, probably aged one and two, in 1937.

Below: Me in 1938 in Connemara, in Southern Ireland, aged three, rowing the boat which took us across the lake on which the house we spent our holidays stood. My adoptive mother sold it during the war after the death of my adoptive father.

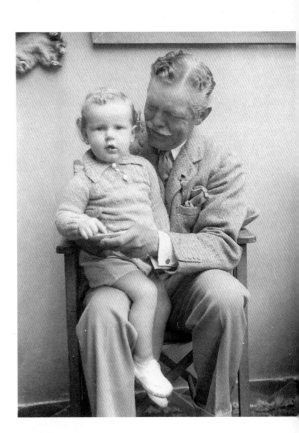

Right: My adoptive father, Alexander Hamilton Wheeler, 'Alec', with me on his knee in 1936.

Left: My adoptive mother, Betty Lydia Wheeler.

Left: Me in 1953, when I was Captain of the Oppidans at Eton. I automatically became a member of the Eton Society ('POP') and was thus entitled to wear a fancy waistcoat.

Below: The Loders Club was a drinking and dining society at Christ Church, Oxford. This photograph from 1958 shows; *standing* – Adrian Berry, me, Bryan Stevens, Edward Cazalet, Robin Furneaux, John Semple. *Seated* – Nikita Lobanoff, David Winn, Jacob Rothschild, Constantine Mano, Paul Channon.

Right: Robin Furneaux, my greatest friend until his untimely death in 1985.

Below: My university friend Edward Cazalet, on 'Nameless Hero', being led into the Winner's Enclosure in 1957. We became close at Oxford, where he and I had fun, and made a lot of money, betting on horses together when we should have been working.

Above: Me at an event in a West End Club in 1973, a couple of places away from the infamous Lord Lucan. I was with him two nights before his disappearance. [Trevor Humphries/Shutterstock].

Left: Jimmy Goldsmith, supreme entrepreneur, fearless gambler and prolific lover. He certainly made an impression on you when you met him. [Associated Newspapers/Shutterstock].

Above: Me in 1987 in Binion's Horseshoe Club, in downtown Las Vegas, playing in the World Series of Poker.

Below: Cramped, tense, but very exciting. Another scene from the 1987 World Series of Poker.

Above: An image of me, captioned 'Wheeler Dealer' used on the front page of the *Mail on Sunday* in November 2008. Gambling is not always this glamorous.

Above: My wife Tessa, a talented photographer, a few years before I met her.

CHAPTER 7

ELEVEN HUNDRED TO A THOUSAND, STUART?

There was a point in my life, while I was at Oxford, when I was far more earnest than I am now, and far more worried about sin and morality and so forth. I was a Christian then, or at least I still believed I should be more of one. It was this that led me, on a number of separate occasions to seek out clergymen whom I hoped might reassure me on one point. The issue that was bothering me was this: I was trying to win money from other people, without giving them anything in return. Was this not rather un-Christian?

They did not answer the question I had asked. Instead they tried to talk to me about what they saw as a far more important subject: the impact that a person's addiction to gambling could have on a family. This was all very well, but it was not the problem I had gone to them with, nor was it something I was thinking about at that time. So I went away without an answer.

Over time my anxieties about the rights and wrongs of gambling gradually dissolved. This was just as well. I moved to London at a time when it absolutely teemed with opportunities for making, or losing, lots of money at the tables.

In the late fifties, John Aspinall, one of the most infamous, flamboyant figures in the history of British gambling, was running high-stakes *chemin de fer* (or 'chemmy') games in private houses. These games had a rather ambiguous legal status, and John Aspinall, clever and enterprising, exploited it. The 'house' took a substantial rake, and the size of the bets was usually large, so that he was making a lot of money. In 1958, the police raided one of these games. They arrested Aspinall and a number of his 'customers', including his outraged mother, Lady Osborne, (always known in these circles as 'Lady O').

In the trial that followed, Aspinall's legal team, led by the celebrated Gilbert Beyfus, QC, somehow found out the details of the brief that had been given to the prosecution, including all of the relevant papers. This gave them a significant advantage, especially when cross-examining prosecution witnesses. Aspinall and his associates were duly acquitted. This led to a free-for-all in the gambling world – it became clear that nobody was going to be prosecuted.

Once this precedent was set, it was inevitable that an attempt would be made to legitimise and regulate some forms of gambling. The Betting and Gaming Act of 1960, which, among other things, effectively legalised casino games, changed everything. Previously, if you had wanted to play games such as blackjack or chemmy, you were forced to do so in semi-legal gambling clubs set up by some dubious characters. They were run with quite a lot of razzle-dazzle, but there was always the nasty possibility – especially for someone like me, who was starting a career as a barrister – that your game might be broken up by a police raid.

The new legalisation included a certain amount of regulation – designed for the most part to protect gamblers from themselves – but one important rule required casinos to allow their punters to take the bank if they wished. This opened up all sorts of new opportunities, including at Crockford's, which had previously been simply a high-quality bridge club, but was now able to operate as a casino.

And so in the early morning of New Year's Eve 1961, along with a couple of other friends, I took the bank for five spins of the wheel at a very crowded roulette table. It felt exciting and very glamorous to do so – I remember one girl in particular, who gazed at me in a most admiring way as I handled the impressive sums of cash involved. But I lost more money in two or three hours than my annual salary.

There were two things that helped to land me in this sticky situation. The first was that because it was not in the interests of the club for people to take the bank – the edge that a casino normally had was now working on behalf of one of the customers – some croupiers paid out a number of losing bets as if they had been winners. I caught one of them in the act, but I rather fear I did not catch them all.

The second was that Jacob Rothschild guaranteed to the casino that our losses would be paid. This happened late on in the evening, after he had already returned home and we had found ourselves in the middle of a bad losing streak. He was roused from his bed by a phone call from the club, who wanted to know how much he was willing to back me for. 'Unlimited,' he replied, and condemned us, as it turned out, to still greater losses.

We made some of the money back on subsequent evenings at the same venue. I also chipped away at the debt by winning small sums like £30 in games of bridge at the St James's Club, where the standard of play was abysmal. I was only half-heartedly pursuing my career as a barrister by this stage, and so I had time to devote to getting my bank balance looking a bit more respectable.

There were, however, times when we enjoyed more success taking the bank at Crockford's. I remember a particular spin of the wheel. The entire table was covered with an absolute flood of chips. There was only one number that nobody had bet on, and, after the ball had jumped round the wheel for what seemed like an agonisingly long period of time, the ball landed on it.

There was also at least one occasion when I took the bank at blackjack – playing alone rather than in partnership with others. Because the croupiers did not do the dealing for me, I had to be the dealer myself. There were quite a number of people playing and not only did they all seem to be putting on large bets, but they all seemed to have very promising totals like 19 or 20, whereas I, the bank, had a total of 13. I then dealt my card, which was a miraculous 8, giving me 21. I won everything. One of the players said to me in a highly sarcastic way, 'Well done!' He quite plainly, and completely wrongly, thought that I had somehow found a way of cheating.

Before long, I began to go to some of London's other new casinos, including the Clermont. Aspinall had set it up as soon as the laws changed. It was a beautiful place (as were the women who got taken there, if not the men who took them).

Aspinall – Aspers to his friends – named the club after Lord Clermont, an infamous gambler who had once owned the club's premises at 44 Berkeley Square. There was a raffish sort of atmosphere, and it was home to some attitudes that even then had probably disappeared from society elsewhere; for instance, the very old-fashioned opinion that you could take as long as you wanted to pay bills to tradesmen like tailors or wine merchants, but gambling debts had to be settled immediately.

John Aspinall and his business partner James Osborne, (the man who described himself to David Cameron as the skeleton in the closet of his nephew, the former chancellor George Osborne – 'the dreaded casino operator!'), had a real talent for getting on with the rich and powerful; so one felt quite privileged to be there, even if one was downstairs playing backgammon away from the actual casino. John Aspinall was very amusing, and surrounded himself with fascinating people, and it was nice to *feel* as if one was a friend of his; even though I do not think I was, not really.

Exclusive as the Clermont was thought to be, it was not too difficult to get into if you could persuade those who ran the club that you were likely to have enough money to lose a bit, or were interesting enough to help boost the club's atmosphere: Aspinall wanted a certain type to be seen to be active there, in order to attract the rich Arab gamblers who really underpinned the business.

I fell somewhere between the two. I had just enough money to lose to the club to make it worth allowing me in, and although I was not one of the wittiest or most amusing characters there, I was entertaining enough to make it worth having me around. So I joined that lucky group of people who were allowed to play backgammon downstairs, away from the casino games, without being charged. Drinking and chatting in an attractive setting made the whole thing very agreeable.

There were lots of gamblers making jokes, which seemed amusing at the time. People like Joe Dwek, a friend of Aspinall's, and sometime European backgammon champion, and another expert backgammon player, the American Gino Scalamandre. They would joke about the gamblers around them, as they played. I remember once Gino, who was watching television, called over, 'Joe, you'll love this, there's a guy hitting a cripple.' It was nonsense: we all knew Joe would not enjoy seeing a man hit a cripple. But, while not everyone would find that incident funny, all this sort of joking helped to get the atmosphere right.

You were always likely to run into famous people at the Clermont, but the way that celebrities played at the table did not always match their public personas.

Ian Fleming was a good example. James Bond may have been

the hard-living daredevil type, but Ian was an extremely cautious bridge player.

Omar Sharif, the famous film star, who was well known both for being very generous, and for being very nice to other players, was a bridge obsessive. On at least one occasion, however, he was certainly the (unwitting) beneficiary of a conspiracy to ensure he won a bridge competition.

The Ladbroke Club, another gambling establishment, decided to have a bridge competition between thirteen world-ranking experts and seven amateurs. I was one of the seven. It was an individual competition, and one played five hands as partner of each of the others in turn. One of the other contestants was Omar Sharif, and so I played five hands as his partner. He was perfectly nice, charming really. Unfortunately, I made a mistake in the play of a hand, and it cost a vital trick. He was obviously disappointed, and did (as he was perfectly entitled to) ask me why I had done what I had done.

Later that evening, I played against him with a French international as my partner. The Frenchman needed to make ten tricks, which was extremely easy on the hand, but he only made nine. He turned to me afterwards and said, 'I'm so sorry, Stuart, I miscounted the trumps.' International players do not miscount trumps, it simply does not happen. So there is no doubt in my mind that he failed on purpose in order to allow Sharif to do well.

There had been a lot of betting and speculation about the results of the competition, and evidently it suited a lot of the people for Sharif to win, which he did end up doing; but I am not saying for a second that Sharif was involved, or knew anything about what was going on.

The financier Jim Slater was another interesting character. He used to say that when you are starting out you need money to pay for the things you want in life, but after a while it is just a means of keeping the score, a way of seeing how well you are doing compared to others. Jim knew this as well as anybody else himself, having been both one of the most successful (and notorious) figures in British finance, and also a 'minus millionaire'.

I first met him a little after he had 'escaped' from Singapore, where he had done something that, if not exactly illegal, was certainly highly dubious. His business partner had been arrested, charged, and convicted, and sent to prison. The Singapore authorities wanted to get their hands on Slater, too. But as he was already in England at the time, they had to bring an action to get him extradited to Singapore. The Singapore authorities briefed Derry Irvine (who was not yet a QC: he was assisted by Tony Blair and Cherie Booth, who was to become Blair's wife). The extradition proceedings took place in January 1977. Slater won, thus allowing him to avoid a trial in Singapore.

He kept his freedom, but at around the same time he lost all his money. He had convinced himself that because the supply of land was limited, its value could only go up, and so he rashly announced that he was going to carry on buying it until it reached the sea. He borrowed a lot and when the property crash arrived, he came badly unstuck.

He was not so badly unstuck, though, that banks stopped lending him money. They extended him credit, and in due course Slater paid everything back, with interest. (Banks are often foolish; in this case their decision to support Slater when he was on his uppers paid off handsomely.) It does seem that those who go bankrupt owing very large sums often remain close enough to the sources of money, and to the men who control it, to recover.

When I had just started out at IG Index, I took a client for lunch at Scott's restaurant in Mount Street. He was a highly important client, which is why I was willing to draw on our not-at-all-large reserves to take him somewhere so expensive. And yet there, sitting in the restaurant, as if they had not a care in the world, were two men whom I knew to be bankrupts or nearly so:

William Stern, the one-time property tycoon, and my one-time boss Pat Matthews, of FNFC.

In an unhappy contrast, the business of an extremely nice local printer very sadly went bust fifteen or so years later. There was nobody around to save him, or even to take him for a meal at Scott's.

I am certainly not a person who feels compelled to make big bets to show other people what a hell of a guy I am. But Slater was a great friend of both Jimmy Goldsmith and Selim Zilkha (founder of Mothercare and one time chairman of the Portland Club), men who loved to play for high stakes, and he tried to keep up with them. Once I said to Slater, who was not at all a good bridge player, 'Jim, you don't need to play so high to be acceptable.' Eventually he did learn to play for lower stakes, though I do not think he ever lost his taste for a flutter. He was once told by a fortune-teller to avoid games of chance, so he immediately challenged her to double or quits on her ten-shilling fee, and won.

I used to run into Jimmy Goldsmith at Aspinall's, which is what the Clermont Club became after it had moved to Curzon Street. He was a tremendously wealthy, incredibly successful businessman, a true tycoon, who had an appetite for risk that I have never seen in anybody else. People used to say that he would not be interested in a deal unless it had the potential to break him if it went wrong. (His energy was not confined to his business dealings; he was also absolutely mad about women and had to have sex all the time.)

He was known to be ruthless and a bad person to have as an enemy – he is said to have hired people to go through the bins of his business rivals – but he could be charm personified to his friends. I liked being in his company, and he in turn admired my own willingness to take risks.

We had a strange deal between us. When he saw me, Jimmy

would greet me by saying, 'Eleven hundred to a thousand, Stuart?' He would then toss a coin, and I would call heads or tails. If I got it wrong, I would pay him £1,000 – close to £20,000 in today's money – if I got it right, he would pay me £1,100. It suited me because the odds were in my favour; it suited him because he knew that I did not have much money and he liked to see me scrabbling around on the floor to see whether I had won or lost.

One day in 1978, I took a girl out on our first date. We went to Aspinalls. The only people in the restaurant were John Aspinall and Jimmy Goldsmith, having dinner together, and two Iranians, one of whom I knew.

'Eleven hundred to a thousand, Stuart?' Jimmy called over to me.

'Okay, Jimmy.'

The coin flipped up into the air. I called. I lost.

Inevitably Jimmy followed up by asking, 'Double or quits, Stuart?'

'No, not that, Jimmy, eleven hundred to a thousand again.' (Double or quits would have meant an even money bet, not 11 to 10.) He agreed.

I lost once more.

'Again, Stuart?'

'No, Jimmy.' By now I was more or less ruined, but at least I had the presence of mind to tell John that he must put me on his club's free lunch list.

The girl I was with, who was already mystified by what she had just witnessed, was even more mystified when one of the Iranians came over to us and said, 'Don't worry, Stuart, you won a hundred pounds really.' This was a very short-hand way of making the point that if one carried on ad infinitum making the bets I had just made with Jimmy, I *would* have come out roughly a hundred pounds up on average for every couple of such bets.

Baffled the girl may have been, but perhaps she was a little impressed as well because, in spite of my apparent idiocy, and the fact that the bet had cost me a small fortune,[12] she became my wife a year later, by far the luckiest thing that ever happened to me.

The most infamous (in the end) of all of the characters I used to run into at the Clermont was Lord Lucan. I knew him quite well, as I played bridge with him at the Portland Club, and gambled with him at the Clermont. It was beating him in the final round of the Clermont poker competition that gave me the £8,000 I needed to pay the deposit on my first house.

His great tragedy was that he had made a hopeless and very sad marriage; there was nothing in it for either him or his wife, Veronica. By the time I knew him, Lucan had given up a career in banking, which he found indescribably boring, though he was said to be quite good at it, and was spending all his time gambling, which was far more congenial to him, if not more profitable. (One night, playing *chemin de fer*, a game that requires no skill, he had made a huge amount of money, enough to convince him, absurdly, that he had what it took to become a top-class professional gambler. One cannot be a professional chemmy player. One is bound to lose in the long term.)

He would spend every afternoon in the Clermont, and soon lost whatever fortune he may have had. He was, however, a friend of John Aspinall, and John allowed him to stay on at the Clermont as a house player, which meant that the casino took all, or almost all, of his winnings and losses. People may not have known he was a house player, but Lucan, who was good-looking, and an earl, and who knew how to behave himself at the table, provided exactly the kind of casual, aristocratic atmosphere that was so

---

12 I think altogether Jimmy and I had this bet eight times, with me winning three times and losing five times. The five losing occasions cost me £5,000, and the three winning occasions made me £3,300, making me overall a loser by £1,700. But over time, I won quite a lot more than that from Jimmy by beating him at bridge.

central to Aspinall's appeal. In return, Lucan was given free meals and, I imagine, a certain amount of money.

It is possible that he felt humiliated by this role – I know I would have been, but then he was a difficult man to read.

I was at the Portland Club with Lucan three days before the terrible events of 7 November 1974 (when his children's nanny, Sandra Rivett, was murdered in the dark at his house in Belgravia by someone who thought she was Lady Lucan, and Lucan went on the run). I was playing backgammon and Lucan was sitting behind me, occasionally throwing good-humoured advice in my direction, and doing a very good impression of a man with a completely untroubled mind.

He had an extremely good poker face. He was famous for never showing emotion when gambling, whether he won or lost, which is all the more impressive considering that we know now that he really was in a terrible financial situation.

I think it just possible that Lucan is alive – I would not lay 100 to 1 against it – but highly unlikely. I knew Michael Stoop, whose car he borrowed that evening, very well. Michael received two letters from Lucan, both written after the nanny was killed. Although I do not know what was in those letters, I know that Michael was completely convinced that Lucan was dead and so I tend to take this view too.

Michael's opinion was that Lucan probably got on a cross-Channel steamer and threw himself into the water and drowned: he thought the reason the body was never found was that the propellers cut it up.

One sometimes saw deplorable things at the Clermont. There was a night when a rich punter, drunk and losing thousands at *chemin de fer*, vomited copiously onto the table. An earl, whom I shall not name, gestured to one of the attendants, and said, 'Take him away, clean him up and bring him back.'

On another occasion, a major backgammon competition was being played in the club. One room was set aside for people to play their matches. At the time when play was due to start, a very rich, keen gambler called Nomikos, arrived. He was an ageing backgammon enthusiast, but no great player. He almost always lost, and when he did so he would say, 'You have to subtract ten per cent from what I owe you and give it to my charity.' There was always a considerable clamour to be able to play against him.

That night he was escorted into the room where the backgammon boards were by a group who wanted to take his money off him. The sharks were so anxious to have the mug all to themselves, that they locked the doors so that none of the players in the competition could get in to play their matches.

Dishonesty in the big backgammon competitions was fairly widespread. Players were put up for auction ahead of the tournament. If you bought the player who won the competition, you would receive a good percentage of the auction pool: so the better the player, the more people were willing to pay for him. Players often bought a percentage of themselves from the person who had bought them. It was common for thousands of pounds to be invested on one player. Perhaps it was not surprising, with so much money at stake, that some people succumbed to temptation.

In one competition in which I played, I was drawn in the first round against somebody I knew quite well. He made it very clear to me that if I gave him a certain sum of money, he would be prepared to throw the game. I was by no means a brilliant backgammon player, but I was better than he was. So I would not have been tempted to take the bribe, even if I had had no moral scruples, and indeed I did beat him.

There was so much dishonesty that eventually these competitions, which were otherwise highly enjoyable, came to an end.

It has been alleged that the dishonesty was not confined to the players; that Aspinall himself was running a crooked game of chemmy. I cannot know whether that was true. Certainly, he operated a ruthless policy of extending large lines of credit to foolish young men who liked to gamble. The point was that if the young men were not able to pay their debts to him, their rather grand parents would step in and pay up.

For instance, in order to save tax, Henry Vyner had been made by his parents the owner of a family estate. The very large estate in North Yorkshire included Fountains Abbey and Studley Royal, and had been in his family since the thirteenth century. Vyner then lost so much money at Aspinalls that he had to sell the estate (which his parents later bought back). There was nothing illegal about any of this, but it was a rough way to run a business and Aspers had no compunction about it.

Over time, more allegations have been made about the Clermont Club and the way it was run. There are some quite persuasive accounts alleging that the eternally spendthrift Aspinall (who did after all own a zoo stocked with all manner of exotic animals) entered into a gambling con called 'The Big Edge' with the gangster Billy Hill. A combination of employing card sharps, and subtly bending the cards so that those in the know had an edge, is said to have enabled the club to swindle its members out of very large sums, perhaps even millions.

I am not in a position to know the truth about all this, but even if the allegations are true, I am confident that, apart from Aspinall himself, no one in senior management knew anything about it. No one was ever charged. It is rather an irony that the one time that the authorities really had tried to bring Aspinall to book they had helped, unwittingly, to legalise casino gambling.

For better or for worse, those days are well and truly gone.

CHAPTER 8

OH GOD, IT'S THE CAR I WAS BEING RUDE TO EARLIER

When I was seventeen, I took my driving test. I failed the first time because I very nearly had an accident. I took it again some time later. This time I did have an accident That prevented me from failing! I hit a car head-on midway through the test. The other car was moving, and that was important, because if you hit a moving car during your test, the examiner cannot fail you; he would be prejudging something that might be going to come before the courts. Furthermore, under these circumstances, you do not have to wait the normal period before you can take the test again. Four days later, I took it again and passed. It was only after this had been confirmed that I told the examiner what had happened earlier. He was irritated, but could not withdraw the pass.

Ever since, I have given the same advice to people who are about to take their driving test: if you think it is not going well, hit another car, but do make sure it is moving.

In the years since I passed my test, I have got myself into a few scrapes behind the wheel. My car is now an absolute tapestry of dents and scratches. I get them by hitting walls, which often seem to come out of nowhere quite carelessly and hit me. I am not a good parker.

One evening, there was a dinner at the Portland for which we had all to wear dinner jackets, and I became so drunk that I realised it would be financial suicide to carry on playing. So I drove home.

For some reason I had borrowed my wife's car that day. As I was driving over Chelsea Bridge, I heard the wail of police sirens behind me, and stopped. The policeman came up to me and asked, 'Have you been drinking, sir?' I said, 'No, well, at any rate not too many I hope, officer.'

Very politely he asked me to get out of the car. Because it was Tessa's vehicle, I could not work out how to do this, so it felt as if things were going really badly. But when I did manage to extricate myself, he simply told me, 'Right, sir, I'd be a bit more careful in the future if I were you.' I think that something much more urgent had come over their radio, which was very lucky for me.

That was not the only time I had a brush with the law as a result of my driving. There was another occasion when I was driving around Hyde Park Corner and I got really irritated with another car. I flashed my lights and peeped my horn and thought the incident was over. A few minutes later, I realised that a car behind was flashing its lights at me. Oh God, I thought, it's the car I was being rude to earlier. There's going to be a row.

So I accelerated and went in and out of various roads to try to lose it. But it stayed on my tail. Finally, it caught up with me and forced me to stop. The good news was that the driver did not have road rage. The bad news was that he was a policeman.

The policeman said I had to take a breath test. 'Well, okay,' I said, 'I'm not very good at blowing into these tubes, but I'll do my best.' I blew into his machine: no good. 'You haven't given a proper specimen,' he told me. So I said, 'I'll try again, shall I?'

And he replied, 'No, we're arresting you.' I certainly was a bit drunk. Things looked bad.

I was driven off to the police station, and had to leave my car behind. The police told me that I had the right to make one telephone call, and I rang Tessa, who, I suspect, had mixed feelings. On the one hand, she felt that it was probably about time that I was done for my terrible driving. On the other hand, it would have been a real nuisance if I ended up getting banned.

This happened not long after the Guildford Four, or it may have been the Birmingham Six, had been cleared. So the police, who had been heavily criticised about the way they had handled that case, were being meticulously careful in how they handled me. They explained what my rights were in great detail and then told me that they would perform two tests, and the more favourable of the two to me would be used. I passed the first, so I said to them that there was not much point in having the other one. They did not agree, so I took the second test, but I was not told the result of that one. I was then driven rather sulkily back to my car. I am not proud of having driven while drunk. A stupid, dangerous thing to do. I am delighted that today's younger generation disapprove of drink-driving, and do not usually do it.

About five or six years ago, I had a head-on collision with a police car, while completely sober. It was at six or seven one evening at a roundabout with five entrances. I went across, and straight into a car, which I realised only after we had all clambered out was being driven by the police. For what it is worth, I really do think it was their fault on this occasion, and my opinion is bolstered by the fact that a bystander, who had seen what had happened, very kindly came up to me and said that he would be willing to give evidence on my behalf.

Policemen are not allowed to investigate incidents in which they themselves are involved, so we had to wait for another group of cops to come to interview me. I had to wait for ages, because the police who were on their way to my incident met another police car that had been involved in an accident, and had to investigate that one first.

They asked me if I had been drinking. I told them that I had had one glass of wine at lunch, but that I was sure that I was all right by now. They insisted on checking anyway, and everything was fine. I did not pursue them for the damage to my car. It seemed unwise to push my luck. It is not unknown for the police to stick together.

One thing you can definitely say for me is that I do not suffer from road rage. If, however, someone in their car hoots at me like mad while I am driving, or simply crossing the road, I have been known to make a quick calculation as to how likely I think they are to get out and whack me; then, if I feel safe, I will stick out my tongue at him.

I am not one to pick a fight with someone who might actually hit me over the head – it is similar to those situations when you see two dogs who find themselves on opposite sides of a piece of glass and feel safe to bark at each other with tremendous ferocity, since they know there is no chance they will actually come to blows. I have probably done this half a dozen, maybe even ten times, which I am aware is half a dozen more times than most other men of my age.

Many years ago, when I was running IG Index, I took out for three very expensive lunches a man who was in charge of deciding whether we would be allowed entry into one of the regulatory bodies of which we needed to be a member. At around the same time, I had an irritating encounter with another car, and stuck my tongue out at the driver. It was only a little while later that I realised he looked very much like the regulator whom I had been taking such pains to butter up.

CHAPTER 9

WE DON'T CARE FOR THAT TYPE OF PLAY HERE

imagine that the population of the world could be divided into two parts: those who love Las Vegas and those who hate it. Two thirds of the world would hate it and one third would love it; I doubt that anyone would be neutral. I am firmly among the one third who love it, though I would not like to live there.

I love the opportunity to play blackjack, twenty-four hours a day. Blackjack is the casino name for what, among friends, is known as *vingt-et-un* or pontoon but some of the rules are different. I love the wonderful shows in Vegas: the expertise of any person performing there is unsurpassable. (Though the girls who perform amazing acrobatic feats are far from generously paid, they are so proud to be performing that there is great competition to be selected.)

I also love the fact that there are, for those who can afford to go to them, a number of absolutely top-class restaurants. Most of all I love the uninhibited assumption that it is fine to spend all day or night having a marvellous time, and that is what everyone is there to do.

The best time to arrive in Las Vegas is after dark. Your senses will already be on the alert after a flight that crosses desert mountains, often the Grand Canyon too, and then, suddenly, you see the most incredible amount of light that you can imagine. Downtown is just one mass of luminescence and, stretching out for three or four miles is the Strip, a road flanked on either side by colossal casino-hotels, each one more dazzling than the last.

Day and night make little difference in this twenty-four-hour culture and it is hard to adjust oneself, during the first couple of days, to the nature of your new existence. Time becomes irrelevant: one tends not to notice as the minutes and hours slip by; casinos rarely contain clocks lest they remind a player that he ought to be leaving.

There is a uniformity about the atmosphere in the casinos. They all have air-conditioning that ensures cool air billows through the vast rooms, in striking contrast to the ferocious heat that attacks you the moment you step outside. If there is a difference, it tends not to be the result of the décor or type of clientele, but rather in the number of people: whereas many casinos are successful and are full of punters, others are depressingly empty, so that you wonder whether they will go broke before their customers do. Often they do.

There is what seems to be a never-ending stream of visitors to Las Vegas: newcomers and veterans; families stopping by for the hell of it, and gamblers who cannot help themselves; loud-voiced, garish-shirted chancers and those, like me, who believe they have a winning system.

The air of unreality is exacerbated by the fact that the insides of the casinos are invariably loud, garish and confusing. The first thing you notice is the countless number of people playing on slot machines (believe it or not, these, to me, unbelievably boring devices are the largest source of profit for the casinos). It seems impossible that there can be so many machines in one place.

The constant noise of the slot machines as they pay out winners with a jingle of coins, and the unearthly light they emit, can feel overwhelming – even more so when you witness the zombie-like behaviour of the players. They play hour after hour, as if in a trance. All they seem to be doing is putting money in, and pulling or pressing a lever, all the time hoping that they get something like three sevens in a row that will pay them out some change, or possibly some far more unlikely combination that will pay them millions.

You will hear the yells of triumph and despair coming from the craps tables well before you see the clamouring crowd that surrounds each table. The players all watch hungrily as the dice are thrown, and shout for the numbers they hope will come up.

The roulette tables are a little more orderly, but even they possess their own air of contained chaos. You see people eagerly making bets on any of the thirty-eight numbers, or on combinations of the numbers, and then the dealer[13] starts to spin the wheel saying, 'No more bets' – in France, the expression is *rien ne va plus* – but in fact allowing people to put bets on hurriedly until the ball tumbles into what will be the winning number.

The casinos always seem to throw up little scenes that you know will not be repeated in any other kind of venue. It is fun, for instance, to watch how, when someone is winning heavily, he swiftly becomes surrounded by gun-wielding security guards charged with keeping everyone else away from the pile of $500 and $1000 chips on the table.

Las Vegas is lots of things, but what it definitely is not, is consistent. For instance, while prostitution is legal in the state of Nevada, it is not so in 'Sin City', otherwise the home of so much crudeness and excess. And heaven help the underage drinker. Some years ago, I was having dinner with Charlotte, my youngest

---

13 They do not use the word 'croupier' in Vegas.

daughter, then aged twenty years and six months. I ordered wine for the two of us. 'How old is that lady?' asked our waitress. I am not a habitual liar, but I said, 'Twenty-one.' 'ID please,' the waitress said, implacably. Charlotte got no wine.

There are, of course, elements that are unsavoury, or cruel. Although they are no longer as dominant as they once were, the Mafia does still have a considerable influence. One would not be wise, for example, to try to knuckle in on the laundry business in the casino hotels. And if you were there for a computer industry conference, you would be ill advised to try to stop the people whose job it is to move the computers from where they are dropped off to where they will be on show in the hotel. When a friend who attended said that his own staff could easily transport their computers without assistance, he was advised that if they did that, they might suffer an accident.

So although I do love it, I know that it is a ruthless place, and there is little or no sympathy for those who get themselves into any kind of difficulty. The city's lack of sentiment is well illustrated by the following. There was a casino known as Wilbur Clark's Desert Inn, and I happened to be in the city when Wilbur Clark died. The casino wondered how to mark this sad event. The answer? They stopped all gambling ... for two minutes. It is also said that in the main hospital in Las Vegas, staff make bets about how long their patients will live. This would be a bet too far for me.

My first visit to the city took place in 1964. I had been travelling to America on business for some time, when Robin Furneaux came back from a trip with exciting news. He told me that Edward O. Thorp, a professor at the Massachusetts Institute of Technology (MIT), had shown how a gambler who was prepared to learn the system, and count the cards that had gone from the pack (and could not therefore be dealt again until the pack had been shuffled), could establish an edge against the casino.

Thorp, an expert on probability theory, and also the 'father of the wearable computer', had caused great excitement when he gave a lecture to the American Mathematical Society in June 1960, entitled 'Fortune's Formula: A Winning Strategy for Blackjack'. He was somewhat unworldly and he was unprepared for the coast-to-coast sensation his talk caused, but he took up the offer made by two millionaires, out of many, to back him, and set off for Vegas to test his theory in practice.

The reaction of the casinos was as arrogant as it was predictable. 'We send limousines to collect people with systems,' they boasted.

Not for long. Thorp was so successful, and so quickly, that the casinos changed the rules to make it more difficult to win. When players responded by refusing to tip the dealers, the dealers went on strike, and the casinos were forced into an embarrassing U-turn. Soon, however, Thorp became a victim of his own success, and increasingly found himself unwelcome at the tables; he did try a number of highly unconvincing disguises to get around this, but the casinos were not deceived. Do not feel too sorry for him: he went on to make a fortune in the markets by the use of what is called stock index arbitrage.

I bought Thorp's book, *Beat the Dealer*, as quickly as I could, as well as a record he had made on the same subject. An exploratory weekend in Las Vegas, in the middle of a business trip, yielded a small profit. I knew I would be back before long.

I returned in 1965 for a two-week summer holiday with $1,500 in my pocket. My great enthusiasm was not shared by my friends, who told me that I was crazy to fly 5,000 miles with the 'ludicrous' object of using a maths professor's system to beat the casinos.

In those days you had to change planes twice, at New York and Chicago, before catching one to Las Vegas. When I stopped off at New York, I had to choose between two flights to Chicago, both leaving and arriving at the same time. I do not know what made me pick one over the other, but while the plane I took landed safely, the other came down in Lake Michigan. There were no survivors. So, both Edward Cazalet and I were lucky at different times not to be on an aeroplane which crashed, killing everyone in it.

As soon as I was settled in my motel, the Tally Ho, I made a call to Edward Thorp, to arrange an appointment with him at the University of California, to which he had moved from MIT.[14] He was kind enough to share some of his expertise with me, much of it about cheating dealers. (As he made clear in his book, the ordinary punter, like you or me, has no chance at all of detecting whether a dealer is cheating or not. The experts of the Nevada Gaming Control Board, whose whole job in life is trying to catch cheating dealers, can be watching a dealer whom they suspect of cheating, and yet, if the dealer is good enough, even they cannot tell.)

Thorp had shown how it was possible to beat the casinos at blackjack. They hated him for this, but they were utterly wrong to do so because he was, I am sure, responsible for making them hundreds of millions of dollars richer. His book encouraged a huge number of people, who might not otherwise have gone, to travel to Las Vegas and try to use his system. They spent money on rooms, food, drink and shows. Even more importantly, they lost enormous sums of money in the casinos.

The problem was that although what they had learned from the professor's book may have helped them to play a little better than they had previously, only a tiny proportion of them were

---

14 I cannot remember how I got hold of his number. I think I may have written to him c/o the publisher of his book, to ask whether I could come to see him. I imagine he was quite surprised to hear from me, but we got on well when we met and he was extremely helpful. I went on to help him because, in the second edition of his book, he had a chapter on how blackjack – which had only recently become a legal game on our side of the Atlantic – was played in England. I provided him with all the information in that chapter, other than his calculations of the percentages.

self-disciplined enough to break even, let alone make a profit.

It is not particularly hard to follow Thorp's system, but it does require effort. You cannot be drunk. You cannot be tired. You must not be trying to impress your girlfriend. You must not allow yourself to be put off by what other players do or say; they will almost always be talking nonsense. Those who do know what to do realise that it is not sensible to advertise the fact.

It helps that one of my odd characteristics is the willingness to persist in a basically boring activity for a long time, if I think there is a good reason for doing so.

The best method of counting the cards is as follows: You assign the value of 0 to the neutral cards: 7, 8 and 9. Tens, jacks, queens, kings and aces are assigned a value of -1, and 2, 3, 4, 5 and 6 are assigned a value of +1. As the cards are dealt, you keep a running total. Broadly speaking, if the total is positive, the odds have moved in your favour; if it is negative, the odds have moved in the casino's favour. Never mind why: it is what computer analysis tells you!

Most people are not methodical, and amidst the fizz and the neon and the noise, they quickly forget themselves. It was very easy, I found, to get too excited if the count required one to bet one's maximum stake. One can become so absorbed in the excitement of a hand on which one has made a large bet that one 'loses the count'.

There was a minority, of course, a very small one, who were able to execute Thorp's system successfully. It was this minority that the Mafia-run casinos were determined to stop. The Mafia are ruthless, especially when they have been cheated. Professor Thorp told me a story about a 'conjuror' who, at a private gathering to which Thorp had been invited, showed that when throwing the dice, he could roll a double six far more often than it would come up at random.

That evening, Thorp happened to be in the casino where the

'conjurer' was about to throw the dice at a craps table. So Thorp had a bet on double six, which indeed came up. Thorp sensibly stopped playing and left with his winnings. The conjuror, Thorp told me, with remarkable *sangfroid*, was later found dead in the desert.

The most common way by which in the past the casinos tried to stop you winning was to use crooked dealers; they were completely unembarrassed about this. A regular method of cheating was for a blackjack dealer to hold the pack of cards in his hand in the normal way but, at his choice, deal the top card or the second card or the bottom card, having found out one way or another – this was part of his skill – what the three cards were. Professor Thorp's book made it clear that the ordinary punter had no chance of detecting whether a dealer was cheating.

A dealer capable of cheating would be paid more than those who were not. He possessed, you see, an extra skill. After seventy years of playing cards, I have never – even had I wanted to – been able to effect the manipulations necessary, so one could take the view that they deserved the extra.

So in any given casino, only a small proportion of the dealers would be capable of cheating. The casinos needed only enough cheats on each shift to be able to handle a system player who threatened to win too much, and possibly a mug punter who had got lucky and might switch casinos before losing his winnings. Hiring more cheats would be a waste of money, and casinos do not like wasting money.

Thorp's advice for dealing with crooked dealers was never to allow yourself to lose more than five times your maximum bet in a single casino in any one session – if that happens, they may be cheating. For a different reason, you should never *win* more than five times your maximum bet in any one session, because you may attract attention to yourself and that may tempt the casino to cheat. All major casinos have holes in the ceiling through which their staff can, unseen, watch carefully what a punter is doing. The eyes in the ceiling probably miss very little. They know what they are looking for.

Another precaution recommended by Thorp was to keep a notebook in which, after every session, I could record whether I thought the dealer was honest or not. I remember that one day at the Stardust casino (closed long ago), I sat down to play against a dealer whom I had previously noted as apparently honest. To pass the time of day, I asked him what kind of form he was in.

'I don't know,' he replied, 'I've only been on for a couple of minutes.' He did not last much longer before he was removed from my table. That was significant because a dealer's shift would normally last at least twenty minutes. He was replaced by a man I did not immediately recognise. After going out to my car and making a quick check of my notebook – which showed that he was one of the dealers I had identified as being suspicious – I sat out the next few hands, until the first dealer was brought on to another table.

Almost as soon as I started playing at his new table, he was moved again. It was only after the whole farce was repeated that I realised the casino was determined I would not be allowed to win. I cashed my chips and headed off elsewhere. As I walked out of the room, I glanced back to see the friendly, honest dealer settling down, cards in hand, at the table I had first left. It was not subtle, but then it did not need to be.

A couple of days later I was playing alone – card counters like being the only player at a table, as the action is much faster – and lost two hands in a peculiar fashion. It was enough for me to decide to leave. As I got up to go, one of the pit bosses shrugged his shoulders at me and said, 'That is what is going to happen if you play alone at the table.'

It was a small incident, but when I thought about it more, and about the ghastly way that the Mafia had dealt with some of the other gamblers who had crossed them, it was enough to make me anxious. I was genuinely concerned, but sometimes I also enjoyed behaving as if I were taking on the Mafia, who might really be after me. As I drove back each evening to the Tally Ho, I would drive several hundred yards past it before turning back, scrutinising my mirror to see if any other car did the same.

I was highly disciplined in those days. To start with, I would bet a minimum of one dollar and a maximum of five dollars. It was only when I had made a reasonable profit that I would move up to 2 and 10, and then 5 and 25, and so on. By the end of my stay, my minimum had risen to $25, and my maximum to $125 – a pittance as far as the casinos were concerned, but more than enough for me.

I treated the whole process as if it were a job, sometimes playing for eight hours at a time. I did not drink until the day's gambling was over. I made sure I never got tired. I did not chase my losses. I always changed casinos after an hour's play or less.

These days I am far from the ascetic I was during those first visits to Las Vegas, but I still approach playing in a similar way. When I am at the table, much of my focus is on counting the cards and trying to get it right. One can easily go wrong and let emotion cloud this process. I also need to consider whether the dealer is one who suits me – you do not want him or her to be dealing so fast that you cannot keep the count easily, or so slowly that you cannot get enough hands in per hour – and I do my best to ignore whatever other players may be doing or saying.

As far as one's own chances are concerned, what other players do is irrelevant, except that slow ones hold the game up too much. Some people complain if they think that another player has mistakenly chosen to take a card, or failed to take a card when that would have been the right action. But whether or not another player makes a misguided move makes no difference at all to the probabilities for the other players — anger directed at them is irrational.

Some may find my approach boring, but blackjack is basically an extremely boring game. The attraction to me is that one can, if one concentrates, expect to beat the casino, which is impossible at most games. The odds in the other games are always bad. So if you want to make money, blackjack is the only game to play.

Admittedly, I have occasionally enjoyed playing roulette for fun but, because the odds are bad, I would not play for serious money. There are (in America) thirty-eight slots into which the ball may fall, but winning bets are paid as if there were only thirty-six. So if you put your money on a single number there are thirty-seven numbers into which the ball may fall, on which you will lose, and only one on which you will win. If the odds were exactly fair you would, when you got lucky, be paid thirty-seven times your stake, but you are in fact only paid thirty-five times. There is no system, short of making a foolish alliance with a crooked dealer, that will work.

The two weeks I spent in Las Vegas in 1965 were as good a reminder as any that life as a professional gambler is far less glamorous than you might think. It will not open the door to a vast fortune, but it probably will give you the keys to a moderate income, but a pretty numbing, soul-destroying existence.

Anyway, having started out with $1,500, I came away with $4,500 a fortnight later (it would have been more, but I am almost certain that on the last day a dealer cheated me out of $1,200). So absorbed had I been in the gambling that I actually stayed in Las Vegas a bit too long. I found that I could not get an economy class flight that would reach London in time for me to get to work on Monday morning. Now, however, I upgraded myself to first class and it was great to enjoy the luxury and gloat that it was Las Vegas that had paid for it.

What I think of as the pinnacle of my gambling life took place when I returned to Las Vegas a few years later – how could I not? It was six o'clock on a Sunday morning (a strange time of day to be playing cards anywhere but Vegas) and I was playing at one of several full tables at Caesars Palace, the famous casino that had not even been built when I first went to the city.

I was counting the cards, as usual, and doing my unsuccessful best to hide the fact that I was playing the system.

The casinos are generally either too lazy or too ignorant to count the cards themselves, but they do have a simple way of handling a player who is counting. When he increases his bet, the pit boss calls over to the dealer, 'Shuffle up.' By shuffling the pack and starting the deal again, the dealer gets rid of a situation that the casino assumes was in the player's favour.

Thorp worked out how to counter this. I was to make my maximum bet right at the beginning of the pack of cards, when the odds are so nearly even that it makes little difference. If the odds turned in my favour, I was to continue with the same size bet. That would obviously attract no attention. If, however, the odds moved in the casino's favour, I would, instead of, as usual, reducing the size of my bet, I would substantially increase it. The idea was that when the pit boss saw that, he would tell the dealer to shuffle the cards and start the pack again. I would thus fool the casino into getting rid of what was in fact an unfavourable situation for me. It worked.

But there is a fine art to playing when you know that you have an advantage: there are situations where you have to be as cautious about the way you appear, as you are about the way you play. Professor Thorp was a master at appearing unconcerned and jolly rather than studious. Moreover, you should also avoid altering your stake in a way that makes it clear that you are playing the system.

I had shown in different circumstances that I could hide my excitement. On the night of the 1966 general election, when the

Liberals had been expected to make substantial gains – winning forty or fifty seats – I was in the Ladbroke Club in London with Rodney Leach. About three quarters of an hour after the polls closed, when two or three results were known, I saw on the television that a prediction had flashed up, for a matter of seconds, that the Liberals would win only about fourteen seats. There was a representative of Ladbrokes, the bookmakers, in the club. I went over and asked if they were still taking bets on Liberal seats. He said that they were, in groups of five.

I asked him the odds for the group eleven to fifteen: he rang through to his office on one of those old-fashioned telephones and told me 16 to 1. It was clear Ladbrokes had not seen the TV prediction.

I had to decide quickly what the largest bet was that would not alert Ladbrokes.

'I'll have a couple of hundred on that, please.'

He telephoned through again as I stood there, trying to appear calm.

'Yes, that'll be fine, sir.'

I was just in time: within sixty seconds they had changed the odds to evens.

A few minutes later, as I sat with Rodney in a corner, gloating over my expected triumph, we were accosted by Boris Schapiro, who was running the club at the time. Boris could always sniff out even the smallest chance of making money, and something about my manner attracted his attention.

'What have you been doing, Stuart? What's all this about?'

For once in my life I did something quite shrewd. I explained the situation to him, and offered him £10 of the £200 bet. I did not want any difficulties when it came to getting paid, and having the man who ran the club on my side seemed a good idea. The Liberals took twelve seats: so I had won.

However, in the curious artificial light of that summer morning in Caesars Palace, I was not so good at hiding my feelings: I *smiled*. The pit boss beckoned me over to him and said: 'You're not losing. We don't care for that type of play here: just cash in your chips and collect your cheque.'

You may be inclined to think that Caesars Palace was behaving badly. I do not. They were straightforward and honest. Since at that time Las Vegas was still largely run by the Mafia, it is likely that most of the other casinos would simply have cheated me out of my money rather than banning me from playing. I regard the incident as a feather in my cap.

Sadly, though it served well for quite a long time, Professor Thorp's system is not nearly as effective nowadays. This is largely because casinos, reacting to the success of his system, tend to use six or eight packs rather than one, which makes it far harder to count the cards, but also makes the swings in the ratio of low cards to high cards left in the packs, still to be dealt, which are crucial to the system, much less.

They also stop dealing when there are only one or two packs left. That is the point at which the swings from the pack being more favourable to less favourable *or* vice versa, are more extreme, and it is therefore when the system player is most likely to find favourable situations. Even so, a dedicated follower of Thorp's system should come out a healthy winner over a period.

A development more in the punter's favour is that these days the big outfits are run by accountants rather than the Mafia, and so it would be rare now to find a cheating dealer, at least in the big casinos. The Mafia's loss of control over Las Vegas was a revolution brought about by the eccentric billionaire businessman Howard Hughes. He was so enamoured by the city that he moved there and bought eight of the city's biggest casinos, and in the process broke the gangsters' stranglehold.[15]

Las Vegas has changed in other ways, sometimes spectacular, over the years. There is now a replica Eiffel Tower, as well as fake

Venetian canals. And many of the casinos have disappeared. I well remember taking my wife and daughters to see The Dunes blown up (deliberately) on New Year's Eve 1993. Thousands of people watched the amazing spectacle, with cannon shots from a nearby ship timed to coincide with explosions within the casino. Eventually the whole thing was engulfed by a gigantic fireball. It was most dramatic.

That night my eldest daughter, Sarah, who was a teenager and therefore should not have been playing the slot machines, did play on them in Caesars Palace, and won something like $500 in 25-cent coins. She had about 2,000 of them, but she could not ask the casino to change them into manageable dollar notes, as one would normally have done, because they would have realised that she was not old enough to be entitled to play. By a piece of good luck, she met me in spite of the crowds of people milling around, and I was able to get the coins changed for her.

Some of the changes are very much for the worse. In 1965, I was able to whip from one casino to the next at will with no difficulty at all; within a couple of minutes of having finished playing in one casino, I would have driven to the next, parked my car, and started playing blackjack. Now, Las Vegas is one colossal and very tiresome traffic jam, so that getting from one casino to another is a major task.

There is a more striking change, and much for the better. When I first went out to Las Vegas in the sixties, there was no question of there being any black guests gambling in the casinos: African-Americans might be there to clean your shoes, but it was

---

15 When Rodney Leach – who amongst his many other qualities was very persuasive – was working for Rothschilds, Howard Hughes, or at least his team, approached him and told him he was considering setting up a bank in England. This was at the time when I was out of a job, and Rodney suggested that I should be their man. It was absolutely crackers. I am not sure that Hughes even knew what had been suggested, and of course nothing came of it.

unthinkable that they should take a room in a hotel or be allowed to play at the tables.

The racial prejudice in the United States in those days was extraordinary. When I travelled with my family in the early eighties to see my American cousins in Dyersburg, Tennessee, we had a black nanny for our then ten-month-old Sarah. The nanny was badly treated by my relatives. But worse, much worse, was to come. My cousin's son had invited us to see a property associated with his father's business. A black man had drowned there a few days earlier. The boy enjoyed saying: 'Two dollars! Two dollars to see the drowned nigger!' He thought I would be amused.

My mother and my mother-in-law, both in their eighties, were with us on this trip around America, which of course took in Las Vegas. I think they were probably quite curious to see the strange place I had visited so often in my bachelor days. We spent two nights in a very large suite in Caesars Palace, with my mother and mother-in-law installed in rooms of their own. As soon as they had settled in, the two ladies decided that it was time to go for a walk. There is nowhere in Las Vegas where one can go for a walk.

Meanwhile I was operating my winning blackjack system with great success. Although I was not betting heavily, I had a great run of luck and I won enough to pay for the whole trip round America.

One night, when I had not yet come upstairs from the blackjack, and Tessa was in one of the suite's rooms, with Sarah and her nanny in another, the fire alarm went off. This caused considerable consternation, because more than eighty people had been killed in a terrible fire at the MGM Grand Casino three months earlier.

I was travelling up in the elevator. When I reached our floor, men were peering out of their rooms with their girlfriends or tarts saying, 'What the hell is going on?' My wife and the nanny were completely unperturbed. The film they both happened to be watching showed a fire, and they thought the alarm sound was part of the film.

Somehow, strange coincidences do seem to happen in Las Vegas.

CHAPTER 10

LET'S GIVE IT NINE MONTHS

One day in an English lesson at Eton, we were asked to write a poem beginning, 'I think I know what I should be, if they would leave the choice to me ...' I wrote, 'I shall be a bookie-bold, blah-blah-blah, blah-blah-blah,' never for a moment thinking that I would end up doing anything so disreputable.

In a sense, though, I did not have much of a choice. I had abandoned a career as a barrister, and while I had made a go of being a merchant banker, that industry had pretty much had enough of me.

I was already a customer of Coral Index, the spread-betting subsidiary of the major bookmaker Joe Coral, so I approached Ladbrokes, and then William Hill, to see if either of them might be interested in setting up a subsidiary to compete with Coral.

Neither of them actually said no, but neither of them said yes. There did not seem to be much enthusiasm at their end, and so when a good friend, Tommy Richter, suggested that we should use the idea of spread-betting to enable people to bet on the price of gold, I thought, why not?

What Tommy had cleverly noticed was that there was a big

speculative boom in gold at the time, and yet there was no sensible way for UK citizens to get involved without buying so-called investment dollars at a significant premium to the normal exchange rate.[16] So it was a fantastically expensive way to deal, and meant, in effect, that British citizens could not buy gold. What we planned to offer would be a great deal cheaper – our customers would not be purchasing gold. They would be *betting* about the price of it, and the investment dollar premium would not be involved. A further advantage for our clients was that we enabled them to bet about smaller quantities of gold than catered for by the normal markets.[17]

Tommy had made a worthwhile amount of money working at Warburg's, before setting up on his own. He went about raising the capital we needed – around £100,000, some of which came from friends and colleagues of his – but he also put in £30,000 of his own money. I could not afford anything to speak of.

There were quite a few challenges. One was to find a suitable name. As we planned to bet exclusively about the price of gold, we wanted to call our company the London Gold Index. But the Bank of England and the Treasury both objected – they apparently thought that it might lead people to think that we were in some way government-sponsored.

So we asked if we might call it Investors Gold Index. That name was also rejected. Rather oddly, however, they were perfectly happy for us to use the initials. So IG Index was born. Given that we barely traded in gold after the first year, it has long been a meaningless name; but now that a brand has been

---

16 Gold was always priced in dollars, not pounds.

17 One lot of silver is 100 ounces and when silver was priced at about £100 per ounce, it meant that one lot was worth £10,000. It was certainly an attraction to some people that, when we later started betting about silver and other commodities, they could bet in volumes that only represented about 2 or 3 ounces.

established, it would be a mistake to change it.

We had a more important problem. Because we were British, like our own clients, we could not ourselves buy gold without paying the investment dollar premium. So it would have been prohibitively expensive to hedge our clients' bets. In an attempt to find a solution, we visited three or four of the five members of the so-called London Gold Market. Most refused to help, but Mocatta & Goldsmid said, 'Well, all right, you can't be our client, because you can't own gold, but when you want to hedge, we will be IG Index's client, betting about the price of gold with you, the bookmaker.'

But for this, the company would never have started. Why on earth did a major company like Mocatta & Goldsmid agree to accommodate a tiny outfit like us? I cannot be sure, for I never asked, but I do not think it was a coincidence that Jock Mocatta and Harry d'Avigdor-Goldsmid were both members of my bridge club. I suspect one or the other of them had a word with whoever at the firm was responsible for making this decision. I am very glad that they did. I also realise now that the fact Harry was a shareholder may have had something to do with it. Curiously, this never occurred to me at the time.

I think Tommy and I were both aware that although *we* thought that we had a good idea, we would need to persuade people to do business with us. So we arranged a drinks party in the City, at which Tommy announced that we had an agreement with the *Financial Times* that they would carry our quotation about the gold prices every day. This was clearly very important.

We were horrified, therefore, when we got back to our office, to find a message from the *FT* saying that the editor had decided we were not the sort of company his paper wanted to give space to. We were simply bookmakers with an outlandish and perhaps unworkable idea. It is to Tommy's great credit that he got hold of the *FT* and persuaded them to visit us and investigate. We passed.

Very soon after this, the *FT* published a very favourable article about us, and this, along with some advertising, helped to get the word out. Even so, it still did not really take off. We were a tiny, unknown bookmaker selling a concept that was completely new and which most of our potential clients did not understand.

People of my age, and many much younger, were brought up on odds betting: if you put £1 on a horse at 3 to 1 and it wins, you come away with a profit of £3; if it loses, you lose £1. Spread-betting works in quite a different way and even some very intelligent people struggle to understand it. I find the easiest way to explain spread bets is to use an example from cricket. How many runs do you expect England to make in the first innings of their next Test match? We might quote 270 to 280, which means that you would be able to 'buy' at 280, or 'sell' at 270.

If you expected England to get a lot of runs, you would 'buy' at the higher end of our quotation, i.e., at 280. We would ask you what size of bet you wished to make. You might say £10 per run. So we would confirm to you that you had made a £10 per run bet that England would get more than 280 runs.

If they make 281 runs you win, but as you are right by only one run, your profit will be 1 x £10. If, however, they make 380 runs, you will be right by 100 runs and so your profit will be 100 x £10. But if England do badly and score, let us say, only 200 runs, you will be wrong by 80 runs, and so you will have lost 80 x £10.

If you had expected England to do badly, you would have 'sold' the runs at the lower end of our quotation, i.e., at 270.

A bet on a share price works in exactly the same way. We might quote a price of 150 to 152 pence about what level share A will close at on a particular day. If you think that the price at the end of that day will be high, you buy at 152 and you might choose to bet £20 per penny of the share price. If it closes at 182 pence you will be right by 30 and so your profit will be 30 x £20. Crucially the £600 you win will be free of all tax, whereas if you had dealt in a normal market it would have been subject to Capital Gains Tax.

Whether you are betting on cricket scores or share prices, the principle remains the same: the more right you are, the more you will win, the more wrong you are, the more you will lose. One of the other attractions of spread-betting, besides the fact that winnings are tax-free, is that you only have to send us as a deposit (in case you fail to pay) a small fraction of our possible loss. In order to win, or lose, fortunes, clients can speculate, putting up a relatively small deposit.

Having done most of the legwork in setting the whole thing up, Tommy did not want to be involved in the day-to-day running. So this was largely my responsibility. In the first year, I had only one day's holiday.

Tommy Richter could be very mysterious. One never quite knew what he was doing, and he never talked about his private life. When we set up the business, we worked from his office, and so I sat in the same room as he did, using his secretary, which she was not that pleased about. I would hear him discussing his business, but he never talked about it to me, and it was all a mystery to me.

The most successful financial thing he ever did, I think, was to buy the freehold of his house in St James's Place, where for a very long time he had his office. I imagine it rocketed in price and turned out to be a tremendous investment.

There was one thing, though, that did become clear after a bit. Tommy talked every day to his mother about his father, who was obviously ill and, I gathered, getting worse. One day, it seemed from what Tommy was saying on the telephone that his father might have died. We happened to have a meeting elsewhere in London that afternoon and in the taxi on the way back, I was bold enough to ask Tommy, 'Has your father by any chance died?'

'Yes,' he said, 'but don't tell anyone!'

On our first day's trading, we had two customers. One was Selim Zilkha, who placed a bet on gold through his partner, Mary Hayley. The other was an Irish jeweller (later, I am sorry to say, murdered by the IRA).

But over the weeks that followed, the phone barely rang. The boom in gold, which we had set IG Index up to exploit, was founded on the expectation that at the beginning of 1975 Americans, who were going to be allowed to buy it for the first time, would rush into the market. This did not happen. The first of January was greeted by a plunge in the gold price, and there was almost no sign of Americans buying it.

By 1 May 1975, when we opened our doors, the boom had come to an end, and we struggled to attract clients. We had very few expenses, so we did not lose much, but I was not taking a salary and was still surviving on what I could win at bridge.

At the start, Tommy had said, 'Let's give it nine months. If it doesn't work, it won't have cost us anything and we can just get on and do other things.' After nine months it was indeed not working, or at least not at a viable level, and so he said, 'Right, as we agreed at the beginning, I want to call it a day.'

The whole thing was entirely amicable and we would stay friends until Tommy, who was only a little younger than me, died a few years ago. He made no request to keep shares or anything like that. It must have been very galling for him later on to see the company go on to do miraculously well. I know I would have felt less than happy had it been the other way around, but he never expressed the slightest resentment. I think he was a nicer person than I am.

When he did pull out, it was natural that most of his friends and connections, whom he had persuaded to put up money, would do the same. I was keen to keep the company going, and calculated that we needed to retain at least £35,000 in the business. I went round some of these shareholders asking them to leave in the company what they had invested when we started.

Harry d'Avigdor-Goldschmid agreed to keep his money in, but told me he was not persuaded to put up more. I also approached my friend Robin Birkenhead, formerly Furneaux. Other early investors included an American member of my bridge club, Roger Lapham, Lizie Byng, as she then was,[18] Robin's sister Juliet Townsend, Robin's first cousin Nicky Berry, and Mary McDougall, a girl Robin, Nicky and I all knew well. One of the other people I approached was Selim Zilkha, whom I asked to invest £5,000. He told me, with great charm, that to be honest an investment of so small a sum really was not of any interest to him.

I went home with my tail between my legs, ready to accept defeat, until in an uncharacteristic moment I wrote to ask him to put up the £5,000 as a favour to a friend. He agreed, and though I had only managed to raise £30,000 altogether, I decided to give it a go.

Things began to look up when Nicky Berry suggested to me that I might be able to scrape a living betting on gold, but I would not be able to make any real money, and the business should expand to take in commodities such as coffee, lead, zinc, cocoa and sugar.

We began to get much more business because I had noticed that the small number of clients we did have betting about the gold price got their winnings, if any, free of tax and that the same would apply to those who bet about commodity prices. As the reader will know, you pay no tax on your profit if you back the winner of a race, and since our transactions were, at this time, all

18 She rather lengthened her name by marriage, becoming the Countess Hervé le Bault de la Morinière.

bets, the same rule applied.

One weekend, not long after we had begun to allow clients to speculate on commodities other than gold, we took a bet that the price of silver would go up. Normally, in these situations, we would have hedged by buying an appropriate quantity of the commodity in question. The problem was that you were not permitted to buy or sell less than a whole 'lot' of silver. One lot was 5,000 Troy ounces, and our client's bet was worth about only a third of that, so if we bought one lot and the price of silver went down, we would lose the equivalent in money of two thirds of a lot of silver, an enormous sum.

The other option, which of course we took, was to stand the risk that the client was right, which only involved taking a risk on one third of a lot. This still meant that going into the weekend we had taken a position that, given we only had £30,000 in the business, was extremely precarious. As it was, the price of silver went down and we made £16,000; a marvellous stroke of luck, and one of the many swings of the pendulum that was to be a feature of life in IG over the years.

The incident showed how exposed and vulnerable was a fledgling outfit like ours. It also showed, to be honest, what a risk our clients were taking in doing business with us: if we lost more than our capital, we would not have been able to meet our commitments to our clients.

In our first year, 1976, we showed a profit of around £12,000. In the second, we lost almost exactly the same amount. It was a tense period for me. I could not pay myself a salary and the only income I had was what I could win at bridge. Once a week I would calculate *exactly* where I was financially, and try to see if I could stay afloat for the next seven days.

I had survived during that period of my life in extreme financial danger, and so I drew up a list of the ten people I considered most likely to be willing and able to lend me money if the worst happened.

And then the worst *did* happen. I went to the first friend on the list. He told me that he would not lend me any money, but that he was willing to let me stay in his flat free of rent.

I did not want to do that, so I approached my second friend, Sebastian Yorke (the son of the writer Henry Green). He quickly agreed to write me a cheque for £1,000, if and when I needed it, and indicated that he could probably give me one or two thousand more if necessary. Of course, I was very keen to avoid having to take his money, but I realised that if I were to go to my bridge club and lose, I would not otherwise be able to pay unless I accepted his offer..

I went to the Portland that evening with my friend's cheque in my wallet, knowing that I would have to cash it unless I won £600. It was extremely unlikely that I would win that much in one night, but somehow I did. Of course, I am still overwhelmingly grateful to Sebastian.

It was very important to me that IG Index should be an honest organisation.

I remember that when I was at Hill Samuel, I was sent to see a bank in Switzerland that they were considering buying. In the course of a chat about the way they ran their business, they told me that if a client asked them to buy shares in, for instance, ICI, they would start by purchasing them at whatever was the lowest price they could find. Then the next day, they would look in the *FT* to see what the highest price was at which the shares had changed hands, and they would always charge their clients that price. They were very proud of that. I cannot remember whether Hill Samuel bought them. I hope not.

I am confident that from the beginning IG did have a reputation for being straight, and I always valued this. It sounds awfully pompous, but being trustworthy, and knowing that people could be confident that the firm would pay its debts, was very important to me. When many years later it became clear that I could make a lot of money out of the business, Edward Cazalet wrote to me saying words to the effect that, 'Above all, the reason you've done so well is because of integrity.' There are all sorts of ways – some large, some small – in which a company like ours could have been dishonest, but I believe the fact that our clients trusted us was a significant element in our success.

Honest we may have been, but the beginning of IG Index was all very Heath Robinson. For a long time, after I had moved the business from Tommy Richter's house to my new house in Lamont Road in Chelsea, in 1976, IG Index consisted essentially of me sitting by the phone in the attic of my house, waiting for clients to ring. My only employee was my wonderful former girlfriend, Katie Sachs, who worked for two hours a day.

It was a very unprofessional set-up: a mass of files containing details of clients' bets, manual typewriters and a little box-file with all of our clients' details, including, to the great surprise of Lizie Byng, one of our earliest employees, that of her ex-husband, George Sulimirski. We brought her in as a secretary, fresh from four years modelling in Paris, and she left the company as our chief dealer. This process – people starting in a junior capacity and then getting promoted – was to be quite a feature of our business.

There was space for six people, as long as they did not mind being squashed, and so we started gradually to add new members of staff. The first to join was my friend Robert Sheehan, a world-class bridge player, and a member of the gambling crowd that I was part of, who is highly intelligent and a very good mathematician. He had said to me one day in the Clermont Club, 'Do tell me if you ever need anyone to help when you're on holiday or anything, even if only for one day. I would be happy to stand in for you.'

His logical mind and experience of gambling meant he was quickly able to get his head around what we were doing. So he started coming in regularly and was an important member of the team for a number of years. Because at the time the company was worth virtually nothing, and I could not afford to pay him any salary, he got six per cent of IG Index's shares in return for the work he put in. He also got some more cheaply from an original investor who had fallen on hard times and, of course, Robert did very well out of it.

Annette Rye was my secretary for a while. She was very charming and highly educated, an excellent secretary in all ways but one: she could not arrive on time. It was not a question of occasionally being ten minutes late, rather consistently turning up two hours after she was due. So that was a bit annoying and she lasted only a year. We called her 'the Moo', though I have forgotten why. She eventually married Robert Sheehan's regular bridge partner at the time, Irving Rose. There was also, very sadly, a temp that came to us who, we discovered later from the newspapers, was murdered.

We were far from busy in the Chelsea days — we did one transaction every three weeks or so at the start — and there was, for several years, very much a family feel about the business, which was one of the enjoyable things about a small company.[19] I had always been at sea in large outfits. When I was at IG Index, I found even the most alarming episodes, when the very future of the firm looked under threat, less worrying than those moments at Hill Samuel when I had to ask a secretary, very diffidently, whether she might have a spare minute to do my typing for me. I liked the closeness and informality of working in a tiny organisation, and the way we would all muck in together.

We would often go down the road for lunch at the Man in the

---

19 Funnily enough, there was a point in the early years at IG Index when, of the twelve members of staff, three of us were adopted. To put that in context, in Britain as a whole, only one person in a hundred is adopted.

Moon pub (though we never recognised Christine Keeler, who I found out later, had been a regular). I would eat steak and kidney pie and talk about old bridge hands with Robert Sheehan. Later, when we had moved to Clapham, we went down to the basement to eat with Tessa and the infant Sarah, my first child.

Some of our clients were friends, but the majority were not. Because we were introducing a new, rather peculiar financial product, we did attract some real chancers. We had one very good client who was a respected figure in an investment company. Quite often he would bet with us that a particular share was going to go up. In hindsight, I fear that he knew perfectly well that his firm was going to buy large quantities of that share, thus pushing the price up. I was too naïve to realise it at the time.

Another man, who wanted to establish a tax loss, proposed that at the same time as he bet that the price of a particular commodity would go up, he would make an equal bet that it would go down. He wanted the winning transaction to be the profitable one (and tax free) but his losses to be regarded as tax-deductible. It was intended to defraud the taxman and, when we made it clear that we would not backdate the transactions (which was an essential element in his scheme) the plan was dropped. It was an idiotic idea, and morally indefensible.

Generally, we could trust our customers to pay up when their bets lost. There were, however, a handful of notable exceptions. I remember that Cyril Stein, who ran Ladbrokes, once telephoned me to ask what our odds were on a particular political event. He wanted to make a bet. I said, 'Yes, brilliant, but the trouble is, Cyril, you're not actually a client of ours. We can't legally accept a bet from you until you are. However, if you can assure me that you want that bet, we can get the formalities sorted out in the next hour or so.'

'Fine,' he said. But during lunch-time, a poll came out that made the bet he had wanted to make look far less attractive, and so he did not go through with it. This was not much of a shock. It was a standing joke among bookmakers at the races that someone from Ladbrokes would phone up and make bets with another bookmaker, and if the bet won, they would be told, 'That one was for Cyril Stein'; if it lost, they would be told, 'That one was for Ladbrokes'.

Mostly, however, we could trust our clients. What I found surprising was the extent to which some people trusted us, even without knowing anything about the company. This was extremely fortunate for IG. One man sent us a cheque for £10,000 as a deposit, and he went on to become a very good client. But he had very little reason to expect that he was going to get things right,[20] and he did not. As he was a very good client, I invited him to lunch in my house in Chelsea and buttered him up a bit. I treated him perfectly fairly at all times, but I was shaken when he asked me one day whether in the event that 'anything happened to him', I could ensure that the money in his account would go to his wife.

Especially in the early years, one of my main ways of ensuring client–bookie relations stayed friendly was to take our best customers out for lunch. I have always found one-on-one lunches quite easy to handle, but I found it impossible to tell at the end of the meal whether it had been successful or not. There were times when I felt that we had got on like a house on fire, but nothing came of it, and other times when I left with the impression that they had been neither interested nor impressed, but then walked back into the office to find they had placed a big order.

And yet as important in their own way as these lunches were, our real business was always done on the telephone. It was the

---

20 Virtually nobody, except perhaps a minute proportion of people who have inside information, have any good reason to think that they are going to get commodity prices right. Remember that getting it 'right' means getting them more right than all the other people who, in effect, created the current market price.

one piece of technology that, in the years before the Internet, we were absolutely reliant on. It would have been extraordinarily difficult to conduct our business without it.

We moved into a new 'office' in Clapham soon after my marriage to Tessa in 1979 – a room right at the top of the house. It worked well, because we were virtually shut off from the rest of the house, and so we were not disturbed by the noise of babies or any other non-business activity.

We had direct lines to two of our commodity brokers and because it was crucial that they should work on the Monday morning after our weekend move, we took every possible step to make sure that the Post Office (who were then in charge of telephones) would organise things properly. I lost count of the times that we were assured that, yes, everything was in hand. It did not happen, and for a few days we had to try to operate without the direct lines that we relied upon so heavily.

I sent what eventually added up to an armada of motorcycle couriers with handwritten letters to the chairman of the Post Office, complaining about the intolerable effect this was having on a small business like ours. In response, a stream of men came round to try to fix the problem, but to no avail. One day, I collared one of the unfortunate engineers who had been dispatched to our office and told him about all the bikes I had been sending to his boss. 'It doesn't seem to make a blind bit of difference,' I said to him. He looked at me, and with some emphasis, he replied: 'It DID. I can tell you it DID.'

I wish I had known more about business before I started one. I had a vague hope that IG Index might go on to be very successful, but no clear idea about how this might be achieved. Others had lots of thoughts about how we might grow, or expand our offerings. I did not, because I am apt to focus very closely on the thing I am involved in at any particular moment, and I do not step back and look at the wider picture. I just went on with things as they were and hoped they would develop okay. I always think that if I had spent even a year in a business school, I might have acquired this sort of knowledge, the lack of which I am sure inhibited me, and by extension IG Index.

Nevertheless, we *did*, over time, become a very great success. While in 1977 we made a loss before tax of just under £3,000, by 1978 our profit before tax had risen to over £21,000. I think there were a number of reasons why we thrived. Our clients' profits were tax free. That was, and still is, the company's main selling point: we pushed it as far as we could.

We always treated people fairly. And I took a great deal of trouble, particularly at the beginning, with our tiny number of customers. I would write to a client, for instance, sympathising with him that things had gone wrong in 'difficult markets', and once I travelled all the way to South Wales to see an important client.

We were careful when we needed to be, never allowing our exposure in any part of the market in which we were dealing to exceed the limit we had set for ourselves. It made no difference in principle whether a bet was about the Dow Jones Index, the price of sugar, or anything else. As soon as a client's actions pushed us past this limit, we would hedge by going into the real market and buying or selling as appropriate: otherwise we could have lost more than we could afford.

But one must not be too careful; it would have been a bad mistake to do too much hedging. In the real commodity markets, there is a difference between the prices at which one can buy or sell, and in the long run this difference represented, when we hedged, a cost to IG Index. If a client's bet, or a combination of clients' bets, were not large enough to put us at risk of a loss that we could not afford, we avoided hedging because it would have involved an unnecessary cost.

Persistence was another factor in our success. We kept going; we stuck to it when things got tough. Perhaps I was more willing than most to do this, because I had already had a couple of false starts as an employee and I did not have anything to fall back on. There was no other option for me, really. I *had* to make a success of IG Index.

CHAPTER 11

WELL, AT LEAST HE IS WITTY

I have spent less time contemplating my adoption, and its consequences, than most people would expect. When asked about it, I tend to give answers that are probably very different from the conventional response.

It is hard for anyone who has been adopted to know quite what it is like *not* to have been adopted and, of course, vice versa. My guess about my relationship with my adoptive mother, Betty, is that it was not very different from the relationships that people have with their natural mothers. So I find it hard to judge to what extent adoption has actually affected me. I was not self-confident at Eton, but I believe that was due to a range of factors unconnected with adoption. It never occurred to me to be ashamed of being illegitimate, something that was obviously not my fault.

Perhaps I am more vulnerable, more afraid of rejection, than I might otherwise have been. On balance, though, I am inclined to think it unlikely that my adoption had a major effect on my character.

I did not, for a long time, make any consistent attempts to track down my birth mother. I suppose I was not really sure how much it mattered. In 1975, however, when the Children Act gave adopted adults the right to get a copy of their adoption certificates for the first time, I did apply for mine.

Shortly afterwards, an envelope arrived at my house on Lamont Road, Chelsea. There was not much in it, no mention of my father, only my mother's name: Chrissie Cleland. That was all. I did not know who she was, or how old she had been when she gave birth. I did not know whether she was still alive. To try to establish this basic detail, I went to St Catherine's House in Holborn, where birth, marriage and death records for England and Wales were held, and went through the death certificates. I remember getting very nervous as I looked through them, hoping very much that my birth mother had not died.

I did not get anywhere because, as I learned later, she had died in Scotland (in 1969), so that her death was recorded there, not in the English and Welsh records.

When one draws a blank like this, one becomes quite willing to follow up loose ends, even if the chances of them leading to anything useful are very low. On one occasion, I happened to go to a physiotherapist who practised the Alexander Technique. He told me that I looked fantastically like one of his patients. As I was still quite young at the time, it was conceivable that he was talking about my father. I was interested enough to pursue it, but it came to nothing.

When I started my efforts to trace my birth mother, it became obvious that my mother, Betty, was uncomfortable. She was not at all nasty about it, but understandably she was not enthusiastic.

I knew she loved me very much and doubtless she did not want anybody to usurp her place. I was very fond of her, and was unwilling to do anything that might hurt her. It is possible that had I asked her, she could have provided details about the adoption society she had used all those years ago – for eighteen months or so, she had even sent the adoption society photographs of me so that they could be sent on to my birth mother. This might have led me somewhere closer to finding my birth mother, and yet, for one reason or another, I never did ask her.

Apparently, it is typical of adopted children that they try quite energetically to search for their birth parents before giving up and forgetting about it for years. Occasionally, I would tell myself, I must go back to this when I have a moment, but that moment never came. I never really thought of it as being that urgent. Somehow, I was always too busy – running and then expanding IG Index was hard work – and the search never made its way to the top of my list, especially after I got married and became involved in bringing up a family of my own.

In 1958, my final year at Oxford, ten of us drew up a list in which we each predicted the order in which we would get married. The poll showed that I was expected to be ninth, and Robin Furneaux last. Twenty-odd years later, when I tied the knot, I was indeed the ninth to get married and Robin never did.

In the two decades before I did finally get married, I had had a number of girlfriends. One summer when I was still a bachelor, I found myself without anybody to go on holiday with, and no clear idea of what to do, so I decided to spend the week in London and invite a different girl out for lunch each day.

One them had been my first real girlfriend, Katie Sachs, granddaughter of Lord Goddard (known, variously, as 'The Tiger', 'Justice-in-a-jiffy' and, to Winston Churchill, 'Lord Goddamn'), the Lord Chief Justice who had presided over the famous trial of Craig and Bentley, in which Derek Bentley was wrongly convicted (as it was decided about fifty years later) and hanged for murdering a policeman. Katie and I had been quite close until about six months before her marriage, after which we stayed in friendly but chaste contact. When I asked Katie to lunch, she said, 'Well, I happen to have a couple of steaks in the fridge, why don't you come here?'

We ate lunch in their basement kitchen (where we behaved impeccably), before going upstairs for coffee. While we sat drinking our coffee in a window seat that overlooked the street, her husband rang to tell her that he was *en route* from his office to Heathrow, but that he was just going to pop in, 'as long as that would not be inconvenient'. 'Yes, of course,' replied Katie.

I told her that if one thing was certain, it was that I was going to stay there until he came. I had realised that he must have seen us from the street and must naturally have been somewhat alarmed to see a man, who had not that long ago been his wife's boyfriend, making himself comfortable in their sitting room.

I was not always so clever. It helps, when you are taking girls out, to be able to remember their names. But I am terrible at this. On one occasion I took a girl out, and we had a good time (or at least so I thought). The next evening, I had been invited to a house party for guests who were to go on to a dance. At the dance, I was with a girl from the house party when I bumped into my date of the previous evening. As I looked at her, I realised that I had no idea of her name. She was not amused. My rule since then has been that if I think the odds of me getting somebody's name right are three to one on or better, I risk saying it. If not, I try diplomacy.

This was not the only instance when I failed to notice something that should have been obvious. There was a very nice girl called Joanna Hare, who later married Stephen Breyer who became one of the nine justices of the US Supreme Court. I must have fancied her a lot at the time, because I took her out for dinner one night and then had lunch with her the following day.

At lunch, she said, 'Can you notice anything different about me?'

Oh my God, I thought to myself, having noticed nothing different about her, I wonder what it could be?

'Is it your hair?'

'Yes, but what about my hair?' she said.

'Well, have you dyed it?' I was doing my best. In fact, she had cut about a foot off.

Until I was forty-two, I had not thought much about getting married, but then I decided I should make an organised attempt to find a wife. I had realised that I would probably be happier if I did get married, and I needed to take some steps to make it happen. So I decided to take a different girl out on each night of one week. It is a sign of how seriously I took the enterprise that I even included Monday night, normally reserved exclusively for bridge. Girls were asked, dates were made, and I always enjoyed myself, but things went no further.

Then one day in spring 1978, a much younger girl asked me to make up the numbers at a dinner party where a guest had dropped out, and I found myself sitting opposite a photographer called Tessa Codrington, who laughed a lot and was a magnificent storyteller. (She used occasionally to be referred to as a 'society photographer', which she herself hated; it did no justice to the range of her talents or the breadth of her interests and sympathies.)

There are competing accounts about what happened next. My own version of this story, which is the true one, is that I asked the hostess for Tessa's home telephone number and then called her in the morning. 'Who? What? Can you ring me in the office?' came the slightly unpromising reply.

Another version, quite untrue, but perhaps considered more entertaining, is that I called Tessa in her studio, and that she told me she was awfully sorry, but that she did not remember meeting me and had no idea who I was.

Tessa spoke in a manner I had never encountered before – amusing, confident and fearless, but never cruel. I do not think she ever said an unkind word. She was a great friend to all kinds of people, and she was very good to anyone who was in trouble.

She was never afraid of any social situation. She was always completely undaunted, and she did not care if you were a duke or a dustman.

She was not conventional, and had little time for conventional people – she always used to say that she just knew she did not want to end up as a secretary. Tessa had been right at the heart of the sixties and a lot of her friends were quite different from mine. Often they, and Tessa too, would all be smoking dope while I sat, perfectly happily, in a corner. Her friends were intrigued that she had found what one of them, an American, called her new beau. I suppose they all saw me as a seven-foot gambling fiend, who ran a business that only a handful of people understood. I think Tessa liked the fact that, in my own way, I was a bit unconventional and not completely like other people from my background.

We got engaged in March 1979, and four months later, in July, were married – we both thought that we had better get on with it. My major contribution to the wedding was champagne. I thought my mother-in-law to be was being a bit stingy by suggesting some other sparkling wine, so I put a bet on the Conservatives to win the election that took place that May. I needed £1,400 to pay for the champagne, but the Conservatives were hot favourites and I had to risk £5,000. The day after I placed my bet, an opinion poll came out that, for the one and only time in the campaign, showed Labour ahead. A nasty moment, but Margaret Thatcher did it.

I also took considerable trouble preparing my wedding speech. Some people can speak brilliantly *extempore*, giving the impression that they have barely thought about what they are going to say, as a flood of articulate, moving sentences spills out of their mouths. I am not one of them. So, using a tape recorder, I practised the speech and played it back to myself at least a dozen times. Apparently, it worked. One guest, perhaps having some doubts about my other characteristics, said, 'Well, at least he is witty.'

During the months before we got engaged, a friend said to me, 'You know, before you get married, you need to consider those long times when it will be just the two of you at home. Have you got things that both of you like talking about to each other? Have you got similar interests at all?'

Our friend did have a point. Shared interests are undoubtedly an important part of many relationships, but not all. Tessa and I had virtually no interests or hobbies in common, but things certainly worked. We had both led very independent lives before marriage, and neither of us thought that there was any reason to change. One other curious thing is that I have a rather nuanced sense of humour. It is quite black; sometimes I stray quite close to the line. I hope not too close. Tessa seemed to be the only person who could never tell whether I was serious or joking.

There is an incident that illustrates both how difficult it was to shock Tessa, and how little interested she was in some of the things that I liked, such as gambling. It also happened to be the occasion of the biggest win of my career as a gambler, although it came in dreadful circumstances.

By early September 2001, IG Index had gone public, so I was worth a lot of money, £30 million or so. I made a big bet that the Dow Jones Index would fall, which it did, quite heavily. I doubled up, and it fell again; I doubled up once more, and it carried on falling. By the eleventh of the month, I found myself in an extremely large short position. Nobody in their right mind would ever wish for an event like the destruction of the Twin Towers to occur, but – let us put it this way – the timing, if it was going to happen, was perfect. The market crashed.

As it happens, the attack on the Twin Towers found Tessa and me in Tangier for my annual bridge week. We were all in a restaurant, the Mirage, enjoying an excellent meal, when the news came through. I never normally discussed my gambling and on this occasion I realised that it would be best to remain extremely quiet, no matter how extraordinary my win. But ten days later I did go to Tessa, who was in bed, and said, 'Darling, I thought you might like to know I've just won a million and a quarter pounds on a bet.'

'Well done, darling', she said, sounding very bored. 'Now,' and at this point she became animated, 'about the flowers.'[21]

Tangier was a place Tessa adored and it was an immensely important part of her life. Her grandfather had been the British Resident in Zanzibar. When he retired, he was all set to move home to England, but he soon decided he could not stand the British weather. Instead he went to Morocco, where he built five houses, one of which Tessa eventually inherited. She had been taken there regularly from a young age and she fitted in perfectly. It was a place that made her very happy, and she was loved by the traders in the fish markets and the Souk, where she was apt to chatter away in some mix of pidgin English, French, Italian, and a spot of Arabic. Apparently, she made perfect sense to the traders.

Before she met me, Tessa had been living in Tangier for a year or so with a man called Rashid, who was quite closely connected to the Moroccan royal family. Everything remained amicable between them after we were married, and he once came to stay with us, but he was given to saying quite alarming things. 'If the roles were reversed,' he told Tessa, 'I'd stick a knife in his back.' I used to joke to Tessa and her friends that, having had a chance to be the queen of Morocco, she had had to settle for marrying a bookie.

I was reluctant at first to spend much time in Tangier. I thought it hot, uncomfortable and dirty, and I did not like the food. In any

---

21 One person whom I did not tell about my bet was a Chicago-based American futures and options trader, Shelly Natenberg, who had come to my bridge weekend in Tangier for the first time. I knew that he had lost close friends in the disaster, and I knew too that it would have been highly distasteful if I had boasted to him of my good fortune.

case I am not fond of big cities, unless they are London or Las Vegas. One day, however, Tessa suggested that I might like to invite some of my friends there to play bridge. 'Oh no,' I said, 'they would not want to do that.' I could not have been more wrong. My bridge week there in the autumn has become a great annual event, and in the two years since Tessa's death, our great friend Sandy Campbell has kindly fulfilled the role of hostess magnificently, with help from her partner, Ed Abelson; though it will never be the same without Tessa.

Steadily I got to know some of Tessa's Tangier friends, partly bohemian and artistic ex-pats, partly a number of locals. There was her major-domo, Abdul Latif – a great character who looked after her for thirty-four years. He had come up to Tangier from the desert unable to speak English, or to read or write in any language. But he was highly intelligent and learnt to speak very good English, taught by the well-known author Gavin Young, who often rented Tessa's house for long periods. Abdul Latif became a vital part of life in Tessa's house even if, from time to time, he was mysteriously absent.

A few years ago, while Tessa was still alive, he came to her and said, 'You don't love me anymore.' So she agreed to sit down with him to talk about pay. Before their meeting Regis Milcent, a great friend who happened to be in the house, tried, with me, to prepare Tessa for the meeting. We got her to accept that she should not agree to anything on the spot. What happened? Out she came: 'Stuart, I've given him a forty per cent pay rise!'

An important member of the household, in the early days of our marriage, even before Abdul Latif had arrived, was the housekeeper, Malika. She had a very grumpy husband, Abdul Garni, but the very annoying thing about Malika was that our guests' possessions had a habit of going missing. We learned in time that all we had to do was mention to Malika that we could not find, for example, a piece of jewellery, and it would mysteriously reappear. Eventually there was a parting of the ways. Not long afterwards, Abdul Garni won the Moroccan lottery. Plainly there is no moral to this story!

I am far from being a perfect father, but fatherhood was never a problem for me; it has always been a pleasure. I am extremely lucky to have my three wonderful daughters.

Our first child, Sarah, was born on 9 July 1980. When Tessa and I were shown round the hospital where Sarah was to be born, I asked whether Tessa would be allowed to be with the new baby at night, and was told that on the whole they were fairly 'lenient' about that. I am rather glad the hospital has since closed.

During labour, when something seemed to be wrong, faulty machines were failing to give clear information. When I expressed concern, the nurse said, 'Leave the worrying to us!' Some time later, however, when the obstetrician was summoned, he had clearly been told that something was seriously wrong. He jumped out of his car in a frantic hurry and performed a Caesarean.

Some five months later, my doctor, Ann Coxon, found out that all was not right. Sarah was examined by a specialist. She had got hemiplegia, which affects one side of the body. On learning this, I telephoned my friend Rodney Leach in distress, nearly but not quite in tears. I have been told by doctors that when a baby has hemiplegia the most likely cause is that something had gone wrong before birth rather than at birth. But that is not certain and I shall always have the nagging doubt whether something might have been done that would have prevented it, if I had made more of a fuss when the machines were failing to give clear information.

One wants one's children to live happy and fulfilled lives, and I was naturally worried that Sarah's chances of doing so might be limited. I should have known better. She is a wonderfully happy person.

Of course, it is very bad luck to have hemiplegia. About one child in a thousand has it. But the degree of severity varies greatly. Sarah was at least fortunate that she had it much more mildly than most. She coped very well and managed to go to a normal boarding school and so on.

She made a great success of managing the photographic side of an auction house and has become expert on the subject of old photographs with a much praised recent exhibition in London. She now divides her time between London and Morocco, with many friends in both countries.

Sarah adores coming to Las Vegas with me, and playing poker and eating in expensive restaurants. On the other hand, she is equally at home in a small village called Rohuna, in Morocco, whose inhabitants must be among the most backward, impoverished and uneducated in the world.

Sarah's birth was followed on 16 October 1981 by that of Jacquetta. From an early age, Jacquetta was a ferocious competitor and I watched with great pride her triumphs at all sorts of sports. But the memory I treasure most is of her, aged eight, absolutely flinging herself into my arms when I went to collect her from her boarding school for a weekend at home. When she was sixteen, she was spotted in the street by the famous photographer Mario Testino, and before we knew it, she was being called a Twiggy for the twenty-first century. *The Face* described her as the face of 1999, and the *Evening Standard* called her the most wanted model on the planet.

I remember thinking, after Jacquetta became famous, that when I was a young man, I was so shy that I would not have dreamt of saying anything to a pretty girl, let alone a model, especially a supermodel. Yet here I was with the supermodel being my own daughter.

It is very remarkable, however, that in spite of Jacquetta's success, she has never put on any airs whatever, and does not seem to think she is anything special at all.

Our last child, Charlotte, arrived on 24 January 1985, six days before my fiftieth birthday. Tessa had always said she would not have a baby after the age of forty. Charlotte was born when Tessa was forty years and three months. So we always told her that she was a mistake.

I have strong memories of seeing Tessa breastfeeding Charlotte and Charlotte's cross look as she went gulp, gulp, gulp, as if she was in control of everything and could tell everybody what to do. This is perhaps why I was not too surprised when she promised that she was going to be prime minister by the age of thirty-one. What was disappointing is that she let me down and, with her thirty-first birthday been and gone, she is not leading the country. She would, like almost anyone else, have made a much better job of it than Mrs May.

Charlotte has a very strong sense of right and wrong, which I am delighted about. I once foolishly expressed a view that she was not the most tactful of people. She was furious and accused me of 'character assassination'.

I used quite frequently to give my daughters and their friends riddles and number problems to work out. By a coincidence, one of my favourite probability problems came up in Charlotte's maths scholarship paper for King's School, Canterbury, and so she did extremely well in that paper. Too well, I feared. I wrote to the school to explain that the very high mark she had obtained in the notoriously tough scholarship exam did not really reflect her ability at maths. I felt she should not be put in too high a class in that subject. She tells me now that she thinks I was right to do so, though I am not sure she was happy about it at the time.

Tessa was never much interested in the idea of me finding my birth mother; it was another of the ways in which she was easy-going. Other people might very naturally have been quite concerned about their husband being adopted: what diseases they could have inherited and all that kind of thing. But Tessa did not think along those lines.

However, in about 1988, I began to realise that perhaps there was only a limited amount of time left if I wanted to make another serious attempt to find my birth mother before she died. My adoptive mother was, by then, terribly afflicted by senile dementia, and would die two years later, on 30 April 1990, so this probably also had an impact on my thinking.

My adoptive sister Susan's search for her own birth mother had ended in a heart-breaking way. She too had been looking for quite some time, and her efforts had finally led her to the woman who had given birth to her so many years earlier. Susan discovered who her birth mother was, also that she was still alive, and where she lived. But the organisation that had helped her had also spoken to her birth mother's doctor. The doctor had told them she was so ill that the shock of meeting my sister would have been too much for her. One has to bear in mind that very often the birth mother, having married later, has not told her husband that she has had a child.

I started my search by writing letters to those in the London telephone directory whose name was Cleland, asking if they could help me. They could not, though several tried. I was disappointed, but persevered.

One day I drove to Uvedale Road in Enfield and parked fifty yards away from the house in which I had discovered my mother stayed while waiting to go into labour. I sat for a while in my car, simply looking at the house. I did not really expect anything to happen; it was just interesting to think that my mother had been living in that building while she was waiting for me to be born.

Afterwards, I went to see a civil servant who kept the records I needed to see. While I was there, he took a call from a friend who had been alarmed by the fact that a strange man had been lurking outside his home on Uvedale Road for rather a long time.

But it was not long before I had a piece of luck. Someone on Uvedale Road – I cannot remember how I met her – remembered a woman who had once lived on the street, and put me in touch with her. I got to know this lady, Margaret Seward, who had known my mother well. She even had a photograph of her. She told me that she herself had been adopted by a couple, Jack and Mary Mitchell, who had been friends with Chrissie at Kilmarnock Academy in Ayrshire, where they all grew up. It was them to whom Chrissie had turned when pregnant, and my mother had stayed with them until she went into labour.

Chrissie and the Mitchells remained friends, attending school reunions together. After Mary Mitchell died, Jack stayed in close contact with Chrissie. They went on holiday together, and he would go to visit her in Scotland. Margaret told me how devastated Jack had been when he heard that Chrissie had died. What is terribly sad is that Margaret had no idea that my birth mother had any living relations. So although I learned a lot by talking to her, the trail, in a sense, went cold.

The next breakthrough came about almost by accident. I had written an article on torture for the *Mail on Sunday*, and was taken out for lunch by the editor who had commissioned it. In the course of our conversation, I happened to mention that I had been adopted, and he said that there was a girl on the paper's staff who moonlighted by helping to trace the mothers of adopted children. Her name was Claudia Joseph. It was through her that I was finally able to find out about my own birth mother.

Perhaps the biggest surprise to me was that Chrissie had been forty-two when she gave birth to me. I had assumed that she had been a teenager who had made a silly mistake. Chrissie belonged to the generation that grew up knowing that because so many young men had been killed in the First World War, there was a shortage of potential husbands. In the thirties, unmarried mothers were strongly disapproved of and Chrissie would have had a very difficult time if she had brought me up alone. I understand her decision to have me adopted.

Chrissie Cleland's family was Scottish, and she was one of eight children. They were not rich, but all had respectable jobs, such as being a doctor or teacher. Chrissie's father was a teacher and she was born in the schoolhouse of Grougar School, Kilmarnock. When she was four, her mother died of tuberculosis, which left her father to bring up his sons and daughters alone.

By 1934, when she became pregnant with me, she too had become a teacher and lived with her father, together with two of her sisters, who were also teachers, in a house her father had built in Cliftonville, near Margate in Kent; quite close, as it happens, to Chilham Castle, my present home.

Because Chrissie's father was blind and he was never told, he never knew that his daughter was carrying a baby. Indeed, nobody apart from the two sisters knew, and so when later I made contact with my natural family after the sisters who did know had died, my existence came as a great surprise to them.

The identity of my father has never been established, though there are a couple of contenders. Tessa believed that it was the headmaster of the school at which my mother taught: why else, she argued, would he have been willing to give her so much time off in which to have her child?

Another possibility, which I am slightly inclined to believe is the right one, is Jack Mitchell, who, along with his wife Mary had come very close to adopting me. After Mary died, Jack went on to spend a great deal of time with Chrissie, and so maybe something was going on. I do not know, and I have never spent too much time trying to find out. I have a diary owned by another person who knew Chrissie well, which may be covered in traces of DNA. That may contain the answer, or it may be too late.

After I was born, Chrissie returned to Cliftonville, and the three sisters, all unmarried, lived there until 1956, when they moved back to Kilmarnock. Chrissie died on 26 November 1969, aged seventy-six.

It was while they were researching Chrissie that the *Mail on Sunday* tracked down a surviving member of my family, an eighty-seven-year-old first cousin, Mabel MacDonald. I went with Tessa, Sarah and Jacquetta to Edinburgh to meet her and twelve other relations. We had lunch together in the Sheraton Hotel and then we went to Mabel's flat. Here we watched some grainy clips of Chrissie, taken in 1956 when I was still at Oxford and she was a sixty-two-year-old spinster.

What astonished my family was that she moved in a strikingly similar way to me – walking in a very upright way with her hands behind her back. Much later, Margaret Seward told me that she had seen me twice on television. 'It's uncanny,' she said, 'your gestures are precisely the same as your mother's.' There was also a striking resemblance between my daughter Jacquetta and Chrissie.

It turns out that Chrissie, like me, had been a keen bridge player, though there were other respects in which we were completely different. The family were typical Scottish Presbyterians, so they were teetotal and certainly did not go in for gambling. There was also a suggestion that at the end of the thirties, my birth mother held strong communist sympathies. Not a characteristic that I have inherited.

It would have been fascinating to meet Chrissie. Plainly I inherited some physical characteristics, and perhaps some mental ones too. I imagine she would have been able to tell me things that might have shed light on my character, and it would have been interesting to ask her why she gave me up for adoption. But I do not feel that I have missed out on some sort of 'closure', or that I am somehow incomplete because I did not track her down in time.

Most of all, I am reluctant to spend too much time

contemplating the other routes my life could have taken: in those alternate lives, it is unlikely that I would have met my wife and had my three girls, and why on earth would I ever want that?

CHAPTER 12

GET OFF THE LEDGE AND
GIVE US THE MONEY

By 1987, IG Index was doing very well – we had made
£700,000 before tax in the year ending May '87, and by the
end of September we had already made the same again, enough
to make us start thinking about going public with a stock
exchange quotation.

Then came the great crash, and IG Index very nearly went
under.

On the night of 15 October, the south of England was torn to
pieces by a storm that swept across the country. Those who
managed to sleep through the hurricane woke the next morning
to see trees flattened, and roofs and windows smashed; thousands
were left without electricity. I happened to have a physiotherapist
appointment in the morning. I decided to treat myself to breakfast
at the Ritz. 'Sorry, residents only,' they said. 'Why?' I asked. 'Look
at the ceiling.' It was not there.

This carnage was mirrored on the stock market, where the
crash began in Hong Kong and quickly spread, first to Europe
and then the States. That Friday, the Dow Jones Index, which had

never before fallen more than 100 points in one day, fell by 108. Worse was to come. On the following Monday, it plummeted by a devastating 508 points. In percentage terms that was a bigger drop than in the 1929 crash.

At IG Index, we had been allowing our clients to bet about stock indices (such as the FTSE index or the Dow Jones Index) for a long time, and that autumn most of them had bet that prices would go up. So we had hedged heavily by buying in the real markets.

As we surveyed the wreckage on Monday, it was obvious that many of the clients who had gone long had lost far more than they thought possible. Naturally it was appalling for them. It was also appalling for us. Some of our clients made it clear that they were unwilling to pay their losses; others indicated that they were unable to do so. We in turn were being pressed by the brokers with whom we had hedged; they wanted us to come up immediately with the money we were losing on our hedging transactions.

Everyone in the office worked flat out until 9 p.m. when the American markets closed; nobody even thought of leaving. It was marvellous. Our staff were doing everything they possibly could. You could hear this crescendo of noise rising from the dealing desk – shouting, arguing and telephones ringing constantly – with the odd comments escaping the general din: 'Just get off the ledge and give us the money!' Had the situation not been so desperate for us, it would have been entertaining to watch.

In spite of the stress, I had time to feel enormously impressed and grateful to our team. A week or so later, when the dust had settled, I put a £100 note and a bottle of champagne on each of their desks. At the end of the day, Tessa came into the office; it was one of those situations where I really appreciated her no-nonsense personality. 'Come on, darling,' she said, 'let's go home.'

Just before the crash, one of our richest clients had made a big

Left: Portrait of the author as a young entrepreneur. A press shot taken by Tessa in 1993 during my time at IG Index.

Below: Me on the dealing desk of IG Index. I had just created a stir by donating £5 million to the Conservative Party. [Shutterstock].

Right: My three daughters Sarah, Jacquetta and Charlotte with me (in a hammock) at Dar Sinclair, Tessa's house in Tangier, in 1989.

Below: The drawing room at Dar Sinclair. The picture on the wall is of David Herbert, the 'Queen of Tangier'.

Left: My birth mother, whom I never knew, Chrissie Cleland, in 1915. People tell me that she and my middle daughter, Jacquetta, who has enjoyed much success as a top model, look strikingly similar.

Below: My three daughters. *Left to right*; Sarah, Charlotte and Jacquetta.

Above: William Hague and me in 2001, not long after my donation. He never had much success as leader of the opposition, but I think his 'second act' was highly impressive.

Below: You know that you have achieved a certain level of fame when you find yourself the subject of satirical cartoons. And, almost two decades on, perennial Tory leadership loser Ken Clarke and I are still no closer to agreeing about Europe

TORY DONOR RULES OUT CLARKE

" IF YOU'LL GIVE £5m NOT TO HAVE ME AS LEADER, HOW MUCH TO STOP ANNE WIDDECOMBE

Above: Lady Thatcher and me in 2004 with her portrait which was painted to mark the twenty-fifth anniversary of her becoming Prime Minister. I had just bought the picture in a 'silent auction'.

Below: Me with Nigel Farage. He is a tremendous mix of good and bad qualities, but his influence on the course of British history has been incalculable. [Alan Davidson/Shutterstock]

Above left: Me with a voter in Battle, Sussex, campaigning for election as an MP in the 2010 general election. I had created my own party, the Trust Party. I did not win.

Above right: Rodney Leach was an influence on me throughout my life, and his death in 2016, during the Referendum campaign, was a great sadness to me. [Alice Leach]

Below: The Vote Leave battlebus, with its controversial spending commitment. [Andrew Parsons/Shutterstock]

Above: Chilham Castle, near Canterbury, in Kent. My home after 2002. I enjoy filling it with friends almost every weekend.

Below: Me in my study in Chilham Castle, where I retreat when I get tired of the friends I have invited to stay.

Above: Tessa and me in Morocco, a place she dearly loved.

bet that the market would go up. He lost a million pounds. I very badly needed him to pay quickly. I called him the next day to ask what he proposed to do about it. He intended, I was relieved to hear, to settle his debts as quickly as he could. He told his bank in Switzerland to transfer the million pounds to his London bank. So far so good: he had behaved impeccably. But his bank in London 'lost' the money for twenty-four hours, a day that brought us to the brink of disaster.

We were saved by a tremendous stroke of luck. When we asked our clients to settle their debts, we received a series of letters from solicitors 'informing' us that their clients were not liable, because the debts were gambling debts and therefore unenforceable. That would have been true but for the Financial Services Act of 1986. I was thankful that I was able to point them to section 72, which had for the first time made these transactions enforceable by law. Miraculously, *this* part of the act had already been brought into effect.

Also miraculously, a different part of the act had *not* yet been brought into effect. The crucial point was this. Most of our clients were required by us, when they opened a bet, to let us have a cash deposit, to protect us against the client's possible failure to pay his losses. We, in our turn, had to put up money to the brokers through whom we hedged, to protect them against a failure by us to pay our losses. We used our clients' deposits with us to provide this money. Part of the act stipulated that we could no longer pass our clients' deposits on to the brokers with whom we had hedged. If this part of the act had been in force, we would very probably have been unable to pay our brokers, and that would have been the end of our business.

Of course, we still had the most appalling week. Our accountants came in on the Thursday to assess whether we were insolvent, in which case we would have had to close. They crawled all over our books before they decided that we were just about all right, but they recommended that we should raise half a million pounds to make sure that people would have confidence in us.

This was easier said than done: I had not got any part of it. I called up our biggest shareholders. Selim Zilkha, easily our richest shareholder, declined to help. But friends such as Robin Birkinhead came up with around £420,000, which meant that I needed 'only' to find £80,000 to avoid having to accept a most unwelcome dilution in my shareholding.

I had had dinner with my friend Torquil Norman on the Friday of the hurricane. That was a coincidence, as I had not seen him much for years – with the notable exception of an unannounced trip to watch me play poker in Las Vegas (of which more later). He called me on the Wednesday after the Monday crash. 'I see there've been some rather violent movements on the stock market. I happen to have quite a large sum of money on deposit doing nothing, I just wondered if that might be of any help to you?'

I replied that it was an incredibly kind offer, and that had he asked me the previous day, I would probably have bitten off his arm to take it, but that actually *today* things were looking better, so I probably did not need it.

The following day, things went badly wrong for us again. Something went awry internally, so that a measure we took, thinking it reduced our exposure, in fact increased it. I spoke to Torquil. He agreed to lend me £100,000 on marvellously generous terms – no interest, no date by which it needed to be paid back, no contract, no anything. 'A friend in need' really is 'a friend indeed'.

Six months later, I repaid his loan and I asked him to become a director of the company.

In those moments when I was not completely absorbed by meetings or the very immediate worries that were crowding around me, I thought, in bookmakers' language, about my own prospects. I decided that it was about 5 to 4 on that we would go under, i.e., slightly more likely than not. I began to consider what I might do if the business did collapse. I knew that my wife, three young daughters and I would probably have to leave London and move to the country, but beyond that it was not clear if there was anything I could do to support them if the worst came to the worst. It was a very alarming time. Anyhow we survived that awful week and the stock market recovered about three months after the crash. We ended up making a small profit in the year ending May 1988.

We did, however, have to shelve our plans to go public, and there was one dreadful morning in 1988 when a lack of business forced us to sack a third of our staff. I think we treated them all well and were generous, but it was awful. The business of breaking the bad news to employees that we are letting them go, for whatever reason, is something I really hate. But once that conversation is over, I feel absolutely fine, which in itself makes me feel rather guilty.

At some point during the eighties we had hired an IT professional who came with a great reputation. It soon became clear, though, that he would have to go. By the time that I had discussed the matter with the other directors and agreed that we needed to get rid of him, he had left for a fortnight's holiday. The prospect of the meeting at which I would have to give him the bad news hung over me grimly every day while he was away, until at last I had done it.

After all the excitement of the Great Crash, Tessa thought that I was close to a nervous breakdown and so she sent me off to the hotel in Penzance run by Jean Shrimpton, the famous model. The experience was the occasion for the only compliment I can remember Tessa ever paying me. After I had been there thirty-six hours or so, we spoke on the phone and she asked me what Jean was like now. I told her that she was absolutely marvellous. 'Oh

God!' came the reply, 'I knew I shouldn't have sent you there.' Why she thought that Jean Shrimpton was likely to leap on me, I cannot say.

I would return, again by myself, three or four more times over the next few years, going for long walks on the moors and having lovely lunches in pubs.

A lot had already changed for IG Index even before the events of 1987.

At the beginning of the decade, in 1981, we moved into our first 'real' offices, in Grosvenor Gardens in Belgravia. Leaving the top floor of my house in Clapham made a big difference to the atmosphere in the office. In 1999, by which time we had over sixty employees, we moved again, to offices south of the river.

To begin with there are only two or three of you in a single room, and you are able to laugh and joke together. Then more join, and they sit in a different room, and then more people join, and they sit on a different floor. When you are all in one room, you have a direct relationship with everyone there. Things change a bit when there are two rooms, but when the staff are spread across a couple of floors, and you have to delegate responsibility for managing junior members to others, different qualities are required of management. A moment arrives (though you may not notice it immediately) when you find that the office is full of young whippersnappers you hope will make pots of money for you, and you realise you do not know any of them.

The change is gradual, but total. Although there was never a moment when I wished that we would be thrust back to being as small as we had been at the beginning, I definitely believe that in some senses it was a happier and more enjoyable place when it was tiny.

This is not to say that it was all work and no play. There was a day when a 'nun' came to Grosvenor Gardens dressed in her full habit, wimple and all. 'I must speak to somebody,' she said, 'something awful has happened. One of our priests in Ireland has lost all of our money through your company, I need to speak to the person in charge.'

Someone shouted over to my office, 'Stuart, there's a nun here who says that one of her order's Fathers has lost all their money gambling with us.'

This seemed like the last thing I would want to get involved with. So I ignored it, hoping the whole thing would blow over without me being involved.

'Stuart!'

'I can't possibly come.'

'Stuart, she simply won't go!'

Eventually I gave in and went over to where she was standing. At this point everything became a bit strange, largely because she had started singing 'Don't cry for me Stuart Wheeler' to the tune of 'Don't Cry for Me Argentina', while also showing me the stockings she was wearing under her habit.

While everyone around me was in fits, I had no idea what was going on. It took me ages to work out that she was taking her clothes off, and even longer to realise that she might not actually be a nun. My wife was responsible for this outrage.

For a long time, I had no office of my own. I sat on the dealing desk, and would often take bets myself. This lasted until well after the crash, when my colleague Lizie Byng, who ran the desk, finally ran out of patience with me and, along with others, suggested it was time I sat away from the rest of the staff. The alleged justification for my move was that they thought I needed more time to think about strategy.

It may be that I continued to stay on the dealing desk (where we speak on the telephone to the clients making bets) for so long because I enjoyed it, but also because I failed to appreciate what the proper role of a CEO was. Everyone else has a very clearly delineated set of tasks, while the CEO is responsible for everything and nothing. Things happen all the time, there are endless meetings, and if you are not careful, all you are doing is reacting to events.

What I should have been doing was what my colleagues wanted me to do – sitting back and thinking carefully about strategy – but I never really got round to it. I remember once hearing that my number two, Nat Le Roux, had said, 'It's not entirely clear what Stuart is doing, maybe it's regulation?' There was a lot of truth in this criticism.

As the eighties turned into the nineties and the millennium approached, our business continued to grow and to change. As well as acquiring our rivals, Ladbrokes Sporting Spreads (in 1997) and William Hill Index (in 2001), over time we expanded the number of things we bet about. In 1982, we offered clients the chance to bet about the level of stock indices, and eventually – thirteen years later – we plucked up our courage sufficiently to offer bets on the prices of individual shares, the first company to do so.

We were very nervous about this. For a time, we had a great respect for, and fear of, the London Stock Exchange. We were afraid that they might get annoyed with us and start making life difficult. When we actually did take the plunge, nothing happened.

Two years later, we added political betting to our portfolio, but perhaps most significant of all was the creation, in 1993, of IG Sport. We had the good fortune to be approached by Ernie Burns, who had been the main sports dealer at our rival, City Index. Later we asked Toby Brereton, an extremely good journalist working for *Sporting Life*, a daily which was at the time a rival to *Racing Post*, to run our sports side. After some hesitation he agreed. We were very fortunate in getting him to come on board.

Another very important hire had been Nat Le Roux, my

number two for a long time, who had a wealth of ideas about how we could branch out from betting on shares to what are called contracts for differences, which became a big part of our business. Nat and I were never going to be great pals – we are very different people – but he understood business much better than I did and his imagination made a big contribution to our success.

Technical developments had, as well as people, a lot to do with our growth, although I myself could never be said to have been an early adopter of technology. Right at the beginning of the company, somebody suggested buying a calculator, but I said, 'Well, that's not necessary, why can't people do long division?'

IG Index had acquired its first computer in 1983. It was to the great relief of the whole staff, who knew how useless I was with technology, that I happened to be on holiday over the weekend when we were to take this bold step into a new era. So if things went wrong, I would not be around to make things worse.

We did not realise then, nobody could have, how colossal an impact the invention of the Internet a decade or so later would have on our business. When people found they could get prices, or make bets, online, it changed everything, and I think at IG we were pretty good at keeping abreast, or even sometimes ahead, of this revolution. For instance, we were the first company to launch an online dealing platform for financial spread-betting. I am told that ninety-nine per cent of the business that IG Index now does is conducted online, and the average deal time is less than a second – it is a world away from the sort of gambling I first knew.

We finally went public in the summer of 2000, a hair-raising experience. Your mind is suddenly swarmed by thousands of nagging questions. Will the price nosedive at the last minute before the great day? Will the so-called institutions (investment trusts and so on) actually want to buy any of our shares? There is a huge amount of administrative work too. You have to hire a merchant bank (or a mini merchant bank, if you are a smaller outfit) to guide you through the regulatory thickets, taking you through the work needed to ensure that you will not make the sort of mistake that will get the company or its directors sued. At the end of all this, the merchant bank that handles the process discusses with you the price they suggest for the shares.

Naturally we did not run a betting book on our own share price; we would have been in breach of goodness knows how many rules if we had, but our rivals did. (We kept an anxious eye on their quotations.)

I also had to do a certain amount to help with publicity, which explains why there are quite a lot of photographs of me wandering around looking rather lost and wearing the French football team's strip (they had just won the European Championships), with our 240p float price emblazoned on the front.

The whole process is very tiring. I was forced to manage on less than six hours' sleep a night by virtue of drinking nothing and eating less than usual. I am used to drinking a reasonable amount, and previously I had found giving up for even a week difficult. I was very anxious to revert to my old habits. I am certainly not unaware of the virtues of abstinence, but if there is one thing that you are *guaranteed* to be told a lot about by the time you reach my age, it is indeed the virtues of abstinence. My problem is that I very much prefer the pleasures of indulgence.

Luckily everything went smoothly, so my sacrifices were not in vain. Our shares were valued at the top end of market expectations; their price rose, and at the end of it I was worth, on paper, between £85 million and £90 million.

I had gained a bit of self-confidence at Oxford, but my very unsuccessful career as a barrister and then a merchant banker, and my failure to make any real money, had left me shy and nervous with people. This changed once it was clear that IG Index had become so successful that I was now worth some large number of millions. The reason it changed was not that I thought very highly of myself just because I had made money; it was because the fact of my success changed the way *other* people behaved towards me.

It is a sort of automatic effect. I do not suggest that people said to themselves, 'Well he's made some money, therefore he must be more worthwhile or a better person than we realised he was,' but it is undoubtedly there at the backs of their minds and makes them think you are more interesting.

Particularly gratifying was the knowledge that I had helped make the original investors a lot of money. For example, all but £100 of an original £5,000 investment was a loan, repaid with interest within about three years. The £100 had become worth about £10 million, and that, I was delighted to realise, was a very great return on their investment – or perhaps it would be equally true to say, a great reward for the favour they had done me by making what, in retrospect, even I consider to have been a mad investment – if they regarded it as a real investment at all.

I can recall very clearly why, in March 2002, I decided to step down as chief executive. One morning, I realised that a great many of the meetings I attended were devoted to technological matters that I did not understand. A CEO should not have to understand every detail about the way that his business operates, but he should at least feel confident enough to be able to ask the right questions. I was not. For a long time, with no help from me I should add, our technology was well ahead of the competition, but recently we had slipped behind. As I almost needed to be told how to turn on my computer every morning, I was hardly the man they needed to put this right.

I was also beginning to realise that I no longer enjoyed running the company on a day-to-day basis. There were 101 decisions to make every day, and I found I did not want to handle them. So, in rather a rush, I decided to quit.

Everybody who is close to me says that I am incredibly impatient. I get upset when I feel that people are wasting my time, or if I am stuck in traffic. But generally, I am apt to take my time making decisions. I will make a list of the plusses and minuses and give them a lot of attention before settling on what I should do. Once I have done so, however, I like to move fast.

My daughter Sarah, who is sometimes right, feels that I implement my decisions headlong. I would say in response that, once one has made up one's mind, there is no reason not to act quickly. My decision to step down was the supreme example: within twenty-four hours, I told Nat Le Roux that I wanted him to take over from me. He took a little time to think about it, and then said yes.

I had given no sign of wanting to leave, and so I suspect it came as a shock (though in the months beforehand, one of our outside directors had said to me, 'You know, Stuart, there's no hurry about this, but I think you ought to be thinking about how much longer you're going to continue.') In fact, I probably should have retired earlier. A decade previously I had written a note to myself saying: 'You must not make the mistake many others do of hanging on too long.' And then I found myself making exactly that mistake.

I remained as non-executive chairman for about a year (which meant that although I chaired board meetings and was consulted on matters of importance, I was not involved in the day-to-day running of the company). I discovered that I was no different to thousands of other men who had founded a business, stepped aside, and then found that they did not get on with their successor.

A point came during the months that followed when the working directors were very much at odds with me. I did not have confidence in the new management of the company – how wrong I was – and I had decided by then that I wanted to sell the rest of my shares. Their response was that if I did insist on selling the shares, I could not continue as chairman. Digging my heels in, I refused to step down, and I told them that while they were free to arrange a board meeting to hold a vote on the matter I would, if they did so, convene an AGM and put the question to the shareholders, which we all knew would lead to a frightful kerfuffle, and an instantaneous drop in the value of the shares.

At this they backed down, and a little while later arrangements were made for a management buyout, although I know that some shareholders, such as the major German bank Deutsche Bank, were keen to keep it as a public company. Similarly, while a number of the original shareholders, including Lizie de la Morinière (formerly Lizie Byng), would have preferred to hold on, they felt loyal to me and so they all agreed to go along with me in selling. Had those who had put up £5,000 originally kept their shares, they would later have been worth about £200 million, something that naturally troubles me.

Two or three years after the sale, I wrote to the six big early shareholders saying that while I thought the decision to sell had been a rational one, I was only too aware that it had turned out appallingly; and so I was sorry that I had been responsible for persuading them to go along with me in that decision. Their reactions were very varied. Three of them wrote me charming letters saying how much money they had made, and how grateful they were. The other three did not reply at all and never have. I think the three that did not reply may have felt that I had persuaded them to sell, and I had sold myself, for reasons that were not necessarily based on the prospects of the company, but more on my own financial situation at the time. They have on the whole, though, remained firm friends.

Of course, I myself would be enormously richer if I had held on. I do not have many regrets. But it is clear that my decision to sell was the worst mistake of my life.

The row with the working directors was all very dramatic and tense for a while, though I was never frothing at the mouth or anything, but my relationship with the company is amicable now. I did not feel the sadness you might expect when I walked out of their door for the last time. IG Index had been thirty years of my life, but so what? I wish the company well, but I do not have a strong emotional connection to it.

Nevertheless, I am proud to think that the firm I founded in my loft in Chelsea, which was staffed to begin with by only me and a quarter of a girl, now has 1,762 employees, customers and offices all over the world, and an annual turnover of some astonishing sum. I may have *hoped*, back in 1974, that something like this would end up happening, but I do not think that at the time I ever really believed it could.

CHAPTER 13

THAT WASN'T A VERY GOOD BET, WAS IT?

I was in bed in my house in Chilham, recovering from an operation, when I realised that Iain Duncan Smith really had to go. It was early October 2003 and IDS had been leader of the Conservative Party for just over two years – during which he had limped from one disaster to the next. His performances had made us wonder why we ever saw him as a potential prime minister. He had been lacerated by Tony Blair on a weekly basis at Prime Minister's Questions, and had generally seemed directionless and incompetent, but it was the conference speech that really did it.

I had watched him (on television) addressing the party at Blackpool. I saw the nineteen standing ovations, and the unconvincingly wild clapping and cheering. Then I listened as he announced that he stood before us 'with the most radical policy agenda of any party aspiring to government since 1979 … my mission is to take the Conservative Party back to government. I won't allow anything or anyone to get in my way.'

'The quiet man is here to stay,' he said, reading robotically from his autocue, 'and he's turning up the volume.'

It did not go up.

I found the whole performance embarrassing. I believe that whatever authority he had managed to cling on to as leader of the Conservative Party virtually drained away for good over the course of those minutes he spent pacing the Blackpool stage.

Almost as soon as the last round of applause had died down, my phone rang – it was the *Today* programme on the line looking for my reaction as a major Tory donor. I felt too ill to talk to them, so I told them, and all the other reporters who called over the next few days, the same thing: 'I really can't say anything at this stage.'

I could not see how Duncan Smith could survive the shambles at Blackpool. After all, the Tories were, as they had proved earlier with their brutal sacking of Margaret Thatcher, completely ruthless when it came to ditching leaders they considered to be a liability. (I only wish they had applied the same policy to Mrs May.) Indeed, as soon as I started to make known my increasingly strong opinion that IDS should stop being leader of the Conservative Party, I was summoned to the office of Lord Strathclyde, the Conservative Leader in the House of Lords, where I was told that I did not need to do anything further, that they had the matter in hand.

But then … nothing happened. We never saw the face-saving compromise deal that Strathclyde was supposed to be negotiating, and as one week rolled into the next, IDS was still at the head of the party. I could see that some people – his successor, Michael Howard, interestingly among them – were already arguing for patience: we should wait for the results of the Hutton Inquiry; we cannot change leaders so close to the local elections; there is still time for the leader to turn things around. The desperate search by rebellious Tories for the twenty-five signatures from MPs, necessary to spark a vote of no confidence in the leader, looked as if it was going to end in failure.

So, as I drank a coffee at Victoria Station, on a Tuesday morning a week and a half after the conference, I decided I had to do something.

I had not always been interested in politics, far from it. I was not oblivious to the subject – Tessa and I used to give general election parties in which people came wearing the colours of the party they supported, and I always voted and watched the news – but for the best part of sixty-five years I had been little more than a spectator. I think this was true even after I made a relatively sizeable donation to the Conservatives in April 2000, when I was asked by my friend Richard Oldfield to a dinner at White's on behalf of William Hague and his party. I was put next to Hague, who had succeeded John Major as leader of the Conservative Party in 1997, and was very much impressed by him – he spoke well, and he seemed honest, and the Tories were plainly in need of financial support.

Until then I had not given more than £100 to a political party but, because IG Index was in the process of going public, and I was feeling unworried about money for almost the first time that I could remember, I gave Hague £15,000. I did not, however, see this as the start of a new stage in my life; I did not realise then how involved I would become in politics.

All this changed once I had stepped down as CEO of IG Index. I was told once that on the morning after his last-minute drop-goal had won the rugby World Cup final for England, Jonny Wilkinson woke up in the grip of a profound depression. Winning the World Cup was the culmination of years of agonising work and sacrifice; he had achieved everything he had ever dreamed of, and it was precisely this that meant he now felt so empty. What next?

I felt something rather similar in the very early days of 2001. One of our investors said to me that there was nothing more depressing than achieving one's life's ambition. I did not experience quite the same emptiness as Wilkinson, but I certainly felt rather flat, and I was determined that I would not fall into the trap of frittering my afternoons away getting drunk and playing bridge – I am afraid I need to remember that now.

My problem was that I was not clear about what I *would* do instead, at least until I decided that I would make a far bigger donation than the one I had given to William Hague earlier. My decision was based on very simple and, I believed, rational principles, though I am aware that in some respects they show how I view the world in slightly different terms from most people.

I happened to think that although Labour, who had a twenty-point lead in the polls, were strong favourites to retain their huge majority in the forthcoming election, it was definitely not certain that they would win. After all, as I was quite fond of saying at the time, Ted Heath had faced equally dismal odds before his 1970 victory. This time the bookmakers made Labour 'only' 10 to 1 on to win (meaning that a bet of £10 would win you £1). So, since bookmakers want the odds to be in their favour, this meant that the betting showed their chances were not thought, by the bookmakers at least, to be as high as that.

Given this, the £5 million I was giving was, I felt, from the point of view of the country, not a high price to pay. If the Conservatives did manage to win the election, the country would be better off by a lot more than ten times the value of my donation. I do realise that this is a very unusual way of looking at things.

Perhaps equally significant was that a great deal had been made in the press of three separate donations of £2 million each that had been given to the Labour Party, something that sparked my sympathy for the underdog. I had just made a very large sum of money, and I knew that the Tory party could not even afford to pay to bring one of their Scottish members down for an important meeting in London. So, while it made little difference to me at that point whether I had £5 million more or less – I appeared to be worth around £90 million, and who needed that much? – it was likely to make a huge difference to the Tories.

As so often in my life, I turned to Rodney Leach. I told him that I was considering giving £10 million to the Conservative Party. He suggested, very wisely, that I should reduce that figure by half. Rodney then arranged a meeting with William Hague, whom he knew quite well, telling him that he had a friend who had something 'interesting' to say to him.

At the time, I still had an exaggerated respect for important people such as major politicians. I also knew what I wanted to say, however, and although I probably gabbled a little, I launched into my little piece before Hague could open his mouth. After giving him my reasons for wanting to offer the Tories my help, I went on to explain that I had no interest in meddling with policy, or in having any say in the make-up of his shadow cabinet. I realise now that this was an absurd point of view.

I added that if I were offered an honour, I would refuse it, since I did not believe people should be ennobled for giving money to a political party – something I felt strongly about then, and still do (it was thought at the time that a donation of even £1 million would guarantee a peerage). Of course, I would now rather enjoy being a peer, so that I could sound off about all sorts of things in the House of Lords.

Hague listened to me carefully before breaking into a smile. 'You must be just about the perfect donor,' he said, 'This is rather like a visit from Father Christmas.'

My family were probably as surprised as William Hague by my decision, but less pleased. I had phoned my wife just beforehand to tell her what I was thinking of doing. She offered no criticism herself, but she did rather swiftly telephone Jacquetta, telling her: 'Darling, we have to face facts. We are now the wife and daughter of a madman.'

While at IG Index, I had been reasonably successful at cultivating financial journalists, but there was nothing about these low-key relationships that could prepare me for the great excitement that my donation created. Suddenly my face and name were splashed across all the papers, and a great scrum of TV cameras surrounded me. I rather liked being at the centre of all that press attention, and the idea that people might be interested in what I had to say. I went on the air to any show that wanted me.

Although I had been explicit about not wanting to buy influence in the party, I was automatically invited to political conferences and think-tank events with top Conservatives, many of whom I came to know a little. I also found myself being ushered into special areas of the Conservative conferences and taken to meet shadow ministers: it was a new life for me.

Although I am sure that I did not think about it in these terms, the money I gave to William Hague effectively meant that I had bought myself into politics. As someone would put it later, that £5 million was a frightfully good investment.

Looking back, I now see that it was idiotic of me to say – and to mean it, which I did then – that I had no desire to influence William Hague's shadow cabinet or his policies. If I did not care about these things, why give them all that money? Some people even speculated that supporting Hague to such a level was the sort of behaviour of which only an eccentric Old Etonian could be capable.

The whole thing caused me to think more seriously than before about how I felt about politics and politicians, and also to decide what issues were most important to me. Almost two decades on, I still do not have anything as coherent as a complete political philosophy, but there are some things I believe in quite strongly.

I am never sure what the terms applied to different political positions mean exactly, but I think libertarian describes my view of the world best. Certainly, I am very right wing economically. The critical point, I suppose, is that I would be slightly in favour of being not all that kind to those who do not have a job (unless they genuinely could not get one), and more kind to those who have low-paying jobs. If the amount you are entitled to through benefits comes close to matching what you can earn, then you are obviously tempted not to work.

I also believe broadly that free markets and low taxation are best for both rich and poor. If competition is allowed to flourish, and the government does not make interventions based on a conviction that it knows better than its people, everyone will, I think, benefit. Why, after all, are people in the West so much better off than those in Eastern countries that deny economic freedom?

I do not, however, think that I am a *classic* libertarian. While I think that the state takes far too great a proportion of people's money in taxes, and that it should interfere as little as possible, I can see how, if you get a tiny number of companies dominating a particular market, they may well use their monopolies in a way that is against the interests of the people, and so I am in favour of regulation to prevent that happening.

I am aware of issues such as obesity, which has a terrible effect on the country (partly on those suffering from it themselves, who I imagine are both unhappy and unhealthy, but also because of its substantial cost to the NHS). So, while one part of me does not hold with rules telling people what or how much they may eat, or regulations constricting food companies' ability to advertise and sell their goods, the other side of me sees that the problem is so great that there is a reasonable argument, for instance, for taxing sugar.

Gambling is another awkward issue. I remember saying to Dominic Cadbury, when he was running the famous chocolate-making firm which bore his name, that neither somebody like me, who had made his money from other people betting, or somebody like him, whose family fortune rested on selling products containing sugar, could be expected to remain balanced in discussions of the effects, harmful or otherwise, of our respective industries. I do not recall whether he agreed.

Jacob Rothschild's father, the immensely gifted and clever Victor Rothschild, was once commissioned by the government to conduct a major investigation into the effects of gambling. He concluded that 99.4 per cent of gamblers were not problem gamblers – most just liked the odd flutter now and then. However, for the 0.6 per cent for whom it was a major problem, the problem was often a *terrible* one. So there genuinely is a very difficult problem. How far should the government go in making regulations that to some extent adversely affect the 99.4 per cent of non-problem gamblers, in order to protect the 0.6 per cent of problem gamblers? I definitely think the government was right in April 2019 to reduce from £100 to £2 the maximum stake permitted in the fixed-odds betting terminals, to be found in most betting shops.

I know that my views on tax are open to accusations of bias, because, as I am wealthier than most, I obviously benefit personally from low taxes. I am yet to be convinced, however, that governments are best placed to know how money should be spent – far better, I believe, to let people spend their own money as they wish. Of course, there are limits, and we do need taxes for a number of essentials – there must be enough money to pay for defence and the health system, for example.

The press would have you believe that my scepticism about global warming puts me in the minority. In spite of the very troublesome demonstrations that have caused chaos to traffic in 2019, I am not so sure about the public. It is worth remembering, too, that only thirty or so years ago there was genuine concern amongst many at the prospect of a new ice age. Scientific opinion does change. How long ago was it that having diesel engines in our cars was considered green? Furthermore, temperatures have only risen by one degree at most in the last hundred years, and this increase is actually beneficial on average, though there will be winners and losers from it.

The amount of money that people want to spend to combat all of this is completely out of proportion to any good it might be expected to do, and it would far better be used fighting malaria and providing clean water in the Third World.

I may spend only a paragraph or two discussing torture, but this does no justice at all to the strength of my feeling on the subject. I consider torture so utterly disgusting and abhorrent that I cannot understand why anybody could *not* feel strongly about it. It is the worst example of man's inhumanity to man. As I have already mentioned, I am quite a coward myself, particularly where pain is concerned, so perhaps this contributes to the revulsion I feel. I can easily imagine how frightful it must be to find oneself the object of torture.

The most compelling argument against it is the moral one, and yet one might also construct a case against it on practical grounds, because it is a highly unreliable and inefficient means of extracting information, which often ends up only generating more hate in those who are subjected to it: it is senselessly cruel. This argument is a very dangerous one, however, because unless it is explained very carefully, it may be taken to imply that torture in support of a good cause is acceptable if it works, which is emphatically not my view.

I have given money and time to a range of charities – such as Amnesty, Liberty, Human Rights Watch, Prisoners Abroad and Reprieve – and I was, I think, the first supporter to make substantial donations to the All-Party Parliamentary Group on Extraordinary Rendition, which was set up in 2005 by Andrew Tyrie. Extraordinary rendition is the shocking practice of many governments, including sometimes our own, I am sorry to say, of sending detainees to other countries knowing or suspecting that they will be tortured. For a long time, torture was the subject I pursued most energetically and publicly (and I am still appalled by it).

Although I liked expressing my views on other subjects in letters to the papers or in questions at think-tank events, I was never really interested in a more organised effort, until I became consumed by the problem of our relationship with Europe.

Even after the £5 million donation, I remained rather diffident.

I admired William Hague a lot at the time. Of course, there were many people who claimed he had taken that top role too soon, when he was only thirty-six, but I believe that when you have the chance to lead a major political party, you cannot say, 'I won't do it now, I'll wait until a few years' time.' When the opportunity comes, you obviously have to take it.

I talked to him a great deal in the months between my donation and the election, and he certainly could not be accused of any lack of optimism or spirit. Whenever I pointed out that he was making no progress in the polls, he would simply react by saying, 'Well, that shows I just have to fight harder, doesn't it.'

But while I liked him, there were occasions when his lack of experience showed, and when he was the Tory leader, he failed to make himself popular enough with the public. The Conservative Party never even looked close to winning the 2001 election, and they did not, managing to win only one seat more than they had in 1997.

The morning immediately after Hague's defeat, I was interviewed by Jeremy Paxman who, with his customary sneer, said to me 'Well, you're a betting man, but that wasn't a very good bet, was it?' I explained to him that it was not a bet; it was a donation.

There is a slight irony to this, in that I had actually made a very good bet on the results of the 1997 election. Scepticism of polls was not invented in 2016. Even though all the polls suggested the Conservatives were on course to do appallingly, the fact that polls had been so wrong five years earlier meant that very few people were willing to put their trust in them. The polls implied that the Conservatives would end up with between 161 and 180 seats.

Bookmakers were betting on how many seats a party would win, offering you the chance to bet in groups of twenty. Ladbrokes were laying 100 to 1 against the number of Tory seats being in that range. So I got as much money on that group of twenty seats as I could. They kept on reducing the odds as I went on betting and in the end the price for new bets had fallen from 100 to 1 when I started my bets, to 16 to 1.

The Conservatives got a mere 165 seats and I won something close to £30,000, but because I had gone to a small local branch of Ladbrokes to make the bet, and they were not allowed to issue cheques of more than £10,000, they had to write three separate cheques. I am not sure how much their rule protected them. It was exciting. I gave everyone in my company a gift when I got back into the office – I think a combination of meat and champagne.

You could say it was a sign that I had become a figure worth cultivating that Hague's successor, Iain Duncan Smith, agreed to have lunch with me within a few weeks of becoming leader. Initially I was rather impressed. He had an interesting background. He was always a committed Eurosceptic. He had remained on the backbenches until 1997, when William Hague brought him into the Shadow Cabinet. He had a reputation for being tough about the right sorts of things – and he was an agreeably indiscreet dining companion.

He told me how during the leadership contest, once the

Conservative MPs had reduced the contest down to the final two, his rival Ken Clarke, the pro-European who had been considered the great favourite, came up to him and said, 'There is not much point in this; I am bound to win.'

What I suspect IDS did not know was quite how close he came to being eliminated in the crucial third ballot of the MPs, the one that decided which two of the contenders would go through to be voted on by the party membership. One of the MPs involved told me later that he had given very serious consideration to voting for Portillo rather than IDS, because while he believed that Duncan Smith would easily make the final two, he had also been very anxious that Ken Clarke should be excluded. In the end, he went with Duncan Smith, which was just as well for IDS, because had this MP opted for Portillo, he would have been out of it. There was only one vote between the two of them.

While I was full of optimism about him when he began his reign, it soon became clear to me, and to a great many other Conservatives, that he was not up to the job. He did not cut a good figure, he did not seem capable of delivering good speeches – in fact he did not appear to have a grip on anything. Then there was the fiasco at the party conference in Blackpool.

Once I had made my mind up that I was going to go public with my concerns, I tried to call Conservative Central Office to let them know what I was planning to do, but the only person around was a secretary, who took a message. My next call was to the BBC. One of the benefits of being such a large donor to the Conservative Party was that once I had decided I wanted to take action, I was prominent enough to get myself a slot on the *Today* programme, where I was able to make my argument that it really was essential that Iain Duncan Smith should cease being leader of the Conservative Party.

I told them, 'He does not come over as a potential prime minister. He comes over as weak,' and 'He is terribly bad at communicating'. Elsewhere, I hinted that the party could expect no more money from me while IDS was the Tory boss.

I thought there would be quite a rumpus. I am not saying that my actions were decisive; perhaps it would be most accurate to say that as the party was already standing on the ledge, it may have only needed somebody to give it a final push.

A few hours after my interview had gone out on the air, Duncan Smith once again failed to land any blows on Tony Blair during PMQs; not long afterwards, he was called into an emergency conference by the chief whip. MPs were seen whizzing around Westminster in a state of great agitation. Later that afternoon, the weekly gathering of the Shadow Cabinet showed the brutality of politics. When a deadly pause followed the end of 'any other business', the silence was broken when Duncan Smith cleared his throat.

Some of the assembled MPs thought for a moment that he was about to resign. Instead he launched into a desperate final appeal to his colleagues. 'I am going to fight the next election as leader,' he told them. 'The party voted for me.' It was as if he knew everything was crumbling around him. Everyone in the room broke into a round of applause, but poor IDS was well aware that several of his senior colleagues were already preparing their own leadership campaigns, or were amongst those actively plotting to bring him down.

Within days he was gone.

I still feel he was absolutely hopeless in that role, but I also feel sorry for him. Ever since he was toppled he has been most impressive, especially in his stubborn advocacy on behalf of the poorest members of society. Like Hague and Neil Kinnock, he has had a good 'second act'. I have great admiration for those people who, having failed in their attempts to win the big prize, still have the guts and determination to fight for a much smaller one.

It is easy to see how Iain Duncan Smith might very naturally have resented my action, but when our paths crossed again later on, he was perfectly civil. I asked him whether he resented me for what I had done, 'Well,' he told me very calmly, 'it was unhelpful.'

Things were less troubled in the two years Michael Howard was in charge. He was efficient in rebuilding Tory prospects, and I gave a further £500,000 to the party. I also became increasingly involved in supporting seven or eight think-tanks, including Civitas, Policy Exchange, Reform, the Adam Smith Institute, Politeia, the Institute of Economic Affairs and the Centre for Policy Studies (the last two of which are very right wing, and had a substantial influence on Mrs Thatcher).

I believe that think-tanks do play an extremely valuable role in politics. They are full of very bright people who have the time to think both about new policies and the arguments needed to support them. Politicians are often too busy running around attending debates, or looking after the interests of their constituents, to do the much more important job of thinking.

I still spend a lot of time going to think-tank events, and I am quite good at putting my hand up and being given a chance to ask a question during Q&A sessions. I try to put a lot of thought in advance into the questions I ask – since you usually get only one bite at the cherry – but I do occasionally make up my interventions on the spot, and this once led me into trouble.

One afternoon in 2013, I attended an IEA event designed to discuss a proposed EU directive that would have imposed a rule on companies that they must have a minimum proportion of women on their boards. The majority of those who spoke were in support, but I thought I had something to add.

'I would just like to challenge the idea,' I said, 'that it is necessarily right to have a particular percentage on a board.

Business is very, very competitive and you should take notice of the performance of women in another competitive area, which is sport, especially the games where men have no strength advantage: chess, bridge, and poker – women come nowhere, and I think that has to be borne in mind.'

This enraged one of the panellists, Dr Clare Gerada, chair of the Royal College of GPs, who called it 'a disingenuous, sexist comment', and then proceeded to point out that her eighty-three-year-old mother had been chess champion in Malta for years. I knew that what I said would be controversial. Tessa was quite cross with me, but not nearly as cross as my daughter Charlotte. She was more furious than anybody else about what I had said.

I still feel my comment was relevant. There are things that I know women are much better at than men, and I accept that intellectually women are as good as men – look at exam results in schools and universities. I still believe, however, that it does not follow that women are likely to be as effective as men in business. I think there is a gap between the sexes in terms of how competitive they are, which was my original point, and why I made reference to games like poker and chess.

There is another point. Women are, of course, the only sex who can bear children, and they are normally the ones to spend a lot of time looking after them. But that does mean that they are necessarily held back in their careers, and for that reason they are less likely to reach the top. Charlotte has also observed that the success of women in, for instance, bridge, is proportionate to the numbers who actually participate in it. I am not convinced.

While Tessa had been annoyed by my initial statements, I think she was quite impressed by the way I subsequently defended them. But then I enjoyed the whole circus of dragging myself around from radio stations to TV studios to explain myself. I have found since entering politics that I very much enjoy talking with political journalists. Though in some arenas I am aware I can come across as shy, and in some circumstances unimpressive, in one-on-one encounters – even if I know they are going to be broadcast on television or radio – I am fine. In fact, I relish them.

This is because I do like to get publicity, whether or not people approve of my views. I do not get upset if people disagree with me (though of course I do try to persuade them), but I do want them to be *interested* in what I have to say; I enjoy being thought worth mentioning. Nor am I troubled by criticism. As long as it is fair and does not seek to misrepresent my views, why should I object?

The only thing I try to avoid is being made a fool of in public on subjects where I am not as familiar on the detail as I should be. This happened to me once when I went to a climate-change conference in Copenhagen. I was part of a panel that was supposed to offer a sceptical alternative to the consensus, but when challenged on the views I had expressed, I found that I was not on top of the arguments necessary to defend them. As *The Times* put it, 'Wheeler admitted to not being an expert on climate change and it showed.'

After Michael Howard stepped down in 2005, following a general election in which the Tories made up quite a lot of ground on Labour, five prominent leadership candidates gave speeches at the conference that year, including Malcolm Rifkind. The journalist Peter Oborne predicted in advance that Rifkind would make the best speech, but that it would do him no good at all. That is exactly what happened: he delivered what was in my opinion the best speech of the conference, but a little later he withdrew from contention, as it had become clear he could not obtain sufficient support.

I do not know to what extent David Cameron was also on Oborne's radar, but the well-received speech he made gave him a great deal of momentum as the leadership election began to gather pace. He needed this momentum, because it was a crowded field, with (at the beginning at least) eleven or twelve pretty serious contenders, including Theresa May and the bookmakers' favourite to succeed Howard, David Davis, who was 3 to 1 *on* to be the next leader, i.e., he was considered to have a seventy-five per cent chance of becoming Michael Howard's successor.

After the conference I did something that, for me at least, was unusually forward. I invited each of the candidates to come, one at a time, to dinners that would be attended by about five prominent political journalists and five major donors. The idea was simply to hear what they all had to say. It was a sort of political beauty parade.

To my great amazement every one said yes, except Kenneth Clarke, who probably knew that as he was a Europhile his views were quite the opposite to mine. He made his excuses and claimed he was busy. Mrs May was one of the people who was invited and came. Thirteen years on, I cannot remember a word she said, though I am not sure if this is the result of my faulty memory, or because she was so forgettable that I have not retained anything of our encounter: perhaps a bit of both.

Ultimately, I decided to support Liam Fox, whom I had found impressive when I had heard him on various subjects, and who reached the last three, along with Davis and Cameron. At this stage, one of the candidates is eliminated in the last vote by MPs, before the decision on which of the final two will become the leader is taken by the party membership. A number of Cameron's supporters may have voted – although I have no evidence – for David Davis, who had come top in the first round (in which serial contender Kenneth Clarke was eliminated), believing that Liam Fox would have been a greater threat than Davis when it came to the membership vote. Much the same thing is alleged to have happened after Michael Gove was narrowly eliminated in favour of Hunt, in the 2019 leadership contest. It is suggested that the Johnson team got some MPs to vote for Hunt, who they thought would be a less dangerous opponent that Gove. I have no idea whether that allegation is true.

As it was, Davis secured only six more votes than Fox in the second round, so this bit of tactical cleverness, if it did take place, may have made a big difference. Cameron duly eased his way across the finish line with plenty to spare in the run-off vote by the members of the party, and became the leader of the party.

I had some reservations about him from the beginning; I certainly thought there was something very 'pie in the sky' about some of his green policies, such as the environmental commission he set up with Zac Goldsmith, one of Jimmy's two sons, a Conservative MP. He was also apt to worry too much about whether one group or another might possibly be offended by his policies, with the result that he was too nervous to go the whole hog and say, 'This is precisely what I am going to do.'

On the other hand, Cameron was young, good-looking, intelligent and energetic, and he gave a decent impression of being tough. Cameron with his back to the wall was always very good. The first time I really saw him in action was when he addressed a dinner for Conservative donors at the Dukes hotel, while he was still Michael Howard's shadow education secretary. I was impressed by the way he fought back against a lot of fierce questioning led by the author Frederick Forsyth.

I would see this quality again and again over time: he was always able to find an extra gear, until, finally, when it came to Europe, he could not.

CHAPTER 14

THIS IS MEANT TO BE FUN

Robin Birkinhead's death in 1985 at the age of forty-eight was a tragic shock: he had a heart attack while changing ends in a game of real tennis. It was a devastating blow to me, and to everyone else who cared for him.

I learned that he had left me £5,000 in his will, or rather in his draft will. It happened that he had completed everything other than getting it signed and witnessed: so when he dropped dead so tragically, the will had no legal effect. His very generous sister, Juliet Townsend, decided, however, to honour his wishes and gave me the money.

My wife Tessa and I discussed what should be done with the bequest. My first idea was simply to reduce my overdraft. Tessa thought that I should, on the other hand, do something much more cultural, like buying a good picture. That held no appeal for me. In the end, we agreed that what would have made Robin most happy would be for me to use the money to play in the World Poker Championships in Las Vegas. So I did. I had played enough poker to know that I was fascinated by the game, and the possibility of winning a great deal of money in the competition was exciting. Also, of course, I loved the city.

As it happened, £5,000 was not enough to cover both the $10,000 entrance fee and the other expenses I would incur: so I speculated with the £5,000 with one of IG Index's rivals and I turned it into enough money to make the trip.

While I was playing, I was astonished to find that my friend Torquil Norman had come to cheer me on. Torquil was the kind of person who admired, or at any rate was very interested in, people who were involved in unusual enterprises. Even so, it was a (very pleasant) surprise. Within a year or so he would save my bacon during what was a very near-death experience for my company. But for the moment he seemed happy enough to watch while, unfortunately, I did not do at all well, finishing only 122nd out of 160. My only consolation was that the famous Texas 'Dolly' Brunson was 123rd. In truth, it did not really matter to me that I had flopped out pretty early. I was hooked, and in the time since I have become rich enough to afford it, I have played every year, except for the time when I was required to celebrate my daughter Sarah's thirtieth birthday in Morocco.

The World Poker Championships is a slight misnomer. Rather than being an official title, it is merely my description of the final major event in a series of smaller tournaments that all fall under the World Series of Poker (WSOP) banner. It is the one everyone wants to win, and the winner's cup, together with the millions of dollars that go with it, of course, is perhaps the game's best-known and most coveted prize.

The whole affair was created by Lester 'Benny' Binion in 1970. He was said to have done for poker what Don King had for boxing. Whether this is a good thing is not for me to say. Old Father Binion, as he was known, was the sort of showman who sported a white Stetson that matched his buffalo coat. Less attractively, he had also been convicted of two separate 'unlawful killings'. After

Father Binion died, the competition was run by his two sons, one of whom was murdered by his mistress. The other, I understand, was made to leave Las Vegas for not being of sufficient moral stature.

When I first took part, the competition was held in Binion's Horseshoe Club downtown — a rather seedy place that ostensibly had a million dollars in notes hanging from the ceiling, though I had my doubts about how much real money as opposed to paper was actually there. But Binion's more or less went bust and for many years now the competition has taken place at the Rio, just off the Las Vegas Strip.

More often than not, one or more of my daughters will accompany me. Sometimes friends come too. It is obviously more fun to have company, but I am more than capable of having an interesting time if I am by myself. Tessa came once, but I think she was pleased to hand the baton over to my daughters. It was not quite her scene, but she certainly took some marvellous photographs of the event.

The first time Charlotte joined me at the World Championships, she was wearing a neck and wrist brace — the unfortunate consequence of a car accident in Malawi. I had wanted to take her to a Cirque du Soleil performance, but the most famous of all, 'O', was sold-out, so instead I booked tickets for another cirque show in town.

When I bought the tickets, I was asked whether I was aware of the content. Of course I was, I replied: who is not familiar with their work? When I came to pick up the tickets with Charlotte, I was asked the same question, and I gave the same answer. By the time that I was asked for a third time as we entered the theatre, I was getting really quite ratty.

I can see now why they were so keen to warn me: I had somehow managed to book seats to watch the cirque's exploration of sex. Charlotte and I sat through hours of naked gymnasts, tons of innuendo and some mad American clowns who kept shouting to the audience, 'Scream like you do when you xxxx!'

Charlotte probably should not have been as surprised as she was. After all, a good few years before, I had gone with my whole family to a show in Las Vegas. When the curtain went up there were six pretty girls, all topless. It was not the whole point of the show, it is just the way things were in those days, when every show was a 'spectacular'. My daughters' eyes were absolutely out on stalks; they had never seen anything like it.

After I was knocked out of the competition, I told Charlotte that I was ready to fly home to England. Charlotte said that she thought it might be rather fun for her to stay on for a couple of days. Tessa was quite upset when I appeared at the airport without the daughter I was supposed to have brought back with me.

Charlotte's reason for staying on was that she had fallen in love with a poker player. He seemed a nice young man, but it turned out that he had had four very unlucky experiences with different women, each of which produced a child.

He had no interest whatsoever in politics, but he discovered that Charlotte did, and so one day he decided to watch a television programme that featured John Redwood, a prominent right winger, whom I myself greatly admired. But after watching the programme, Charlotte's boyfriend told her it had convinced him that he would never, under any circumstances, vote Conservative!

Both Sarah and Jacquetta have been several times, too, and they are always good companions. On more than one occasion they have cleverly managed to obtain press passes so that they can get closer to the action. In 2018 Sarah was particularly good at writing notes, and then giving them to the croupiers and masseuses to hand to me.

In the first few days after I land in Las Vegas, I immerse myself in the subject by reading and re-reading my increasingly battered-looking poker books. I also play in a number of the smaller competitions. But all of it is only a prelude to the main event.

During the eighties, there would be fewer than two hundred in the competition, but now online poker and so forth have raised the popularity of the game to such a pitch that one can expect to face well over 5,000 opponents. A tremendous variety of people enter. You do not need to show any sort of skill or knowledge in order to do so; you simply need the $10,000 entry fee. In fact, the lower the standard of your play, the more welcome you are.[22] Money is all that matters in Las Vegas.

There are, however, quite a few poker celebrities – such as Amarillo 'Slim' and Phil Ivey, who featured in a case in the Supreme Court in the UK, which he lost, perhaps rather unluckily, against the Ritz Casino – as well as many other professional poker players. Their numbers are increasingly matched by swarms of would-be professionals in their twenties: earnest, clever, calculating young men, who come to Vegas having made a big study of the game.

I differ from the majority of the other contestants in two quite significant ways. For a start, I am English, not American. And secondly, I am eighty-four, not twenty-four. I guess the other players must think that I am rather peculiar, but they do seem to like me on the whole. This, and the fact that at my age I have developed a habit of making the odd silly mistake, means that I am often underestimated, which I can occasionally use to my advantage. The fact that it is clear to everyone that I am very amateurish, also enables me to get away with things that might not work if I had a different reputation.

---

22 It is a good competition for an expert player to enter because the contestants' ranks are swollen by people who are not necessarily very talented, but who have put up the money to be allowed to play. If you are a professional, your skill should put you at an advantage compared to the vast majority of the players, which means that the chances of you bringing home a sizeable prize are good.

Repeated trips have taught me that although in theory people can wear whatever they like, in practice there is a kind of Vegas uniform: sandals, white knee socks, corporate-logo polo shirts. Baseball caps are a great favourite, too. Of course, some people like to vary this: it is not uncommon to see people sporting novelty items of clothing such as dungarees, or skiing glasses (which they think will help them gain an advantage during the play by hiding their expressions). I once saw a man in a crocodile suit. Heaven only knows why.

I have been known to wear some jazzy shirts myself, often a Hawaiian (one favourite was always a Warhol-style one that featured lots of pictures of Margaret Thatcher) teamed with quite an old red suit. And while I have never gone quite so far as goggles, a colleague from IG Index was once surprised when visiting me in London on a sweltering summer day to find me wearing a polo neck. I told her that I was practising for wearing it in the heat of Las Vegas. I had read somewhere that one's throat begins to throb or goes red on occasions when one is emotionally disturbed, as one might be when one is bluffing, so I thought that if I could cover this area it would put me at an advantage. I did not put it to the test, though; I never found a polo neck that I liked.

One of the first things you notice as you approach the poker rooms is that the doorways are apt to be wreathed in big billowing clouds of cigarette fumes: smoking is not allowed at the table. The room itself is filled with a scrum of people – cocktail waitresses, massage therapists (charging $20 per ten minutes), journalists, ageing bunny girls holding trays of bottled water and, of course, the players themselves. They all cluster around the tables, which are absolutely crammed beneath a host of punishingly bright lights.

Once the opening proceedings are over and done with, it is not noisy. There is no music, thank God. On the whole it is very silent, because everyone is concentrating like mad. The silence may be broken when a dramatic hand comes up, or occasionally you will have a very tiresome player who cannot stop talking and annoys everyone.

It is easy to mistake the way that many of the contestants slouch, chew gum and fiddle with their phones, as indications of boredom, just as it is easy to think that the busty Scandinavian blonde wearing a T-shirt that reads, 'This is my poker face. Botox rocks', is anything less than serious about the game. But everyone is here to win, including me, and it is hard *not* to begin each new tournament by entertaining thoughts of a glorious victory. In those moments, I allow myself to consider how delicious it will be to take a private jet home when I have picked up the $10 million jackpot, and to remind myself to keep my best pair of white trousers ready for the final day.

The format of the event is simple. We will be playing no limit Texas Hold 'em, the only poker game that I now play in Las Vegas. This form of poker started, as the name implies, in Texas, about a hundred years ago. It only gradually spread elsewhere, but is now so popular that in any major gathering of poker players the last and major event is always the no limit Texas Hold 'em competition. The World Championships are no different.

Each player gets the same number of chips, say 20,000, and he is put at a table with, generally, eight or nine other players. The player to the left of the dealer is required to make a bet, known as the small blind. Next, the player to *his* left is required to make a bet, known as the big blind, which is twice the size of the small blind. As the deal moves one to the left after each hand, it follows that by the time eight or nine (depending on the number of players at the table) hands have been played, each player will have had to pay both the small blind and the big blind.

On any hand when a player is neither the small blind nor the big blind, he does not have to make a bet at all. He can simply throw his cards away and take no part in the hand. To start with the blinds are very, very low in relation to the number of chips you have. This means that you can, if you like, play a very cautious game with almost no chance of being knocked out of the competition for quite a long time.

After a bit, one, perhaps two, of the players at your table will have lost all their chips, and are therefore out of the tournament. At that point, either the table is broken up and the remaining eight players are distributed among other tables where a couple of people have been knocked out, or people from other tables that have been broken up will be added to your table. Accordingly, the number of people at each table continues to be close to ten.

You will be required, on the first day you play, to arrive at either 11.00 a.m. or twelve noon. Each session lasts two hours and then there will be a twenty-minute 'comfort' break. As you can imagine, the queues for the toilets can be considerable, so it helps if one of my daughters can get me a place in the line in advance. Luckily the men queuing do not seem to mind.

Apart from that, one plays continuously, except for a supper break of about seventy-five minutes. I try to run this, as my daughter Charlotte will tell you, like a military operation. We speed out of the main poker room and start the journey (it really is a journey; the corridors are so long that I get far more exercise out in Las Vegas than I do in London) back to my hotel room to eat some cold room-service food that will have been ordered an hour previously. Efficiency is key.

On one occasion a few years ago, I arrived at noon and did not get away until three in the morning. That does make the whole thing rather tiring, at least for somebody of my advanced age.

In 2003, one of the years when I made a reasonable amount of progress – I had to re-book my flight three times and at one point my chip count rose to 150,000 – I played thirty-two hours of poker in three and a half days. I thought this was quite good for a partially sighted, rather deaf pensioner who had not played a single hand of poker since the year before. (There are far more disadvantaged players than me: one competitor, Hal Lubarsky, is actually blind and needs a 'spotter' to help him play.)

What made things somewhat harder for me that year was that the tournament took place during the very lengthy management buyout talks at IG Index. This meant that my sleep was interrupted a lot by taking business calls, which was a bit of a nuisance from the poker point of view. I was so exhausted by the final morning that I could hardly eat my breakfast.

Adrenaline and excitement go some way to helping you keep going, as does the knowledge that a) you have paid a substantial sum to play, and b) a very substantial prize will be yours if you win. But it takes a toll. I know I get tetchy, snapping at my daughters when they offer me bananas in the early hours.

People can get quite emotional in both victory and defeat. There is a lot of money at stake, ranging from at least $10 million that the winner gets, down on a sliding scale to the small profit made by those who get into the top ten per cent in the competition, so people do get worked up, especially when they get knocked out in a big hand. I do not think I have ever seen anyone burst into tears, but I have seen a lot of fury expressed at the luck that fate has dealt a player. And a few years ago, they banned 'excessive celebrations': some people had gone over the top when they won a hand, probably in the hope that the television cameras would catch them.

I have found that during the games themselves, the atmosphere at different tables varies a lot from table to table. Sometimes you get a jolly set of people who chatter away, in spite of the big sums involved, and make jokes and so forth. At other tables, you will find people being quiet and tense, particularly the young. Of course, that is natural: they will have paid a large sum of money to enter and they are playing for an overwhelmingly large first prize. I much prefer the former type of table – a group of unsmiling young men is not my cup of tea.

If your neighbours at the table are reasonably friendly, there can be a lot of conversation. But one has to remember that when your opponents appear to be enormously friendly, it may be an attempt to find out what they can about your style of play.

If you want to win at poker, you must pay a lot of attention to what your opponents do, so that you know their style. You cannot succeed if you focus solely on your own hand. To do well, you have to spend a lot of energy because, even when you are not involved in a hand, you should be observing the way other people play, and tucking what you learn into your memory.

You can make some assumptions even before the first card has been dealt. The way people look can be a good indication of the way that they will play. If someone comes across as brash and aggressive, the chances are that they will play in a brash and aggressive manner. On the other hand, come to think of it, so also do the dour, serious young men who never smile.

When you start at a new table, the people to focus most closely on are the person seated immediately to your left, and the person seated immediately to the left of him, because they play after you and you need to know if they are the kind who will be frightened off if you make a big bet. The next person who should command your attention is the player immediately on your right, and so on, until you feel confident enough to be able to make judgements about the whole table.

What you are trying to find out is how high they bet in certain circumstances, and whether they are inclined to fold when somebody else makes a big bet. The simplest of all 'tells' is that a player who looks ostentatiously bored very likely has good cards, but there are a million other tiny indications.

It is striking how even in a game of Internet poker, when you cannot see the people you are playing against, you can gather information about their styles and temperaments by, for example, observing how long they take to make their bets, how much they raise by, and how often they bet.

Strangely enough, although it is widely agreed that this sort of focus on the behaviour of your opponent is crucial, one often sees large numbers of players apparently absorbed in something completely different, very rarely looking up to see what others at their table are doing. A lot of the players listen to music. Others read poker magazines and newspapers, play on their phones or hand-held computers, or struggle with crosswords. Some chat. Some even order beers for the table; I imagine it helps them to relax.

The most successful players are not only logical and brave, though these qualities are important, they have enough energy to go on concentrating flat out for the up to twelve or more hours in the day when they are at the table. Perhaps that is one of the reasons why poker has become a young man's game.

I think I am probably better at disguising whether I have a good hand or not – which is really a question of preserving the same demeanour at all times – than I am at reading other people. I was quite pleased one year when one of the other players asked me, 'Old man, why so silent? This is meant to be fun.'

I very quickly smiled back. 'But I am having *great* fun.' Perhaps I was doing too good a job of hiding my emotions.

There are various styles of play. Conservative players will bet only when they have got a good hand. The more aggressive players will be ready to enter a hand starting with cards that many others would think not worth playing with, because they are confident that they can outplay the others; taking advantage of things they have picked up from watching them. The most successful players now are the super-aggressive ones, mainly young.

Their approach requires them to be especially alert, because they are playing many more hands than other people (and thus less often relax by sitting out a hand), and they have to maintain a close watch on everyone else at the table.

It is much easier and more relaxing to play against a cautious player, because you can be fairly confident about how he will play. For instance, if he comes into the first round of betting, you can be pretty sure that he has a good hand: a super-aggressive player, on the other hand, may have *anything*.

My approach to the game has changed over time. I used to be rather conservative, but I now realise I have to be more aggressive, willing to get involved in more hands and willing to bluff quite often. But the really important thing is to vary your style.

In addition to this, good players need to be prepared both to set traps and to know when, and how often, to bluff. For instance, if you find yourself with two aces – the best hand you can have – the normal thing is to raise the betting. This would be the strongly recommended course of action, most of the time, but if there are aggressive players to your left, you might just call and bet the minimum amount. In doing so, you would be giving no indication that you had a good hand. When somebody raises, as you would hope and expect, you could bluff by calling again, but more likely you would make a big raise, thus closing the trap.

You could also try to do the same with a hopeless hand, because the strong implication from your betting in that way is that you do have a good hand and were setting a trap when you simply called originally. It is a very dangerous and potentially expensive form of bluff, but likely to work quite often.

One year, quite early on in my career, I had great success in setting traps. I enjoy the cunning and skulduggery of all of this, and the way it combines the analytical elements of my personality with the mischievous ones. I do not know why I do it less often now. Perhaps I am losing my nerve.

This psychological aspect of the game is very interesting, though there are some players who will take it to crude extremes.

One year, a pony-tailed young man from the Deep South tried to put the other players at our table off their games by passing round a locket containing photos of his children, and saying, 'Take a good look at these angels, so you'll think about it before taking my chips.'

Sometimes, it is enough to be lucky, or dumb, or both. During one of the first times I played in the big event, I found myself on a ten-person table with a professional and a woman who was only in the event because her husband had won a competition at his firm, for which the prize was entry to the contest, and he had given it to her. On one hand, all the players except these two had dropped out. On each round of betting the pro raised, and the girl would call. After the last card had been dealt, he raised once more, and once more she called.

'Oh, all right,' he said, 'you win. All I've got is a queen.' He did not even have a pair. We all looked on, fascinated to see what cards his opponent had been playing with. She laid them proudly out on the table: she did not have a pair either, but she won the hand because she had a king.

By some miracle, she lasted until the end of the day, at which point I asked her, 'How did you know that he was bluffing?'

'Oh,' she replied, 'But I had a king!' I imagine she did not survive long.

At the end of the day's play, if you have survived, you put your chips in a specially provided bag, label it with your name, and then the bags are all taken away to some secure place. The next day you will be at a different table, facing new opponents.

You continue playing until you have lost all your chips, at which point you are gone, forgotten for ever, and have to make the long, lonely walk out of this vast room. Whether you feel as if you have been unlucky or stupid, the knowledge that it is all over for another year is terribly depressing. Some people like to stick around after they have been eliminated to see how the rest of the tournament pans out, but most have no desire to do so and like to get home as soon as they can. Me too.

My most exciting year was 2003, when I came thirty-third. For that I got $35,000 for my $10,000 entrance fee. By the time there were only thirty-three players left, each of us naturally thought that he might win. There were not nearly so many players then as there are now, so the prize was closer to $2 or 3 million than the $10 million it is today, but that was certainly enough to be interesting.

As it happens, my neighbour at the table that day – called, rather appropriately, Moneymaker – was the eventual winner. Very remarkably, he had only played on the Internet before, never at a table with his opponents present. One needs a lot of luck to win a tournament like that and he certainly had one very important piece of luck. He had a pair of eights, which is a fair hand, but one of his opponents had a pair of aces, which is the best possible hand. The betting got very high and another eight came up so that he now had three eights, beating his opponent's two aces. 'That's poker,' as they say.

The next year, as the popularity of poker soared, there were three times as many players, so that although I was only 164th, that was still enough for me to get $15,000 back for my original $10,000.

There is obviously a chance I could repeat this, or even improve on it. There is, after all, a considerable element of luck in the game, and if I were overwhelming lucky, I could find myself in the later rounds once more.

Dan Harrington's excellent book on the game, *Harrington on Hold 'em*, written before there were nearly as many players in the competition as now, said that by the time the tournament got down to nine players – the final table always starts with nine players – they would probably all be professionals. In a recent year, however, not only was there not a single professional in the final nine, there was not one in the last forty-five. This is partly because there are such enormous numbers of people playing now. In a field of 8,000, even if there are as many as fifty professionals, the chances are that some poor players will get lucky.

Although I now know more about the game, I have become progressively less successful, probably because I get tired far more easily than I used to.

Dan Harrington, a former winner of the World Poker Series, said to me once, 'Of course, there's no possibility I could win this tournament again, I'm sixty-two!'

Although I am aware that it is mainly a young man's game – only the young have the energy to sustain the necessary levels of concentration for ten hours a day, for perhaps several days in a row – I have not given up hope. After I had crashed out of one tournament ten years ago, I said to my daughters, 'Never mind, darlings, my real goal wasn't to win this time, but in thirty years. I want to be the first world champion over a hundred years old!'

I still have a good number of years to go, but I already know what I will say when I do collect the prize money: 'Well, every little bit helps these days.'

CHAPTER 15

BANGING ON ABOUT EUROPE

There are two kinds of loyalty in politics. You can be loyal to a party or a person, or you can be loyal to what you believe in. Sometimes these loyalties overlap, but a point often comes when you have to choose between one and the other.

In contrast to somebody like Michael Howard, who is intensely loyal to the Conservative Party and the people in it, my primary loyalty is to the ideas that I believe in. I still remember how faithful Michael was to Iain Duncan Smith in 2003 – even on the day that IDS was forced out, he still wrote an article urging patience on his fellow Tories – but personally I do not believe in being loyal to individual politicians or parties if that means backing their policies when I do not agree with them.

This may be because I did not have the emotional attachment to the Conservative Party that some do, for example, Michael Howard and, in particular, Theresa May.[23] For that matter neither did I have that kind of emotional attachment to the UK Independence Party (Ukip). I hugely admire its triumph in causing the Referendum to take place and indeed I have given a great deal of money to it. Even so, I resigned from it on 15 April

2019 because I felt that it had by then changed and got an extremely undesirable reputation for racism, which seemed to me very probably to reflect the truth.

Some people think that there is almost no concession not worth making if it can ensure party unity and prevent Jeremy Corbyn getting in. I do not. I was asked recently whether I would prefer a Corbyn-led government and a 'clean' Brexit, or a Conservative government with a compromised Brexit or no Brexit at all. The choice was easy. I would be appalled if Corbyn were elected, but not as appalled as I would be if Brexit were abandoned or seriously softened, although I realise I shall be first to the guillotine if Corbyn does get in.

David Cameron became leader of the Conservatives in 2005. Four years later, he expelled me from the party. Looking back now, it seems surprising that it took so long, because I was already consumed by a topic that put me almost completely at odds with him and his shadow cabinet: Europe.

It may sound strange, but even after I had given the £5 million to William Hague, there was a long period when I still did not feel particularly strongly about politics. This changed once I began to be concerned about the European Union. The real catalyst was the creation of an organisation called Business for Sterling, which had been established by Rodney Leach. He was worried that Tony Blair and much of the British business establishment were so enthusiastic about joining the Euro.

I hosted a reception at Chilham Castle at which Rodney hoped to secure more backers, and after that he put me on the

---

23 I was never the sort of tribal Tory who will not vote for anybody other than the party in blue. While I have never voted Labour, I have cast ballots for the Abolish the GLC Party in local elections, and once for a Liberal Democrat in a general election (ironically in a tactical attempt to oust Kate Hoey, a politician I now greatly admire, from the constituency I then lived in).

organisation's board. Business for Sterling eventually evolved into Open Europe, a highly influential think-tank.

From a position of knowing very little, I began to try to learn as much as I could, and as I did so I gradually became more inclined to the view that the EU was a disaster. By the time that David Cameron had become leader of the Tories, I was convinced that the only real solution to the problems presented by our membership was to withdraw entirely.

Despite being one of the Conservatives' largest donors, perhaps the largest of all, I still had little to no influence on policy matters – another reason to regret my foolishness in that first meeting with William Hague. So while I became increasingly vocal about my frustration and disappointment at the fact that my opinions diverged sharply from those of the leadership (even though I suspect over half the Shadow Cabinet and a very large proportion of the grassroots were of the same mind as me), I was not really in a position to push things in the direction I wanted them to take.

I was at the Tory conference in 2006 when David Cameron said that the Conservatives were not going to continue 'banging on about Europe in this Parliament'. I cannot recall a more idiotic statement by any politician ever. It was utterly obvious that Europe would be of extreme importance in that Parliament.

My concern mounted once it became clear that Cameron had left too much wriggle room in his promise to hold a referendum on the Lisbon Treaty. By contrast, I felt so strongly about this issue that in 2008 I ended up (unsuccessfully) suing the Labour government, because I did not believe they should ratify that treaty without a referendum.

The Conservative Party's broadcasts for the local and European elections in 2009 showed how terrified they were of the subject. Rather than 'banging on about' the EU, they devoted only five seconds out of a five-minute broadcast to their policies on it. It almost seemed to me that they hoped if they stopped talking about the European Union, all the tiresome problems associated with it would simply disappear.

In January of 2009, I had suggested that the return of Ken Clarke to the opposition front bench was highly undesirable, because of his strong pro-EU views. But back he came, as shadow business secretary. I was not the only person who was uncomfortable with this appointment, which was yet another indication of the fact that the Tory leader was not in favour of leaving the European Union, and also the way in which Cameron and the clique around him made up their minds without regard to the views of their colleagues.

Probably a bit fed up with all the noise I was making, David Cameron invited me to come and see him. Although we had never been at all close, he knew my views, and he knew I had been a big donor, and for both reasons I think he decided it would be worth a meeting. He and his chief of staff, Ed Llewellyn, listened to what I had to say and made comforting noises, but I came away with the impression that nothing was going to change. I do not think that they really believed I was likely to leave the party; they simply thought I wanted to carry on pressing a more Eurosceptic line.

They were half right. Although I had decided that I would begin to donate money to Ukip, beginning with £100,000, as well as voting for them at the upcoming European elections, I fully intended to continue to vote for the Tories in local and general elections. It was not at all uncommon at that time for those who voted Conservative in general and local elections to vote Ukip in European elections.

While I was contemplating making my support for Ukip public, I contacted Lord Tebbit, the highly distinguished former chairman of the Conservative Party, whom I knew to be a Eurosceptic like myself, and asked if I could come and see him. 'No, don't worry,' he said, 'I'll come and see you.'

When he arrived at my flat in Mayfair, I could tell immediately that he was being very careful in what he said, which was no surprise, given his great loyalty to the Conservative Party. When I told him what I was intending to do, I could see him picking his words cautiously before saying, 'Stuart, I do not think that that would be an unreasonable thing for you to do.'[24]

Not long afterwards, I went public. While making a statement about my own position, I also urged others to follow my lead. 'There's nothing to stop you being a member of the Conservative Party (unless they decide to turn you out), and giving money to Ukip,' I said, before continuing, 'It really, really matters what's going on in the European Union and what I want to do is to get a message over to both the main parties.'

I had, shortly before going public, informed David Cameron of what I was about to do. Rumours that I was about to be expelled from the party soon followed. On 29 March 2009,[25] Eric Pickles, the party chairman, emailed me.

I write to you as a courtesy to inform you that you are suspended from membership of the Conservative Party as a preliminary to expulsion. A formal notice of the decision will follow tomorrow outlining your right of appeal.

I replied:

---

24 It is interesting to note that around the same time as the furore surrounding my expulsion, Lord Tebbit was asked questions about who he thought people should vote for. While carefully avoiding specifically recommending Ukip, which would have been a catastrophe for the Tories as they would have had to expel him, he suggested not voting for the three main parties or BNP. Try to spot the difference between that and recommending Ukip!

25 As it happens, ten years to the day before the date on which we were supposed to, but did not, leave the EU.

Thank you for your email, which did not actually come as a surprise as I had been told hours earlier by the BBC!

I expect you are required to give me details of my right to appeal, but in case it helps this is to let you know that I will not appeal.

I felt no anguish at the prospect of leaving the Conservatives. Although for a long time they had been the best advocates for the political causes that I cared most about, now they were not. There was some relief too: I would no longer be kicking against a closed door. Perhaps some people in my position would have stayed within the party and tried to carry on making the case about Europe from inside, but I had a strong feeling that would not work and what might work instead would be money for Ukip.

Politics was not, and is not, my life. I can see that for someone who had devoted most of his life to politics, expulsion from his party would have been dreadful. That was not my situation at all. Most of my friends are not politicians and, as far as I know, I did not lose any friends when I was chucked out by the Tories. (Tessa was a Liberal Democrat who adored Paddy Ashdown, so it made no difference to her one way or the other whether I was a member of the Conservative Party.)

I am not an observant person, but I did not notice anybody cutting me in the days that followed, rather the opposite. Goodness knows how many people, ranging from a vicar to a pensioner, approached me to say that they would be doing exactly as I had recommended. I also received an email from IG Index's finance director, who ages ago had moved to Australia to marry a clergyman. She told me: 'You're "breaking news" down under!'

I knew the whole situation would be rather an embarrassment for Rodney, who was the chairman of Open Europe, and quite close to Cameron. So I took the initiative and went to see him. 'Rodney,' I said, 'I can see that this puts you in an awkward position. After all, most of the other people on your board are very pro-

Conservative. I can see that you might not want me in Open Europe anymore.'

'Oh, no, no, no,' he replied, 'of course we still want you, but I will just have a word with the chief executive.'

When we spoke next, he was a bit embarrassed. 'Now of course we shall still be delighted to give you all our material and anything else like that which you want,' he told me, 'but possibly it would be better if you stood down.' With that my connection with Open Europe came to an end.

There was a curious sequel. Roughly a year after my expulsion, I gave a recorded interview to Anne McElvoy on BBC radio in which I mentioned that official confirmation that I had been given the chop was delivered by an email. Some time later, in the course of an interview with Eric Pickles, Anne happened to mention this to him, and was surprised to hear him tell her that, no, in fact he'd had a long chat about it with me on the phone. I was even more surprised, as I have never spoken to him in my life.

I suppose it shows that there are some politicians who are prepared to lie about almost anything. But why tell a lie that can easily be exposed with a minimal amount of effort, about something which is, in any case, of no importance whatsoever? (This reminds me of some advice given – in jest – by a distinguished friend who shall be nameless: 'If you are going to commit a fraud, do at least make sure it is a worthwhile one.') I still find Pickles's statement baffling, but then if I have learned anything since 2001, it is that politicians can be very – how shall I put it – careless in what they say.

I grew up at a time when it was more or less expected that politicians would show a certain amount of integrity. Their honour was expected to mean a great deal to them. Think of Lord Carrington, who resigned as foreign secretary over the Falkland Islands, even though there was no way that he could have anticipated the Argentine invasion.

By contrast, while there is much about Michael Gove I admire – especially his intelligence, and the tenacity and courage he displayed during the Referendum campaign – I cannot forgive him for the way he put his own political ambitions ahead of the country's best interests, in failing to resign when presented with a Brexit strategy of which he must have strongly disapproved: Mrs May's dreadful Chequers deal.[26]

It was partly in response to what I regarded as some of the worst aspects of politics that, in the general election of 2010, I contested what was at the time the safest Conservative seat in the country: Bexhill & Battle. Ukip had done very well in the 2009 European elections, and so Barry Legg, the chairman of the Bruges Group, a Eurosceptic lobby group, thought I might be able to match this performance, or even improve upon it.

I hesitated, and then I thought, why not? It was initially suggested that I might stand as a Ukip candidate, but there was a bit of a problem. The party already had quite a following in the constituency and although the Ukip member who would otherwise have been its candidate agreed not to stand (thanks to the intervention of Nigel Farage), for various reasons the Ukip backers in the constituency would not allow me to campaign under their banner. So I ended up creating a small party of my own, The Trust Party, with the slogan: 'Politics we can believe in'.

We had one other candidate, Douglas Taylor, who ran in Perth

---

26 Events move so quickly nowadays. In the aftermath of the Chequers deal, I wrote a very strongly worded letter to the *Daily Telegraph* in which I suggested that the prime minister should be sacked, and David Davis replaced by Jacob Rees-Mogg, because I thought David Davis behaved badly by not resigning. But David did resign the following day. I acknowledged in another letter that the *Telegraph* published later that week that I had misjudged him, and wrote that if his resignation did the trick, then the United Kingdom would have reason to be grateful to him forever. Within minutes of the paper confirming that they were going to print my follow-up letter, Boris Johnson had resigned too, so yet *another* amendment was required.

and North Perthshire against the SNP MP, Pete Wishart. We quickly produced a manifesto that emphasised the pressing need, as I saw it, to clean up the 'corrupt' MPs' expenses system. I proposed a new Parliamentary court with the power to jail politicians who fiddled their allowances.

Allied to this, I also promised to show that those experts who claimed man-made global warming was inevitable were wrong, to grab back powers handed over to Brussels, to promote marriage, to improve treatment for injured British soldiers and to prevent the use of torture against terror suspects.

The Trust Party was launched on 29 March 2010 with a press conference and poster lorries that drove past Parliament and the Westminster headquarters of the other main parties. It was all very novel and exciting.

I explained that my primary aim was to restore faith in politics and politicians, quite a big task, of course. I was not, however, completely immodest. As I pointed out in an interview, 'I'm not here to be prime minister, I'm here solely to make a point, which is that the people have not had their say on the expenses scandal, and nor can they when the only choice they are offered is between equally tainted, equally shameless parties. This scandal is not going to be solved by the people who caused it.'

That was quite a pertinent point at the time, because the sitting MP, Greg Barker, had been accused of pocketing £320,000 from buying and selling a flat that he bought with the help of expenses. I saw this as a flagrant example of MPs using rules to enrich themselves, though it was not illegal. He was just the type of greedy MP who, I felt strongly, should be removed from the House of Commons. I saw no excuse for his claims.

We really went for him with full-page adverts in the papers and a leaflet campaign in which we made the argument that he was unfit to represent the town. I was so fierce at the hustings that I astonished my wife. 'Goodness, Stuart,' she said afterwards,

'I never knew you could be like that.' I found other elements of the election process more challenging. I was waiting to have my hip replaced at the time and, since walking was difficult for me, we decided that the best way I could canvass was to plant myself in the middle of a shopping centre, while my small team accosted passers-by and asked them if they wanted to meet the candidate. A certain number did, but perhaps not enough.

Looking back, there were times when I was hampered by my lack of experience. I spent far too much time allowing myself to get bogged down in lengthy arguments, or discussions with one voter at a time. Madness, as experienced politicians know. As Bill Griffiths, my marvellous election agent, said to me, 'We're both like Mr Magoo characters.'

What I found extraordinary, and very touching, was the way in which people who had never met me, and did not know me from Adam, rallied round and helped. There was one man, a former police officer who was by then working for the prison service, who came along canvassing and looked after the telephone for several hours at a time. He was far from alone. There was nothing in it for them; they were doing it purely out of public spirit.

Candidates always persuade themselves that they have a chance of winning, and to begin with I was no different. But as election day got closer, I knew that my chances of winning had receded to practically nothing. In the end I polled 2,699 votes, which put me solidly ahead of the BNP candidate, and not a million miles away from the Labour one, though sadly just short of recovering my deposit. The good news, for me anyway, was that my 4.94 per cent exceeded the result achieved by the television celebrity Esther Rantzen, who had also stood (in Luton) on an anti-expenses platform.

Not long after I had been expelled from the Conservative Party, Nigel Farage had invited me to attend a couple of dinners along with a number of the top Ukip people. It was a soft sell, so soft in fact that a year or so later, when I was asked to become treasurer, I was not even a member of the party. I paused for a couple of weeks before accepting the invitation: I was already at an age when I was somewhat anxious about taking on too substantial a role, and I was not sure that I knew enough about what I was entering into. As it was, I ended up joining the party and becoming its treasurer on the same day, in January 2011.

By contrast, I had never been bothered one hoot by the ways in which Ukip had been described by rival politicians, or certain parts of the press. Generally, we had tried to live with these insults rather than get too worked up about them. When Michael Howard called Ukip members 'gadflies' in 2004, the party immediately started a Gadfly Club – it even has a tie with a gadfly on it.

Similarly, a little later, David Cameron dismissed Ukip members as 'sort of a bunch of … fruitcakes and loonies and closet racists mostly'. I rather think the laugh is on him now – after all it was pressure from Ukip that led to him calling the Referendum, the result of which a) saw Mr Cameron resign and b) will (I hope) change the course of our country's history for ever.

There had never, at that time, been anything about the party in general that made me feel they were people with whom it would be a disgrace to be associated. There had been, it is true, too many incidents in which members had made insensitive or misguided comments, but nothing to suggest that the party as a whole was racist.

My feeling was that Ukip was a radical party, and you do not join a radical party unless you have strong opinions and want to see the country changed in a substantial way. And so, because we had firm views on immigration, it was inevitable that there would be a minority who held positions that went beyond what was acceptable. However, I also believed that they did not represent what the party stood for, and it was important that we made this clear. More recently, however, this has changed. Ukip has become an explicitly racist party, which is why I resigned from it in April 2019.

I know it has been said that, along with the money they knew I would contribute, I brought some aura of respectability to Ukip. It is impossible to measure this – but I can see it is possible that my reputation may have helped. Certainly, there must have been some symbolic weight in one of the larger donors in British politics switching his allegiance so publicly. Perhaps more significantly, I knew people who might become donors – this was always going to be more important to the party than what school I had been to.

Ukip's big problem was that politics is an expensive business. As American politicos like to say, there are only three things that are important when it comes to winning elections: money, money, and money. Even the most basic elements of running a party – such as producing campaign literature, paying permanent staff, or putting up candidates for by-elections – cost an enormous amount of money (a single by-election, for instance, required an outlay of £50,000 if it was to be fought effectively). Ukip needed someone who could both help them raise serious amounts of money, and also ensure that the party did not get into trouble by spending on things they could not afford.

While I had supported the Conservatives, I had been a strange mix of insider – because I was invited to all manner of events and treated nicely – and outsider, because I was never an actual politician. This changed in Ukip, where I became very much part of its organisation.

I was an ex-officio (non-voting) member of the party's national executive committee (NEC), and I think that, as treasurer, I was able to exert a reasonable amount of control to stop them getting into serious financial difficulties. This could be tough. When Nigel Farage wanted something, he was apt not to take it kindly if he was told there was not enough money to pay for it. Membership of the NEC also meant that I had to sit through hours and hours of the most boring meetings. I tried to persuade the committee to introduce rules that would set a limit on how long the meetings could last, but nobody seemed interested.

I was also very keen that they should introduce management accounts, as well as regular summaries of income and intended expenditure. But although the NEC did periodically draw up rules to try to control our outgoings and stop us using cash we did not have, these had little effect on Nigel Farage, who wanted to spend it like it was water. Steve Crowther, the party's chairman, would always assure me that they had all the finances under control. But we were living almost hand to mouth, and it never really felt sustainable. Things did indeed deteriorate after I stepped down as treasurer, and Ukip came close to going bust.

Along with trying to raise money for the party, I was, as treasurer, also responsible for ensuring that what cash did come in was above board and complied with the piles of rules, produced by the Electoral Commission, that govern election spending and the reporting of donations.

Donations to a political party of greater than £7,500 each year have to be declared and made public, and this presented us with a problem when it came to soliciting donations from those prominent Conservative supporters who also happened to believe very strongly that we should leave the EU. They were all, understandably, keen to avoid offending the Conservative government, and possibly being expelled as I had been, but at the same time they still wanted to contribute to a cause they felt strongly about.

So quite a large number of them gave exactly £7,500. One exception was my friend Lord Stevens, my colleague so long ago at Hill Samuel. He pointedly gave a donation of £7,501, just to show that he was perfectly happy to be identified as a supporter of the party. (He became one of the three Ukip peers but he has since, like Lord Willoughby de Broke, and now me, resigned from the party. So now Lord Pearson is the only Ukip peer.)

Because the £7,500 regulation acted as such an inhibition on large donations, lots of people tried to circumvent it. Similarly, the law prohibiting donations from abroad was seen by some as an obstacle to be overcome, rather than a rule to be observed. This meant that I had to spend a substantial amount of time telling some potential donors that although we valued their wish to support us, we could not accept the money they were proposing to send, from France, for instance, nor could somebody based in the UK make the donation on their behalf.

It could be highly frustrating, but I am glad that we were so careful because, quite apart from the moral objections I would have had to the sort of behaviour suggested, these are matters that are coming under ever greater scrutiny. I imagine any breaches would have been discovered eventually, and would have caused Ukip great embarrassment, or possibly worse. Look at the trouble Arron Banks has found himself in.

It was widely believed by us in Ukip that the Electoral Commission was biased against us. We would see thoroughly undesirable characters – some of them convicted criminals – cheerfully giving enormous sums to other parties without even a hint of an investigation from the Electoral Commission, whereas we seemed to be under extremely close scrutiny.

I am convinced that representatives of one of the large pro-EU organisations tried to play dirty tricks on us. I would periodically receive phone calls from people saying, 'You know I'm really interested in what you're doing, and I'm thinking of making a large donation, but the problem is that I'm actually resident abroad, so there are difficulties about how I could do this.'

They would then elaborate a complex scheme that, they said, would enable them to get round the regulations. The callers were so unconvincing, and the proposals they made so clumsy, that it was hard not to conclude that they had been put up to it by someone trying to lure us into a trap.

Perhaps we had become victims of our own increasing popularity: huge success in the 2014 European elections – we got more seats than any other party – made it far harder to dismiss Ukip out of hand. It was a staggering triumph. It showed how fed-up people were with various aspects of the EU's control over their lives.

What made us seem an even more potent new force in politics was our great coup: persuading two sitting Tory MPs to defect. For the first time in its history, Ukip had a presence in the House of Commons.

Since I had been associated with the Conservative Party for such a long time, and especially with those elements within it that took the same line as I did on Europe, I was involved in this. At the beginning of 2012, I sat down with Nigel Farage and we discussed the names of the eight or nine Eurosceptic Conservative MPs we thought might possibly come across to Ukip.

I wrote to each of them asking them to lunch, assuring them that I would not reveal the fact of our meeting to their party, or to anybody other than Nigel Farage, and that we would eat in the kind of restaurant where we were unlikely to be spotted together. Two declined, saying that it would be 'inappropriate', but the rest said yes.

The conversations were perfectly friendly; after all, we were interested in the same things. We discussed the EU, and David Cameron's leadership, particularly his vacillations over Europe that a lot of them found highly unsatisfactory. I am not sure I ever used the word 'defect', I simply asked if they might be interested in meeting Nigel Farage. At that point, a couple of the MPs explained politely why they had no intention whatsoever of leaving the Conservative Party, but others, including the MP for Clacton, Douglas Carswell, were far more positive.

I had already had lunch two or three times with Douglas and so I knew him quite well, but once he had expressed interest, the detail of his switch was handled by Farage, and I did not know of his final decision until it was announced publicly. Nigel had been amazingly good at keeping it secret, and almost nobody else knew either.

When the news broke in August 2014, it hit the press like a bombshell. The next month Mark Reckless, the MP for Rochester and Strood, also came over to us. That was certainly another triumph for Ukip. But the party's success turned out to be pretty well at its peak.

The first-past-the-post system was disastrous for us. Over 3.8 million people voted for us in the 2015 general election compared with about 9.4 million for Labour. Yet Labour won 232 seats, Ukip only one. We came second in 118 of the 650 contests, and secured 12.6 per cent of the vote. Plaid Cymru won three times as many seats as us with just 181,704 votes, or 0.6 per cent of the vote.

There was also the problem that in some people's minds Ukip was associated with Europe, but not a lot else. We always tried, reasonably and rationally, to get ourselves accepted as more than simply a one-issue party, one that had views and policies on a wide range of subjects. But on the whole, people were not much interested in what we thought about anything other than Europe.

There have been many misconceptions about Ukip, but one thing that is unfortunately true is that Ukip is a bit of a ragbag organisation. There was no shortage of enthusiasm or passion, but I do wish there had not been so much chaos. While in theory the NEC was supposed to be responsible for any important decisions taken by the party, in practice whatever Farage wanted more or less happened. I was not the only person who, having expressed an opinion in the NEC, was humiliated after being effectively told to shut up by Nigel. But we continued to get on well, as indeed we still do.

There was too much quarrelling at the top. Nigel's attempts to dominate the party, to always have everything his own way, were a source of great tension. He found the NEC an intolerable nuisance and was not afraid to say so. In his view, they only served to obstruct the things that needed to be done to achieve success. So although Farage was Ukip's most recognisable figure, and undoubtedly its biggest asset, there were nevertheless some in the party who thought he was dreadful.

Nigel is a mixture of good and not-so-good characteristics. He is highly intelligent, highly articulate, extremely well informed, very quick on the uptake and always entertaining – I do not remember ever having been bored in his company. He also possesses massive energy and that most elusive, and potent, political gift, the common touch.

On the other hand, he was apt to treat people very badly – especially anyone who he thought for a single second might have any chance of challenging him for the leadership. When the press began to talk about Suzanne Evans as a possible future leader of the party, he ensured that she was almost expelled from it, and he certainly excluded her from taking any sort of decent job in it.

Something similar happened to Patrick O'Flynn, the party's economics spokesman, and as soon as Neil Hamilton received a standing ovation at one year's party conference (the only other person to do so was Farage), as well as winning the vote for the NEC by an astronomic margin, that was it as far as Neil's prospects were concerned – he has never been allowed to speak at a party conference again.[27]

Nigel was completely disorganised. I remember that when I was travelling back with him one day from an event in Scotland, I was struck by the way in which he had no idea what to do with himself. He made a series of phone calls in which he dithered: should I be here? should I do this? It evidently did not occur to him to go to his office to do something about running Ukip.

Ukip headquarters were in London and were supposed to be the heart of the party, but Nigel was hardly ever in his office, to the point that it was difficult to say exactly *where* his office was – if it was anywhere, I suppose it was his home. It was madness really. You never knew where he would be, or when, and so there was little point in making appointments to see him.

His presence alone had the capacity to create chaos. When I was travelling with him to the event in Scotland, I witnessed the shocking way he was mobbed as he left the pub that we had just been into for a press conference. Admittedly this may have been set up by the SNP. The police bundled us in to a taxi, but the taxi driver, who was afraid his vehicle was going to be torn to pieces, refused to take us. Nigel was put back in the pub by the police and I think he had to leave it by a rear entrance.

Nigel was quite rattled but, curiously, although I am a physical coward, I never really thought we were likely to be hurt. It got to him a bit. (Of course, it was far more likely that he was the one who would be attacked.) Ukip also had to employ protection for Farage after he got bashed over the head in public.[28] He was a real magnet for the rage of his political opponents.

The fact is that Nigel has had a colossal effect on British history. I am certain that the Referendum would not have taken place at

---

27 Interestingly a similar thing happened with Daniel Hannan. He is a very talented politician, but Mrs May blocked his attempt to get adopted in a winnable Conservative seat.

28 We appealed to David Cameron on this subject, saying that since the state paid for his bodyguards, the same facility should be offered to Nigel Farage, who was, after all, the leader of a major national political party. He refused, I do not know on what grounds.

all had it not been for Nigel and the party he led. Whether you think it is a bad thing, or (as I do) a good thing, taking Britain out of the EU (assuming it happens, of course) will have an immense effect on the lives of millions. You could argue that Farage has exerted more influence over the country's development than anybody since Clement Attlee, with the possible exception of Mrs Thatcher, and yet he has never come to power.

Nigel had been able to place such great pressure on David Cameron that the prime minister was forced to offer voters a referendum on Europe. This was his great achievement. But I considered that he was too divisive a figure to lead the campaign that would follow. This would be a task for a different kind of politician.

CHAPTER 16

TAKING BACK CONTROL

I was delighted when it was confirmed after the general election in 2015 that we would have a referendum on Europe. I saw it as the first step towards getting us out of the EU. David Cameron was right to think that calling a referendum would help him win a majority in the House of Commons,[29] but evidently wrong to be as confident, as he apparently was, that he would win the Referendum.

I thought we did have a chance of winning. Indeed it seemed to me to be a toss-up. Although I believed it was important that Britain should leave the EU, I was not confident that the voters would agree. Much would depend on what kind of a campaign the Leave side fought. Luckily for us, we had Dominic Cummings and Matthew Elliott.

By the point, halfway through 2015, when Matthew asked me

---

29 Those who criticise him for calling for a referendum ignore what was overwhelmingly likely: the Conservatives would have lost the election had he not done so. Although the Tories were unlikely to have lost seats to Ukip, in many seats the loss of votes might well have meant that Labour or the Liberal Democrats would have won the seat.

if I would be interested in joining them, Dominic and Matthew had already been discussing for some time the creation of what would become Vote Leave. In October 2015, it was launched officially.

I had met Dominic through Rodney Leach many years ago – he was for a while the campaign director of Business for Sterling, before being poached by Conservative Central Office. He did not get on very well with them and he soon disappeared to the north for a couple of years to write a book.

Dominic is extremely intelligent, and has the great skill of being able to think about things in an original way, and come up with original solutions. He possesses excellent political instincts and thinks logically. But he is not an emollient character, and he is not good at getting on with people. In fact, he is capable of having rows with almost anybody; particularly, as it turned out, Arron Banks. This is not to say that he was impossible, only that he had strong views that he was apt to express forcefully. What I did not know at the time I joined was how close he was to Michael Gove, something that would become crucial later on.

Matthew Elliott, whom I knew through my support of the TaxPayers' Alliance, which he had founded, was a much quieter character than Dominic. His ability to get on with, and gain the respect of, all kinds of people may have been as important to the Leave campaign as Dominic's brilliance. Matthew was able to encourage people to join us in the first place, and to keep the team together at crucial moments.

This was tested early on. Dominic had been in contact with a number of the Eurosceptic Tory MPs, but their attitude was beginning to infuriate him; he felt they were disorganised and too inclined to squabble among themselves, so much so that he was already thinking about walking away and heading back up north to continue working on his book.

I called him up and did what I could to help persuade him to stay on. Eventually, once a number of other people had talked to him, he agreed. My telephone conversation with Dominic may have been the biggest contribution I made to the campaign.

At the start I was both a director of Vote Leave, and one of its three treasurers. As well as giving money myself, I tried to convince others to do the same. An idea had floated around for a while that it would create a great splash if we could persuade ten individuals to give a million pounds each to the Leave campaign – and then, when we won, they would be celebrated as the people who had helped save our country.

I took the City asset manager Jeremy Hosking, whom I had not met before, out to lunch. I explained the concept to him somewhat diffidently, telling him that I understood that a million pounds was a considerable sum of money. Not for him, it turned out: he told me that that would not be a problem at all (he ended up giving £1.8 million). But unfortunately, a million pounds was a bit too much for most of the other people we approached – and not everyone who had said they would produce that sum actually did so – and the plan was quietly shelved.

As well as helping to raise funds, I invited a number of other figures to join our campaign. Some would go on to play significant roles. Others, like General David Richards, who had a reputation for being outspoken and willing to upset the government, did not strike me as doing very much in the end. What he had to lose by coming out for what he believed in, I do not know. He already had his peerage.

At one point, I mentioned to Dominic that I owned Chilham Castle, and told him that if by any chance it would be useful to have a weekend there, I would be happy to host it. In January 2016, we invited a number of the figures who would end up being important to the campaign. Dominic put together the guest list, and I added a couple of my personal friends that I thought could contribute. As well as Dominic Cummings and Matthew and Sarah Elliott, we invited Daniel Hannan, John Mills, David Starkey, Lord Richards, Patrick Barbour and Lord Lawson.[30]

There was no specific purpose for the weekend; the idea was to have a general discussion about the tactics and strategy we would employ during the campaign. It seems, however, that in the months since this weekend took place, a number of misconceptions about it have emerged.

It was not about raising money, though that was discussed. And as far as I am aware it is definitely not true, as has been alleged, that at any point in the weekend anybody discussed getting rid of Dominic. Nor is there any truth in the idea that the purpose of the Chilham weekend was partly to discuss a merger between Vote Leave and Leave.EU. I never heard a single mention of this.

What we *did* talk about was our shared concern about the timing of the Referendum. Even in January it was still not clear when the vote would take place. Our campaign was only just getting off the ground, and so we naturally hoped the Referendum would be scheduled for a date that gave us as much time as possible to prepare.

Dominic believed it was almost certain that the vote would be called for September, that the vote would be to remain, and that there was no way Cameron would call for an earlier vote. The feeling was that the prime minister was pulling a fast one on Britain, first by delaying naming a date for the vote, and secondly by putting the Referendum in such broad terms, with little scope

---

30 Two of the people whom I had asked personally to attend were Ann Walker and her husband, Angus. A long time ago, Ann Walker had been a very serious girlfriend of mine – I had even (unsuccessfully) proposed to her. At dinner on the first evening, Ann, who is very interested in climate change, was sitting next to Lord Lawson, who had written a brilliant book, *An Appeal to Reason*, on the topic. She became so excited that she had a heart attack from which, thank goodness, she quickly recovered.

for knowing what leaving the EU would actually look like.

Dominic, on the other hand, was very keen that we should not try to explain exactly how things should be run if we won. It was up to the government to work that out, he felt, not us, and we should simply concentrate on making the case for leaving the EU.

It seemed to us that perhaps the best we could hope for was a result that would be close enough to allow us to campaign for a second, more thought-out referendum, that included a strategy for how Britain would extricate itself from the EU and what that would look like. And yet, although I do not remember anybody believing strongly that a Leave win was likely, we were confident that the movement was heading in the right direction at a reasonably comfortable rate.

In late January, not long after the Chilham weekend, tensions that had been building for a while came to a head. Although removing Dominic Cummings from his post had not been discussed at Chilham, it had evidently been on the minds of certain members of the Vote Leave board.

There was no actual vote on the Dominic situation. But I was present at a meeting, in the course of which Bernard Jenkin made the case for why Dominic should be got rid of. I am not sure why Bernard did so, as there had earlier been a meeting between him and Dominic and John Mills, which was joined by Matthew Elliott, who then mediated a compromise by which Dominic would take a lower profile with the media and leave the handling of MPs to Matthew.

Anyway, Dominic very quietly and impressively made his reply, and things swung round to him. It was a crucial moment, because he could have been thrown out. My memory of the discussion is that Matthew Elliot's attitude was somewhat equivocal; but at that time I did not know about the earlier meeting. Matthew told me later that he had said nothing because, as he saw it, the matter had already been resolved.

I did not make any kind of crucial intervention, but it was clear from the way that I behaved that I was on Dominic's side. I was of the view that it was not just a question of Dominic's own considerable qualities, important though these were. There was a definite suggestion that if Vote Leave chucked Dominic out, a lot of the staff on the ground would have walked out. With only a few months to go until the vote, this could have been catastrophic.

The meeting did not entirely clear the air, but it did remove any appetite for revisiting the question: Dominic's position was confirmed.

In the following weeks his instincts, and his gift for clear thinking, were to become increasingly important. One of the tools he used a lot, and which to a large extent shaped the Leave campaign, was statistics. He spent a lot of money employing Aggregate IQ, a little-known Canadian tech firm, to do very detailed investigations into what made potential voters tick. They were extremely helpful in getting our message to the right Facebook users.

Part of the genius of 'Vote Leave, Take Back Control' as a slogan was that sovereignty sounds like a pretty abstract concept, but Cummings's slogan sounded very immediate and easy to understand. He pushed and pushed this line, and insisted that our campaign repeat it over and over again. This is something that I feel he got absolutely right.

Of course, immigration also matters a lot to people, but although Dominic acknowledged this, he argued that since there was not anyone in the country who was not already aware of it, you risked unnecessarily inviting accusations of racism if you kept banging on about it and made it the central plank of your campaign.

This was opposite to the view taken by Arron Banks and Nigel Farage, who I suspect still maintain that immigration, and the way that they drew attention to it, was the issue that won the Referendum. They would probably say that it should have been pushed even more. There was another basic difference in strategy between Vote Leave and Leave.EU. Vote Leave believed that there were about thirty per cent of voters who would definitely vote for leaving and thirty per cent who would definitely vote to remain, so that the crucial thing was to go after the undecided forty per cent. Leave.EU, on the other hand, believed the important thing was to emphasise the point that would appeal to the core leave voters: immigration.

From time to time there was talk that Vote Leave might merge with Leave.EU, the organisation run by Arron Banks and Nigel Farage. I do not think that was ever likely. There was bad blood between the two outfits that dated back to well before the Referendum campaign. Just one later example: Banks once approached Douglas Carswell, a key member of Vote Leave, at a Ukip conference and accused him, in front of many other people, of having mental problems and being on the verge of autism. This was an astonishing and idiotic piece of behaviour, considering that Vote Leave and Leave.EU were both fighting for the same outcome in the Referendum.

Arron had, in the summer of 2015, been very much at odds with Matthew Elliott and he was trying to persuade Dominic to join his team. Indeed, Arron had a private detective tail Matthew. Later, when it became clear that Dominic would stay with Vote Leave, Arron fell out even more with Dominic than with Matthew.

Dominic felt considerable animosity towards Arron, but I do not think there would have been a merger, even if Dominic had not been part of the Vote Leave team. There were too many tensions and personality clashes between the two camps, and I cannot see that it would have been possible to reconcile our differences in strategy. But constantly slagging each other off would obviously be highly counter-productive.

I went twice for drinks with Arron Banks in 2015. His reason for suggesting that we meet was to recruit me for Leave.EU, whereas my reason for meeting him was to try to persuade him that as his team and ours were both trying to achieve victory for the Leave side, we should not be attacking each other. Both of us left the first meeting, in June, after two hours, having completely failed to secure our objectives. I met him again in September, this time in the company of his right-hand man, Andy Wigmore, but with the same result.

One of the most significant barriers to a closer union was that Dominic believed that a lot of the MPs, including the Cabinet ministers whose support we knew would be essential, would not touch the campaign if Nigel Farage or Arron Banks had anything to do with it.

This strategy would be justified before too long.

In February, David Cameron went to Brussels to try to secure from the EU a number of concessions that might make continued membership look more attractive to the voters. But the deal David Cameron brought back did not amount to much and everything accelerated later that month, on 20 February, when the prime minister announced that the Referendum would take place on 23 June.

On the same day, six Cabinet ministers — Michael Gove, Iain Duncan Smith, Chris Grayling, John Whittingdale, Theresa Villiers and Priti Patel — effectively became rebels and announced that they would be backing the Leave campaign. Within twenty-four hours, Boris Johnson — who had for a long time seemed to be sitting on the fence — also confirmed that he would be on our side. Their support was crucial. I do not believe we would have won without it.

Two months later, in April 2016, we were designated as the official Leave campaign. I had always thought we would be, and in the months before it was confirmed we certainly behaved as if this was going to be the case, but in retrospect I think it may have been far closer than we had thought.

We were helped, I think, by the fact that Leave.EU and a number of its members were considered dubious. Vote Leave's team, on the other hand, were seen as closer to being establishment figures. We did not want to break things up in a more general way, we simply happened to be against the government on one issue: Brexit.

But far from resolving the tension between the two Leave-supporting outfits, the official designation of Vote Leave seemed only to increase it. This was a great pity, and unnecessary. Both parties knew that winning the Referendum was going to be difficult. Why make it harder than it needed to be?

I played a far less central role once the campaign was underway; I was no longer part of the decision-making body and did not participate in strategic and tactical discussions.

However, as time passed, I began to be very concerned about one matter. We were taking on financial commitments that I was not confident we could meet. Although I raised these issues in a couple of meetings, my deafness put me at a disadvantage, as I could not properly hear what people were saying in reply. It was this that led me on 22 March 2016 to resign from my position as treasurer, and also as a director of Vote Leave – I did not feel I could stay on when I could no longer hear enough of the answers to the concerns I had raised. I need not have worried, as it turned out. We raised more than we needed.

Another thing I was uncomfortable with, though it did not contribute to my decision to resign, was the £350 million that we promised in messages on the side of buses could be spent on the NHS. I pointed out that it was a gross rather than a net figure (if one takes into account the rebate, it would be more accurate to talk instead about £276 million: still a lot of money!), but no one seemed that interested. Although I never spoke to Dominic directly about the matter, it has been suggested that he was anxious to make the promise as controversial as possible, to ensure that it would be talked and argued about. Its accuracy, he may have thought, was not necessarily the most important thing.

What I never saw any sign of at all were the sorts of alleged financial irregularities that have drawn so much attention since the Referendum. I think it was a peripheral issue that made very little, if any, difference to anything. If the vote had been extremely close it might have been a problem, but there is no way that the sums involved could have changed the result.

I must point out that the other side had been doing very suspect things. The spending by the Remain side of £9 million of taxpayers' money on a nakedly pro-Remain leaflet was disgraceful; so for them to then accuse us of overspending by a few hundred thousand pounds, whether true or false, does seem rather rich.

He had thought for a long time that although there were a lot of things wrong with the EU, it could be reformed. I did not see how this could be achieved. It was strange for me. My euroscepticism had been ignited by Rodney, but I had now become far more eurosceptic than he had ever been.

Nevertheless, it was very unclear which way Rodney would have voted. I know that after Rodney's death, Charles Moore published an email that Rodney sent to a friend, which suggested Rodney had, reluctantly, decided to vote to leave the EU, but I am not sure whether he really had finally decided. (Nor, incidentally, did I know which way Tessa voted. I suspect out.)

I remember Rodney that weekend demonstrating high kicks with Dominic Lawson's daughter Domenica, and playing chess with Dominic late into the night. Then on the Sunday evening he left. At noon the next day, in a meeting he was chairing, he had a stroke.

A few weeks later, Tessa and I were away on a trip we had taken from Seattle up the coast of Alaska on a huge liner. Somebody emailed Tessa to tell her that Rodney had died, and so she had the difficult task of telling me the sad news about one of my oldest friends.

As the campaign developed, I became increasingly confident that we would win, though this was shaken slightly by the tragic murder on 16 June – a week before polling day – of the Labour MP Jo Cox, by a Leave supporter.

However, in the final days, and on the morning of the Referendum itself, the polls began to point, in what seemed a decisive way, towards a Remain victory. So I then thought Remain more likely than not to win (polls do get things right more often than the press suggests), but at the same time I thought the odds of 5 to 1, which the bookmakers were laying against a Leave victory, were too high. I put some money on Leave. I was mildly irritated that my eldest daughter Sarah, a convinced Remainer, had backed Leave and had got 6 to 1!

On the night of 23 June, I was invited to a dinner party by Jon Moynihan, an important member of the Leave team, at 5 Hertford Street, Robin Birley's private members' club in London. It was an excellent dinner, but there was no TV screen, which rather spoiled it, and so we all left early. I went on to the IEA.

We had had a radio at the dinner, though, and I felt the same charge of excitement as so many other people across the country, when first the Newcastle and then the Sunderland results crackled through its speakers. By then it was clear to anybody with any sense that the Leave campaign was going to win, and yet for an hour and a half afterwards the bookmakers continued to lay 7 to 4 against Leave. This is a particular type of mistake persistently made by bookmakers. When the result of some event, a horse race, a political vote or anything else, appears likely to be very favourable to the bookmakers, they foolishly offer far too attractive odds about that result, as a hedge. That clearly costs them a lot of money in the long term.

I had spent a large chunk of my fortune, and devoted a great deal of my time, to the Leave cause, and in the small hours of 24 June, following a number of days when it looked as if all was lost, it became clear that the country had voted decisively to leave the European Union. I am not the sort of man to punch the air with glee (by way of contrast, Daniel Hannan, who left the IEA at the same time, was so bursting with joy that he could barely contain himself), but if I say I was delighted, or thrilled, these words do no justice to the relief and pleasure I felt.

When David Cameron resigned on the day after the Referendum, most people thought that Boris Johnson was very likely to become our next prime minister. But one of the first things I did that morning was to write to Michael Gove.[31] I told him that I considered that he had done a very patriotic thing by supporting the Leave campaign even though he was such a very close friend of David Cameron, and that I hoped he would do another very patriotic thing.

I wrote, 'I know that you have repeatedly emphasised that you do not want to be the leader of the Conservative Party. I believe that, BUT I believe – and I guess in your heart of hearts you know – that you would be the best person to be the Prime Minister. Boris would be good, but you would be better. You may not have the vote-pulling power that he has, but that should not be a problem at the next election. So please stand for the leadership. The leadership campaign need not be at all bitter, and it goes without saying that it is hugely to the advantage of the people of this country to have the best possible Prime Minister.'

---

31 That same morning I also wrote to Nigel Farage, saying that he and I had our differences and that one could argue endlessly about who should get the credit for victory, but that it was obvious that without him there would have been no Referendum and that he would deservedly be remembered for ever for that.

I now know that Matthew Elliott handed Michael Gove my letter, but Gove may not have read it; certainly he has never replied. He should have resigned after the ill-fated Chequers agreement in July 2018 – had he done so at the same time as Johnson it might well have tipped things over the edge – but I fear that his own ambition prevented him from doing the right thing. (I no longer think he would be a good prime minister, but I do think he is an excellent Secretary of State. He did extremely well in both Education and Justice, and so I hope he continues in the Cabinet.)

What is curious is that two years earlier he seemed only to discover his ambition at the last minute when, having supported Boris Johnson's campaign for the whole of the week after the Referendum, and right up to three hours before nominations closed, he torpedoed Boris's campaign by a ferocious personal attack on him, stood for the leadership himself, and left us with Mrs May in charge of the country.

CHAPTER 17

A CLEAN BREXIT AFTER ALL?

I think Mrs May has been an appalling prime minister; probably the worst ever, on the basis of the harm she has done our country. But her decision to call the election in 2017 is one thing I do *not* criticise her for – she would have been crackers not to do so with such an overwhelming lead in the polls, which seemed virtually to assure her five years of unchallenged power. Critics should not simply look at the result of the decision; they should consider what the evidence was at the time she made the decision. Unfortunately the campaign she fought was not good enough. This set the tone for what was to follow, and everything else about her has been a disaster.

It is Mrs May, in my opinion, more than anyone, who is responsible for the mess we find ourselves in. Although I think that she did intend to leave on 29 March 2019, the reason we did not do so was her failure to understand the situation, coupled with gutlessness and a lack of basic intelligence. And I do not accept the idea that she was set an impossible task. In my view she was set an easy task, and bungled it.

People say that it was a mistake to trigger Article 50, because

Brexit was too complex a process to be resolved in just two years. Absolute rubbish. I would have handed in our notice the day after the Referendum. People had voted out; let's get out. I do not see what was difficult about it. Civil servants and diplomats can argue about the minutiae, but the principal issues were, and have always been, very plain.

Mrs May's government was absolutely pathetic in its negotiations. To me it has always been obvious what leaving meant. What people voted for was to be completely clear of the EU. Immediately after the Referendum, Mrs May seemed to agree: she made it very plain that leaving the EU meant that we would be leaving both the Single Market and the Customs Union. We would be out and we would not be under any obligation to the EU any more. Over time, though, this clarity gave way to confusion and all that *was* clear was that she saw Brexit as a problem to be managed, rather than an opportunity to be exploited, and that she had utterly failed to see the strength of the UK's bargaining position.

Until the current debate, I had always thought it was an exaggeration to say that because so many politicians had never done anything but politics, they were useless at other tasks such as negotiation. I now realise that I was wrong. Mrs May plainly had not the faintest idea how to negotiate, nor had she any guts in a negotiation. Her dreadful performance has done almost irreparable harm to the people of what I used to view as the country of which I was proud to be a citizen.

It was perfectly reasonable for the EU to have tried (outstandingly successfully to date) to secure the best deal for themselves that they could. What I do not understand is why we did not do the same. It is obvious, unless one is blinded by the Remain press, that the EU needs a deal far more than we do, and yet almost as soon as the discussion had begun, we had agreed a transition period, and to pay them many billions of pounds as part of our divorce settlement. The refrain on both sides was, for a long time, 'nothing is agreed until everything is agreed', and so if we had had a tough negotiator on our side, we could easily have turned the whole thing round and forced the EU to give way to us on the great majority of the outstanding points on trade – on the basis that if they did not, we would have been quite happy to walk away without a deal, and they would not, for example, get their £39 billion.

Mrs May was also outmanoeuvred, repeatedly, by those in Parliament who were determined to thwart Brexit. I accept that securing the backing of other parties in Westminster was always likely to be hard. The Labour Party may in in theory be committed to honouring the result of the 2016 Referendum, but in practice they have only been interested in frustrating what they describe as a 'Tory Brexit'. And both the Liberal Democrats and the SNP are both 'Remain' parties.

However, had she been more gutsy and competent, I am sure Mrs May would have been able to secure the overwhelming support of the Conservatives (with the exceptions perhaps of irredeemable Europhiles like Ken Clarke), who are a party that likes to win, and would not have been forced into the humiliating cycle of concession and failure that has been so much a feature of the last two years.

The hundred or so Tory Remainers have, I believe, allowed themselves to be overly influenced by big business's fear that any change might make things more difficult. People who run successful, or even reasonably successful businesses, are very frightened of any change, such as, for example, a no-deal solution, and are strongly in favour of giving in to the EU on anything, as long as basically things remain the same for them. Out of nervousness they do not want to have to embrace something they know little about. The Tory Remainers have absorbed this perspective without really questioning it.

I believe, though, that a genuine fear of chaos, or of some major economic disadvantage, is only a small factor in their thinking about the prospect of no deal. The panic currently being whipped up in some sections of the press might be compared to the hysteria in 1999 about the 'Millennium Bug', or to the predictions by taxi drivers ahead of the 2012 Olympics that there would be gridlock on the streets of London. Just as computers did not go into meltdown when we entered the new millennium, and just as it has never been easier to drive around London than it was in the summer of 2012, I do not think there would be riots, or shortages of food or medicine, if and when we left the EU without a deal.

As I have said, we do not need a deal. We can simply trade with the EU on the basis of the existing World Trade Organisation (WTO) rules, and strike our own free-trade deals with countries across the globe. But this is not really the point: as much as anything else, the Remainers' opposition to no deal has been a cover to prevent *any* deal being agreed.

A strong, competent leader who really believed in Brexit, and who possessed even minimal negotiating skills, could have beaten back these concerns. If Mrs May had taken a tough stance and got decent terms from the EU, how could anybody in her party have objected?

Instead she produced a catastrophic deal – including as it does the so-called 'Irish backstop', which in practice we could not ever get out of – that would, if we accepted it, leave us as a vassal state; we would not be our own rulers. But though it looked doomed to fail to pass through Parliament, she ploughed on, as if she had even a faint hope of getting the vote through. I felt like asking: does she know something we don't? It turns out that she did not.

What was strange, though, is that when Mrs May's deal returned to Parliament for a third time it was, reluctantly it should be said, supported by a number of those who had until then been seen as strong Brexiteers. Boris Johnson and Jacob Rees-Mogg voted for it, and the excellent journalist Dominic Lawson backed it in his column. The MPs were, I believe, victims of blackmail: the threat being that if they did not vote for this version of Brexit, watered-down and humiliating though it was, they would not get Brexit at all.

I spoke to Jacob and Dominic, both of whom I greatly admire, and told them that although I could not quarrel with their logic, my instinct was that they had to resist this pressure. The damage of staying in the EU was less than the damage of leaving on the terms of Mrs May's deal. In March, I wrote to Jacob:

As the largest ever (I believe) donor to the Tories, and a major donor to Vote Leave, I am hugely dismayed at suggestions in the press that you may be prepared to reconsider your opposition to Mrs May's deal if it gains the support of the DUP.

As far as I can tell neither the Attorney General nor the Star Chamber has changed their view in a meaningful way on the effect of the Irish 'backstop'. So the deal is virtually unchanged and voting it through now would show that the UK would, pathetically, give in to blackmail. There is nothing in the point that we will be letting the voters down if Brexit is not voted through, because the deal is Brexit in name only. Furthermore, even if the EU does grant an extension it is quite possible that, with a new Prime Minister (perhaps you), we could get 'No Deal' or a good deal at the end of the period.

I also think that a most unwelcome side effect of you personally backing the deal would be that it would lead to the end of your political career.

He replied:

Mrs May's deal is a bad one and leaving on WTO terms would be better. If this is the choice it is the one I will make. However, a long delay is a means to stop Brexit altogether. I am afraid that the numbers in the Commons would simply not allow a new leader to get to 'No deal', that was tested in a vote last week and we lost with only one third of the votes.

This means I may have to decide between Mrs May's deal and remaining a member of the EU. Which option ought I to take?

A week later, I emailed him once more:

I ask you to consider who will be considered most responsible for the contempt with which the whole world will rightly regard the UK if Mrs May's deal is voted through, when nothing significant has changed since its massive defeats in the House of Commons. It will not be Mrs May, who (madly) believes her deal to be a good one. No, it will be those, or the one person, who for so long, and so effectively, led the opposition to it, but then succumbed to blackmail.

Even a long extension would be infinitely better. We could at the end of it leave properly, under a different Prime Minister who had the guts and the intelligence to negotiate properly.

The minority of MPs who stood firm were proved right in the end and if, as now seems far more likely than it did (though far from certain), we do get out of the EU on reasonable terms, both Boris Johnson and Jacob Rees-Mogg will have every reason to be eternally grateful to that minority. If they had voted, as Johnson and Rees-Mogg did, and as Dominic Lawson recommended, the UK would now be stuck with Mrs May's awful deal, with no real chance of getting out of it.

Then, in early summer 2019, the thing that for months had seemed at once absolutely inevitable, and yet at the same time somehow impossible, finally happened. On 7 June, Mrs May resigned as leader of the Conservative Party. (Unbelievably, though she was now only a caretaker prime minister, she continued to try to force highly controversial legislation, involving huge expenditure, through Parliament. Quite clearly it should have been up to her successor to decide such matters.)

I was delighted that she had quit, and that we would get a different prime minister, but while Brexit remains undelivered, I remain anxious.

As long as the fate of Brexit is uncertain, the Leavers still have a great deal to fight for, but I am sorry to say that (for good reasons) it will not be Ukip leading the fight. That party has become racist, which it never was under Nigel Farage, and I have resigned from it. I did so with a lot of sadness; it was, after all, Ukip that, under Nigel, got us the Referendum.

The interesting question is: where next? Nigel Farage has already formed his Brexit Party, which has trounced the two main parties, especially the Conservatives, in the 23 May European elections. I was a supporter, but I am very unlikely to wield much influence. One trouble for me is that I really have run out of money for political purposes. I do not flatter myself. I know that the fact I was able to give money to parties or causes was the main determinant of how useful I was to them. My name may have some marginal benefit, but no more than that.

Nigel Farage has used his charisma and energy to exploit, quite brilliantly, the frustration shared by so many about the fact that, many months on from 29 March 2019, Britain is *still* a member of the European Union. Theresa May and Jeremy Corbyn went missing in the lead-up to the European elections; if they did have arguments to make about Brexit, they certainly did not seem to want to make them. Farage, by contrast, was everywhere. In some quarters this has led to the Brexit Party being portrayed as a one-man-show, in which Farage enjoys uncontrolled power.

This, to some extent, overlooks the significant role played by their chairman, Richard Tice — who was one of the people I approached, successfully, for money, when I was the Ukip treasurer. He is a very good guy, whom I have long admired, and if the Brexit rally I attended is anything to go by, he has first-rate organisational skills; there is no way that Nigel Farage could have put something like that on by himself. It will be interesting to see how the relationship between the two men develops, but I do not believe even Richard could handle the problems that would arise in the (fortunately almost inconceivable) event that Nigel became prime minister.

The point that kept being made at the rally was: 'We have only been in existence for five and a half weeks, look how far we've come.' This is all very well, but once time lengthens, and problems arise, Farage will again get extremely frustrated if anyone in his own party tries to stop him doing what he wants to do. Tice may not be able to prevent this.

Our 'first-past-the-post' electoral system means that, even if they can sustain their tremendous success, it is highly unlikely that the Brexit Party will ever be able to win a majority in the House of Commons by themselves. This is just as well. My support for them is strictly limited to the vital objective of getting a clean Brexit. The idea of that party governing the country would be absurd. Nigel Farage has done a huge service to the UK, but he would be a hopeless prime minister.

In principle, those of us who want to get out of the EU should consider an alliance between the Conservatives and the Brexit Party. But I am not sure that it would work. Many Tory MPs already have an instinctive dislike of Nigel Farage, and he would only make this worse by wanting to be the boss of everything. Probably an 'alliance' should only be about the two parties agreeing not to stand in certain constituencies.

It is therefore all the more important that, if we want to get an acceptable form of Brexit, the Conservative Party must be led by a convinced Brexiteer. One has to be careful of suggesting that there is nothing else of any importance going on in the country besides Brexit, but Brexit is so much the central issue as this book goes to press that I think it is essential that our new prime minister should be someone committed to leaving the EU on what I would call a 'clean' basis: no fudging, no indefinite commitments. Whatever happens, we must come out on 31 October.

The crucial difficulty the new Tory leader will face is that the Conservative Remainers in Parliament could still prevent us from leaving without a deal.

The new leader should appeal to a mixture of party loyalty and, to be quite frank, fear. I went to a Brexit Party rally three days before the European elections and every speaker made it absolutely clear that a vote for the Brexit Party was also a vote for no deal. The lesson, therefore, of their colossal victory in the European elections is that whoever wants to win the next general election has got to accept no deal if it is the only way of getting out of the EU this autumn. Since a large proportion of the country wants a no-deal Brexit, the Remainer Tories will understand that if they do not support it, a great many Conservative seats will be lost (in many cases including their own), and Labour let in, so they will think: 'Even though I do not really enjoy the idea of voting through an exit on this basis, I will do so, for the prospect of Jeremy Corbyn in power is infinitely worse.'

Unlike Mrs May, her successor must be very clear about what they believe in. They must be resolute, and they should be a person of principle; somebody who does not wait, like Boris Johnson has had a habit of doing in the past, to see which way the winds are blowing before they act themselves.

Conviction is everything. If the new prime minister makes it absolutely clear that he is willing to leave with no deal, and the

EU believes that he can get the legislation through Parliament, then since the EU needs a deal infinitely more than we do (as I strongly believe), they will panic and make us all sorts of offers before the autumn deadline.

There is a further, more important point: even in the event that a deal is not, for whatever reason, agreed before the deadline and we leave on 31 October without a free-trade agreement, I believe a deal will be done very soon afterwards. The EU will say to themselves: 'Well, we have a £85 billion trade surplus with the UK, and we want that £39 billion – we've *got* to get a deal.' In other words, no deal will be followed very closely by a good deal.

There will inevitably be *some* problems in the event that we leave the EU without a deal. If, for instance, the EU decided to impose tariffs, those companies that export predominantly to the EU might find it difficult to carry on doing business in Europe. But because we would no longer be subject in any sense to the European Court of Justice, or anything like that, and because we would no longer have to pay the £39 billion, and because we would be saving the money we currently pay to the EU, our government would be in a financial position to say to those who had been adversely affected by this decision: 'We can afford to compensate you for the next five years.'

Ultimately, as with any major change to a nation's economic and constitutional status, there will be winners and losers, but I am very confident that, for the country as a whole, the long-term benefits will far outweigh any short-term problems.

I have heard it said that the break-up of the United Kingdom is another possible consequence of the sort of clean Brexit I think is essential. Of course, we should make every effort to persuade Scotland, Wales and Northern Ireland not to seek independence, and I would see it as highly regrettable if they did, but if they parted ways with England, it would still, at least for me, be a price worth paying. I do not believe, as others do, that it would affect our influence in the world. It would be a great constitutional upheaval, but far, far, less damaging than remaining in the EU.

On balance, I would say that it is likely that we will get what I regard as a satisfactory Brexit, without a break-up of the UK. Things have not been easy, but Britain has a reputation for losing every battle except the last. With Brexit, it may be that, in spite of disasters on the way, we come through it and get a good result in the end.

Assuming that we do leave on a decent basis, I think the country will very quickly stop talking about Brexit. I cannot see it lingering as an issue. Within a year or much less we will be far more interested in things like tax, education, health and so on. I think this would be true even if there were to be significant disruption for, say, three months (which I do not believe will happen) after a no-deal Brexit. I am also inclined to believe there will not be any sort of great realignment in politics.

With Brexit delivered, the Brexit Party will (I very much hope) fade away, because there would no longer be any need for it, and two-party politics will reassert itself, the Conservatives returning to a position of considerable power with a huge majority (an extreme view, I realise, and I may be completely wrong). What we have seen over the last few months have been protest votes, delivered in very unusual circumstances, and I do not think they should be taken as indications of a more substantial shift in people's loyalties. [32]

If, however, Brexit were abandoned, or delayed indefinitely, then that would of course be different, and we would see some real anger; though not, I think, fighting on the streets or anything like that. The British people are not given to popular uproar.

---

32 I have noticed one change, which I fear is permanent. Newspapers used to divide their pages into those that contained factual 'news', and those that contained comment. This is no longer the case. *The Times* now comments throughout on what a bad idea Brexit is and the *Daily Telegraph* takes the opposite view and argues that we should champion a 'clean Brexit'.

As I write this, Boris Johnson has just defeated Jeremy Hunt in the final round of the Tory leadership contest, the poll of Conservative Party members, and he will succeed Mrs May as prime minister.

Boris Johnson is, I believe, likely to fulfil his promise that he will get us out of the EU by 31 October this year, and I think he is more likely than any other potential Tory leader to beat Jeremy Corbyn in a general election. Recent polls show that.

I am far from blind to his failings. I have not the slightest doubt that there was an element of cynical calculation in Boris's support for the Leave campaign. There is something, surely, in the fact that he did not declare his position until a day after all the other rebel Cabinet ministers, and that in the summer of 2018, he waited until the day after David Davis had resigned before doing so himself. I do think he waits, when he can, to see which way the wind is blowing.

But I would rather have an imperfect prime minister who is likely to achieve a clean Brexit and beat Labour, than one whose principles I might admire but who is less likely to secure these objectives. And anyway, one could argue that delivering the right sort of Brexit is very much in Boris Johnson's interest: if he does not do so he will probably lose any general election he leads his party into. My instinct is that he will go flat-out to get us free, and his appointment of Dominic Cummings as the head of his advisers significantly increases the likelihood that he will succeed.

He was completely right to avoid exposing himself to interviews and so forth during the early parts of his leadership campaign. If you are in a position of great strength, why risk making a gaffe.

I do think, however, that he should have been pushed about what he intended to do if he could not get a no-deal Brexit through the House of Commons. Would he prorogue Parliament? (It is clearly arguable whether this would be legitimate.) If not, what is his alternate strategy? A combination of defections and suspensions have reduced what was already a very tenuous government majority; and a number of senior figures in Mrs May's Cabinet have not only resigned, but they have said they will combat any attempt to force through a no-deal solution. He seems to have inherited a disloyalty problem, how does he propose to resolve it? What will he offer to the irredeemable Remainers on the Tory backbenches to gain their support? Or will he roll the dice and call an election?

These are important questions. Boris Johnson may want to avoid them, but at some point in the next few months he will have to find answers.

EPILOGUE

I am not much embarrassed by being old – though I am frustrated by no longer being able to do things that until quite recently I found very easy, like walking without a Zimmer frame. Luckily, I have managed to arrange my circumstances in a way that suits me perfectly. During the week I live in a flat on St James's Square, within walking distance of the best parts of London. From my sitting-room window I can see my office, which is a hundred yards or so away on another side of the square, and opposite it is the Army and Navy Club, which is where my bridge club meets every Monday.

It is funny, though, how getting older does allow one to take a longer view. While I was in Canada with Edward Cazalet in the fifties, we worked briefly in a broker's offices. We were given an article to read that warned us, in hysterical terms, that in twenty-five years the world would have exhausted all its oil reserves. Twenty-five years on, when we most definitely had not exhausted our oil reserves, I read exactly the same warnings. The same thing has happened at regular intervals ever since, and I suspect will continue to happen well after I have disappeared.

I think I have gradually become wiser, but less so than most other people, and it has been a slow process.

My deafness has had an adverse effect on my life, despite the wonders of modern technology. It is isolating. Broadly speaking, unless things are going exceptionally well with my hearing, I struggle to take part in the conversation at any crowded event (and this can include a dinner party of only six). This makes life less enjoyable to me, of course, and it does the same for those around me. I can generally pick up the main thrust of a conversation, but not all the asides – the whispers, the jokes, the confidences – that are so much part of the pleasure of communicating. On the other hand, I have not made enough effort to use effectively what modern technology provides to help solve this, which is idiotic of me: note to myself to get a grip!

Memory also declines as you get older – some things have a habit of just slipping out of your mind. But I think it is easy to over-interpret what are quite minor foibles and convince yourself that you are in the grip of something far worse. I went to my doctor the other day about another thing, but I also said to her, 'By the way, my memory is atrocious.'

'Oh really?' she said. 'Then let's do the standard memory test.'

She reeled off about six questions, and I did my best to answer them. The next question was: 'Will you please count backwards from 100 going down by seven each time.' Now, if there is anything I am good at, it is that kind of thing, so I rattled through it at great speed, to the astonishment of my doctor. 'Sorry,' she said, 'that was too fast for me, could you do it again?'

This was followed by about twenty questions – simple ones, like 'Where are we now?' – and another look of astonishment from the doctor, who said, 'Nobody has ever got 100 per cent on this test before.'

'Well, it must have been a rotten test,' I replied, 'since I have an appalling memory.'

She conceded that it was as much a test of cognitive function as of memory, but it was still a relief. Words that I need do not come to me quickly enough now, although I might be more worried had Tessa not said to me, about thirty years ago, 'You're nothing like as on the ball as you used to be.'

Later I saw a programme on television that claimed the Americans had made two discoveries about dementia, neither of which would have been the slightest use without the other. First, how to detect it much earlier than before, and secondly, even if you cannot cure it, how to arrest it. So I thought to myself, well, if that's true, I had better find out if I do have it.

I went to a specialist, who subjected me to all the tests, and was told that I had passed with flying colours. Just to make sure, I went to the same person again five years ago, and admitted to a number of lapses in my memory. He listened to me carefully, and then said, 'Nothing you have told me gives me the slightest cause for concern.'

The future of the world generally does not frighten me; on the contrary, it excites me. People are getting better off, and though there remains much that could and should be done to relieve the effects of poverty, the poor are far less poor than they were even fifty years ago. Capitalism is not perfect, but it has driven the greatest increase in living standards in history.

The pace of technological change is more rapid than at any time, and likely only to get faster, so that I think it has become very difficult to predict what might be achievable even in ten years' time. I think astonishing things are going to happen over the next hundred years. The idea of flying to the moon would have been regarded as completely fatuous in the time of Christ. Now even the idea that we might soon be able to learn what people think without them opening their mouths no longer seems outlandish.

Things that enable you to do things you have not been able to do before are on balance beneficial, even though there are some very serious problems sometimes when they are put to appalling uses.

I appreciate the concerns that have been expressed by Liberty, another charity I support, about the erosion of privacy, and how governments or corporations might use or misuse the unprecedented amount of information about us that they are now able to gather, but it does not trouble me. I think people's anxieties over these issues are way overdone.

I think that both our government and our laws need to accommodate the lightning pace of technological innovation. Our institutions and legal code are, as it stands, much better prepared to cope with the challenges of the twentieth century than they are of the twenty-first. But these matters will get sorted out. They are interim problems.

The only really massive danger, as I see it, to this constant progress is a nuclear holocaust. Without any real logic at all, I feel the odds against this happening, or something else as devasting, are considerable.

I wonder if the fact that I am very optimistic about the world in a general way explains why I do not think about death all that much, perhaps less than you might expect, given that I am eighty-four. The chances are that in ten years or so, or maybe quite a lot less, I will die. What concerns me more is the process of death – the idea that I might end my life in pain. A friend of one of my daughter's once told me that death is usually not handled well, that many people feel great discomfort, even agony, as they near death, and so I do want to make it as sure as I can that my own departure from life will be as free from pain or worry as possible.

I have made a living will in which I have stated that to a greater extent than most people I am keen that if I am suffering quite badly, I do not want treatment to continue. You could say that I have been consistent on this point throughout my life: when I was young and used to say my prayers, I would say, 'Dear God, please protect me from pain, and also from the fear of pain.'

Perhaps my feelings on this subject have been affected by the devastation I felt after Tessa's death in 2016. She had for almost twelve years been afflicted by carcinoid cancer; a rare, slow-moving form of the disease.

In the first years after Tessa's diagnosis, it did not particularly alter the way she went about her life. She had to be very careful and take all the medicines she had been prescribed, but she continued doing all the things she wanted to: riding and going to Tangier and so forth. It was only a year or so before her operation that her illness began to affect what she could and could not do.

I took Tessa's care, and the appointments we had with her doctor, Martyn Caplin, very seriously, and would bring a colossal file with me each time, so that I could note down everything that had been discussed. About a year and half before Tessa's operation, I had asked Dr Caplin whether he thought surgery might be a good idea. He thought that it was not the right time to operate. There were different drugs and injections that stood a fair chance of working, and these were preferable to what would inevitably be an intrusive and difficult procedure, which would seriously interfere with her ability to enjoy a happy, active life.

Each time we saw him, he would write a report, which I would then file away. Over the fifteen months since I had asked the question about surgery, there is no mention in these reports of that possibility, until I raised the subject again, asking him whether surgery was out of the question. 'It isn't out of the question,' Dr Caplin told us, 'we should be considering it.' From that point on things moved quickly, and within a month the decision to operate was taken.

This was, I still believe, the right call – it had become clear that she would have deteriorated rapidly without an operation – but I do wonder whether I should have been more insistent a year earlier, when Tessa was already losing weight and weakening, at a pace that seriously worried Dr Caplin. She would at that time have been better able to withstand an operation.

It was at this stage that the medical profession's gift for euphemism came into its own. 'Well, yes,' one of them said to me, 'it's true that Tessa's illness is now in a more complicated stage.' It was not, in fact, more complicated, it was just worse.

I discussed this all with Dr Caplin a few months after Tessa's death. He was, as he had been throughout the time we had known him, humane and reasonable, pointing out the advantages and disadvantages of the courses of action we did and did not take. 'It's possible,' he concluded, 'that would have been the better route, but these things are difficult.'

The operation itself was long and difficult, and it showed that there was another large, previously undetected tumour close to the liver, which they decided would be too much to deal with at the same time. (So perhaps no operation would have been enough.)

I went to see her every day in the six weeks after the operation, much of the time in Intensive Care. I was hugely touched and pleased when the children told me that she was always asking, 'When's Stuart coming?' At one point a nurse asked her – why I do not know – if her husband was a good man. 'Yes,' Tessa replied, apparently with some emphasis, 'he's a *very* good man.'

I had always been slightly more willing to talk about emotional things than Tessa and she did not like to get bogged down in serious discussions about the children and what school they might go to and so forth. Now, as she lay there in her hospital bed, it became incredibly important to me that I should talk to her in a way that was different from how we had talked before. 'Darling,' I told her, 'I really do want you to realise how immensely I love you.'

By this point Tessa found it impossible to communicate, but her sister, Jane Micklethwait, who was on the other side of the room, told me later that it was obvious that she had understood every word I had uttered, and that she was happy with it. One's mind is so liable to play tricks in these situations; it is easy to end up believing that something has happened simply because one *wants* it to be true.

So the idea that somebody else had witnessed our exchanges, and saw them in the same way as I did, is a source of great comfort. It was not the only time that we had such an encounter. On another occasion, my daughter Charlotte said that the things Tessa and I said to each other brought a tear to the eye of a watching nurse.

At every stage of the process, I had been assessing what I thought were the chances of her survival. It was a very serious situation, but it would have been odd to suddenly completely change the way I looked at matters. By the time the final decision had to be taken on whether to operate, we were told that normally the chances of it killing the patient were about three per cent, but because Tessa was such a healthy person, the chance of death would probably be lower. I found myself thinking that because she had become so much weaker, I reckoned there was a five per cent chance.

Then, in the time after the operation, when things did begin to go wrong, I thought initially that Tessa was heavily odds on to come out the other side; it was only very close to the end that I started to think there was perhaps a 1 in 3 chance she might die. But I still thought she was more likely to survive than not. In the end, she did not. Tessa contracted an infection, and died on 11 December 2016.

Although I am agnostic, after Tessa's death I made more of an effort to determine whether I did believe in God, and if so whether it was the Christian God, or a kind God, and so forth. I read quite a bit about this subject, but very little convinced me. In part, this is because some of the philosophical writing is so obscure that many of the words used do not even feature in the dictionary.

If I had to put a bet on it either way, I would probably wager that extinction is our likely fate, and we will not be reunited with our loved ones. But I do not feel sure about this. This is a source of hope: I should very much like to see Tessa again.

ACKNOWLEDGEMENTS

I have had, and very much needed, a huge amount of help in writing this book. Above all, my decision to approach Josh Ireland right at the beginning to get him to turn my ramblings into a properly structured book was crucial. He had a very tough job. My daughters, Sarah, Jacquetta and Charlotte, who have themselves been immensely helpful, especially by giving an enormous amount of time to Josh, say to me, 'Daddy, you have given Josh an almost impossible task: you can't remember anything!' They are right, but he has managed it wonderfully and put up with my constant nit-picking with great humour.

There are many, many others who have been kind enough to come up with all kinds of memories and/or advice. I am tremendously grateful to them all. This book, and whatever merits it may have, would have lacked a great deal without their help. I shall name but four:

I would particularly like to thank Roddy Bloomfield, a close family friend, for encouraging me to write the story of what he calls my 'most unusual life'. Without his invaluable support and his knowledge and experience, and his finding me a great publisher, this book would never have got off the starting blocks. For this, Roddy, I am immensely grateful.

Sarah Paterson read an early chapter and came up with a

wealth of trenchant and very valuable criticisms which have significantly improved the whole of the book.

My PA, Su Lungley, most ably assisted by Heidi Lloyd, has been crucial. In Su's case, apart from doing a tremendous amount of work, without a shadow of a complaint, she has been very good indeed in forcing me to get on with things, as well as making a wealth of helpful suggestions.

Su's predecessor, Yvonne Carlton, who amazingly put up with me for seventeen years, provided Josh and me with a huge amount of detailed and background information, for which I am extremely grateful, as it was essential, given my poor memory.

Finally, I obviously would not have got this book together if Andrew Johnston of Quiller had not taken the gamble – and, as a gambler myself, I realise full well that publishing an author's first work is a gamble – of publishing it. I am extremely grateful to him and of course to all his team for putting the book together and, in particular, for putting up with my ignorance about how a book gets put together.

APPENDIX

A TEN-MINUTE GUIDE TO PLAYING BLACKJACK BETTER THAN 90 PER CENT OF THE POPULATION

This guide assumes you already know the game of Blackjack. If you do not, please have a look at the account in the glossary.

There is one thing I must explain before coming to the instructions. A hand is called *soft* if it contains an ace, and if that ace can be counted as eleven without causing the total to exceed twenty-one. For example, if you hold (A, 6), you have soft seventeen and you cannot *bust* by drawing another card, because you can then count the ace as one. All hands, other than *soft* hands, are called *hard* hands.

Please not too that I shall refer to kings, queens and jacks, which all count ten, as tens.

Here are the rules:

1. If you have a pair:

- Always split aces except against an ace in the dealer's exposed hand.
- Split eights against two to nine.
- Never split fours, fives or tens.

● Split the other pairs when the dealer shows from two to seven; if he shows anything else, do not split.

2. If you have a *hard* hand without a pair:

● When the dealer's exposed card is two through six, never risk *busting*, i.e., stand at a total of twelve or more.
● When the dealer's exposed card is anything else, continue drawing until your total reaches seventeen; then stand.

3. If you have a *soft* hand:

● Continue drawing until your total reaches eighteen or more; then stand.

4. *Doubling down* on *hard* hands:

● If your total is eleven or ten, always *double down* except against an ace or ten.
● If your total is nine, *double down* if the dealer's exposed card is from two to six.
● Otherwise do not *double down*.

5. *Doubling down* on *soft* hands:

● If your hand is anything from A, 2 to A, 7, *double down* whenever the dealer's exposed card is four, five or six. Otherwise do not *double down*.

If you follow the above rules, the casino will not have any significant edge against you. If you want to have a significant edge against the casino, my advice to you is to buy the 2016 edition of *Beat the Dealer* by Edward O. Thorp (Vintage, 2016).

GLOSSARY

BLACKJACK

Blackjack is a very popular casino game, similar in some ways to games often played at home, called Pontoon or Vingt-et-un. It is played with one or more packs of cards. The objective of the game is to beat the dealer in one of the following ways:

● Get 21 points on the player's first two cards (called a 'blackjack'), unless the dealer also has a blackjack

● Reach a final score higher than the dealer without exceeding 21

● Let the dealer draw additional cards until his hand exceeds 21, in which case he is bust.

Players are each dealt two cards, face up or down; the dealer is also dealt two cards, one up (exposed) and one down (hidden). The value of cards two through ten is their pip value. Face cards (jack, queen, and king) are all worth ten. Aces can be worth one or eleven. A hand's value is the sum of the card values. Players can draw additional cards to try to improve their hands. A hand with an ace valued as 11 is called *soft*. The hand cannot bust by taking an additional card; the value of the ace will become one, to prevent the hand from exceeding 21. Otherwise, the hand is *hard*.

Once all the players have completed their hands, it is the dealer's turn. The dealer then reveals his hidden card and must draw another card until the cards total 17 or more. Players win by not busting and having a total higher than the dealer, or not busting and having the dealer bust, or by getting a blackjack without the dealer getting a blackjack. If the player and dealer have the same total, this is called a 'push', and the player does not win or lose money on that hand. If the player busts, or the dealer obtains a total higher than that of the player, the dealer wins.

Blackjack has many rule variations. The above is typical.

The casino has one very important advantage over the players. The player has to play before the casino, so that, if he goes bust, he loses even when the dealer also goes bust. On the other hand, the player has three advantages:

1. If he obtains a blackjack, he gets paid 3 to 2.

2. If he has a pair, he may choose to split the pair making each card start a new hand.

3. He may, after looking at his two cards, choose to 'double down', i.e., double his stake. But if he does so, he must take one more card and no more than one.

CHEMIN DE FER

Six decks of cards are used, shuffled together. Players are seated in random order, typically around an oval table; discarded cards go to the centre.

Once play begins, one player is designated as the banker; he deals, or the casino deals for him. The other players are 'punters'. In each round, the banker puts up the amount he wants to risk. The other players, in order, then have the opportunity to bet against the bank.

The banker deals four cards face down: two to himself and two to his opponent. The banker and player both look at their cards; if either has a total of eight or nine, this is immediately announced and the hands are turned face-up and compared. If neither hand is an eight or nine, the player has a choice to accept or refuse a third card; if accepted, it is dealt face-up.

Traditional practice – grounded in mathematics, similar to basic strategy in blackjack – dictates that one always accept a card if one's hand totals between 0 and 4, inclusive, and always refuse a card if one's hand totals 6 or 7. After the player makes his decision, the banker, in turn, decides either to accept or to refuse another card. Once both the banker and the player have made their decision, the hands are turned face-up and compared.

If the player's hand exceeds the banker's hand, the player wins, and the position of banker passes to the next player in order. If the banker's hand exceeds the player's hand, the banker wins. If there is a tie, bets remain as they are for the next hand.

THE CHEQUERS DEAL

The Future Relationship Between the United Kingdom and the European Union (more commonly known as the Chequers plan, deal or agreement) is a UK Government white paper about Brexit, published on 12 July 2018 by the Prime Minister, Theresa May. The paper was based on a three-page Cabinet agreement and laid out the type of future relationship between the UK and European Union (EU) that the UK sought to achieve in the Brexit negotiations.

In July 2018, the Brexit Secretary, Dominic Raab, described it as a 'detailed proposal for a principled, pragmatic and ambitious future partnership between the UK and the EU.'

The white paper was finalised at a meeting of the UK Cabinet held at Chequers on 6 July 2018. Brexit Secretary, David Davis, and Foreign Secretary, Boris Johnson, resigned in opposition to the plan. The plan was rejected by the EU in September 2018.

Free movement of people

The agreement said it would end free movement of people 'giving the UK back control over how many people enter the country'.

A 'mobility framework' would be set up to allow UK and EU citizens to travel to each other's territories and apply for study and work.

CONTRACTS FOR DIFFERENCES

A contract for differences (CFD) is essentially a contract between an investor and an investment bank or other firm. At the end of the contract, the parties exchange the difference between the opening and closing prices of a specified financial instrument, including shares or commodities.

CFDs do not carry votes like ordinary stock but enable investors to gain economic exposure to a listed company for a fraction of the deposit required when buying shares. They also escape stamp duty and can be bought in size without triggering obligations to disclose the holding.

A CFD is simply an agreement between two parties – the investor and the CFD provider – to pay each other the change in the price of an underlying asset. Depending on which way the price moves, one party pays the other the difference from the time the contract was agreed to the point where it ends.

So, like spread bets, CFDs involve the investor taking an opposing view to the investment bank, speculating that an asset price will rise, by buying ('long' position), or fall, by selling ('short' position).

Also like spread bets, CFDs incur no stamp duty as they do not involve buying an asset, only agreeing to receive or pay the movement in its price. And because you only have to put down a small deposit on trades, called 'margin', you can make large profits – or losses – on the money you put up, from small moves in the price. So CFDs give you the advantages of owning shares without many of the inconveniences. They differ from spread bets in their tax treatment.

CRAPS

Craps is a dice game in which the players make bets on the result of a roll, or a series of rolls, of a pair of dice. Players bet against the casino. The dice are thrown by one of the players on behalf of all of the players, but the players may, according to what bets they have placed, hope for different outcomes.

FINANCIAL SERVICES ACT 1986

The Financial Services Act 1986 (1986 c.60) was an Act passed to regulate the financial services industry. Its provisions were not all brought into effect simultaneously. There were two provisions of particular importance to IG Index. One of them rendered the result of spread bets (the type of bet used by IG Index) enforceable at law, whereas previously they had been unenforceable because the debts were gambling debts. This provision was already in force when the stock market crash of 1987 occurred. The other important provision forbade spread-betting companies (such as IG Index) from passing on to their brokers, money they were holding on behalf of their clients. This provision was *not* in force at the time of the crash.

HEDGING

A strategy aimed at minimising or eliminating risk, normally involving positions in two different markets, with one offsetting the other. Derivatives – futures and options – are widely used for hedging purposes, because they can protect an investor against changes in the spot value of an underlying asset or currency.

INVESTMENT DOLLARS

Until 1979 there were, in the UK, what were known as exchange controls. A UK resident who wished to buy certain types of asset, including gold, had to buy so called 'investment dollars', which cost more than the normal exchange rate between the pound and the dollar. The difference was known as 'the investment dollar premium'. But when the UK resident sold the asset, he had to pay to the government a quarter of the investment dollar premium which he received from the buyer. This made it very unattractive to own the type of asset concerned.

LIBERTARIAN

Libertarianism is a collection of political philosophies and movements that uphold liberty as a core principle. Libertarians seek to maximise political freedom and autonomy, emphasising freedom of choice, voluntary association and individual judgment.

THE LISBON TREATY

The Treaty of Lisbon was introduced after France and Holland voted against a very similar proposed treaty called the Reform Treaty.

The stated aim of the treaty was to 'complete the process started by the Treaty of Amsterdam [1997] and by the Treaty of Nice [2001] with a view to enhancing the efficiency and democratic legitimacy of the Union and to improving the coherence of its action'. Opponents of the Treaty of Lisbon argued that it would centralise the EU, and weaken democracy by 'moving power away' from national electorates.

MANAGEMENT BUY OUT

When those who are employed by a company buy, often in conjunction with a merchant bank, all the shares of a company from the existing shareholders, the transaction is known as a 'management buy out'.

POKER

Poker is a family of card games that combines gambling, strategy, and skill. All poker variants involve betting as an intrinsic part of play, and determine the winner of each hand according to the combinations of players' cards, at least some of which remain hidden until the end of the hand. Poker games vary in the number of cards dealt, the number of shared or 'community' cards, the number of cards that remain hidden, and the betting procedures.

In most modern poker games, the first round of betting begins with one or more of the players making some form of a forced bet (the *blind*). In standard poker, each player bets according to the rank they believe his hand is worth as compared to the other players. The action then proceeds clockwise as each player in turn must either match (or 'call') the maximum previous bet, or fold, losing the amount bet so far and all further involvement in the hand. A player who matches a bet may also 'raise' (increase) the bet.

The betting round ends when all players have either called the last bet or folded. If all but one player folds on any round, the remaining player collects the pot without being required to reveal his hand. If more than one player remains in contention after the final betting round, a showdown takes place where the hands are revealed, and the player with the winning hand takes the pot.

With the exception of initial forced bets, money is only placed into the pot voluntarily by a player who either believes the bet has positive expected value or who is trying to bluff other players for various strategic reasons. Thus, while the outcome of any particular hand significantly involves chance, the long-run expectations of the players are determined by their actions chosen on the basis of probability, psychology, and game theory.

ROULETTE

Roulette is a casino game. Players may choose to place bets on either a single number, various groups of numbers, the colours red or black, whether the number is odd or even, or whether the numbers are high (19–36) or low (1–18).

To determine the winning number and colour, a croupier spins a wheel in one direction, then spins a ball in the opposite direction around a tilted circular track running around the outer edge of the wheel. The ball eventually loses momentum, passes through an area of deflectors, and falls onto the wheel and into one of 37, in Europe, or 38, in America, coloured and numbered pockets on the wheel. If the player has selected the right single number, or group of numbers, he will win either the amount of his bet, or some multiple (according to the rules) of his bet.

SHORT POSITIONS

A client of IG Index who bets that a price will go down is said to have a 'short position'. For example, if he bets that the price of share X will fall, he is said to be short of share X.

A NOTE ON MONEY

Translating the value of money is never an exact science. But to help you relate prices over the years to today's money you may like to know that £1 at various dates was, according to the Retail Prices Index worth the following in today's money:

1930	1940	1950	1960	1970	1980	1990	2000	2010
£65	£56	£34	£23	£15	£4	£2.26	£1.70	£1.27